How to Communicate Technical Information

A Handbook of Software and Hardware Documentation

(formerly titled: How to Write a Computer Manual)

Dr. Jonathan Price

The Communication Circle
Albuquerque, NM

Henry Korman

WordPlay Communications
Berkeley, CA

ADDISON-WESLEY
An imprint of Addison Wesley Longman, Inc.

Reading, Massachusetts   Harlow, England   Menlo Park, California
Berkeley, California   Don Mills, Ontario   Sydney
Bonn   Amsterdam   Tokyo   Mexico City

Sponsoring Editor: John Carter Shanklin
Production Coordinator: Megan Rundel
Copyeditor: Barbara Conway
Cover Designer: Gary Palmatier
Interior Designer: Dick Kharibian
Compositor: Tony Jonick

Library of Congress Cataloging-in-Publication Data
Price, Jonathan, 1941–
    How to communicate technical information: a handbook of software and hardware
documentation / Jonathan Price, Henry Korman.
        p.   cm.
    Includes bibliographical references and index.
    ISBN 0–8053–6829–9
    1. Electronic data processing documentation.   I. Henry Korman
    II. Title
    QA76.9.D6P74 1993
    808'.066004--dc20   93-7824

ISBN 0-8053-6829-9

3 4 5 6 7 8 9 10 11–CRS–00999897

This book at a glance

How to use this book

Compare the examples of documentation practices

This icon calls your attention to an example of what not to do, or to a document needing revision or development.

This icon identifies an example that illustrates practices we recommend.

Scan a Checklist for an overview or a refresher

Each chapter concludes with a checklist that summarizes major points and issues. Use it to quickly review a chapter or to check off items against a document you're creating.

If you are a newcomer to technical writing

You will learn how to write a manual that other people can really use to master the subject. You've used bad manuals; here's how to write a good one.

To see where you fit in	Turn to Chapter 1, "The Project Cycle—What You Do at Each Stage."
To see what you need to research	Read Chapter 2, "Gathering Information," Chapter 3, "Understanding Your Audience and Their Work, "and Chapter 4, "Learning the Product."
To learn how to decide what to write	Read Chapter 5, "Planning the Documentation."
To set up a schedule and budget	Follow Chapter 6, "Developing a Schedule and Estimating Costs."
For general advice	Read Chapter 7, "As You Work."
To write a particular document	Look the document up in Part Two. Chapters 8 through 16 discuss each type of documentation and each part of a manual, from introductions to tutorials, to glossaries and indexes.
To revise a draft	Read Chapter 17, "Getting Feedback," Chapter 18, "Rewriting Drafts," and Chapter 20, "Updating a Manual. "

To adapt your style	Turn to Chapter 19, "Refining Your Style," for some tips on tone and usage.
To help someone else revise	Read Chapter 21, "Reviewing Someone Else's Manual." It shows you how to give other people advice on improving their manuals.
To do further research	Turn to the Bibliography at the end of the book.

If you are an experienced technical writer

You will learn how to create documentation that goes beyond user-friendliness, to teach, to show people how to accomplish tasks, to help them out of difficulties, to support them whenever they need you.

To see where we're coming from	Please read the preface, "Setting the Scene."
For a new slant on audience analysis	Read Chapter 3, "Understanding Your Audience and Their Work."
To track product changes	Read Chapter 4, "Learning About the Product."
For a thorough documentation plan	Read Chapter 5, "Planning the Documentation."
To set up a schedule and budget	Follow Chapter 6, "Developing a Schedule and Estimating Costs."
For ideas on how to work better	Read Chapter 7, "As You Work."
For advice on a particular document	Look the document up in Part Two. Chapters 8 through 16 discuss each type of documentation and each part of a manual, from introductions to tutorials, to glossaries and indexes. You may want to flip to the end of a chapter to browse the Checklist first.
When you have to revise a draft	Read Chapter 17, "Getting Feedback," Chapter 18, "Rewriting Drafts," and Chapter 20, "Updating a Manual. "
To adapt your style	Turn to Chapter 19, "Refining Your Style," for some tips on tone and usage.
To help someone else revise	Read Chapter 21, "Reviewing Someone Else's Manual." It shows you how to give other people advice on improving their manuals.
For further reading	Check the Bibliography at the end of the book. It is arranged by chapter.

Setting the Scene

Take a look at your bookshelf or desk: How many manuals, guides, or textbooks do you see there? And how many of them have really helped you master a subject?

We look at our own shelves and see hundreds of manuals, advice books, texts, and magazines, all designed to help us master new hardware or software. In an average week we use a few dozen pieces of software, so we often need to learn, or relearn, the programs we don't use full time. And every few months we get an upgrade or a new version and more paper purporting to explain how to use the new or revised features. We have lots of reasons to look up facts in this mass of documentation. But we often find our path blocked; we can't find what we need, or we find only part of it, or if we find the subject, we encounter writing so bizarre that only a Martian engineer could follow the procedure. Why is it that so much documentation is so bad?

Seven years ago in the first edition of this book, we urged writers to shape manuals from the point of view of the customer, not the engineer. Since then we've seen many companies moving toward friendlier, more useful manuals. But there's still a long way to go.

In revising and updating this book over these years, we've seen several main themes emerge:

- We all still face yards of unusable documentation on our shelves. Only a few manuals are genuinely helpful.

- We dream of manuals that can actually increase the user's mastery; we imagine that documentation can actually be more than user-friendly (what an ugly term!). We need **convivial** manuals.

- It's important to rethink what we do. For instance, we must recognize that we need to show people how to use a product to carry out tasks in their own work, rather than just describing the product and leaving it to them to figure out how to use it. We must see the value of taking a diagnostic approach to smoothing away potential problems, and to show people how to diagnose—and solve—their own problems.

Our backgrounds are not academic, although we have both taught for many years at the graduate and undergraduate level and in workshops for beginning and professional writers. We draw upon our own experiences of creating documentation for exciting products (and some boring ones) from companies that sell mainframe, mini, and personal computers and the software that runs on them, plus computerized equipment such as cameras, answering machines, copiers, and video tape recorders. We use many of these products in our own work, but we still experience the same nightmares that users tell us about: trying to find our way through baffling layouts, incomplete indexes, confusing sentences, inaccurate and incomplete information, arrogant attitudes, and indifference to our fate. We too have faced manuals from hell.

Convivial manuals empower people

We have a dream of good manuals. Their writers recognize that the customers' main interests are in getting their own work done, not developing an appreciation for the intricacies of the product. These writers also recognize that at different times during their day, customers want to use manuals in different ways:

- To get some training on what the product can do for them, by playing out some as-if scenarios, or taking a guided tour
- To gain a broad conceptual understanding of the way the product works and how that functioning fits into their own day-to-day work
- To look up step-by-step procedures showing exactly how to accomplish tasks on their job using the product
- To look up what some part of the product itself does
- To get help when they are in the middle of a task and just need an instruction or two to get back to work
- To find out how to diagnose and solve a problem

A well-designed manual—or set of documentation—lets customers use it in all these ways.

Think of the manual for a moment as a tool. Like a hammer that has been weighted so that it balances nicely in your hand or a shampoo bottle with indentations built in for your grip, the documentation looks as if it has been made with you in mind. It's flexible enough to be used in many ways, considerate of your tastes and senses, designed for you, not an engineer, and built in such a way that it helps you understand its own use, and your work, better. In all these ways, it is what the social philosopher Ivan Illich calls **convivial**.

In his book *Tools for Conviviality*, Illich criticizes many of our industrial-strength tools, such as highway systems, as rigid and confining. Such tools demand that we invest a lot of effort in learning to use them, only to find ourselves unwittingly locked into their use.

An individual relates himself in action to his society through the use of tools that he actively masters, or by which he is passively acted upon. To the degree that he masters his tools, he can invest the world with his meaning; to the degree that he is mastered by his tools, the shape of the tool determines his own self-image. Convivial tools are those which give each person who uses them the greatest opportunity to enrich the environment with the fruits of his or her vision.

Convivial manuals, then, empower people to do what they want. Readers tend to come back to such manuals repeatedly. And instead of just learning how to look up a few items, they branch out and explore, learning more than they first intended. They see more in the product than they did before and understand more about their own work.

Rethinking what we do

Traditional manuals have not been designed well, in part because the writers took only one approach as they organized and wrote: the teacher's role. That model, in which the writers teach the readers what the software or hardware is and what it can do, helps readers accomplish only two tasks: finding out what some part of the product does and, perhaps, understanding on a conceptual level what goes on behind the scenes in the product.

To provide more service to the customer, we need to adopt a wider range of models of the interplay between writers and readers.

- The teaching model offers an expert's point of view (the writer teaches readers what the software or hardware is, and can do, much as a professor passes along an interpretation of a play).

- The task model interprets the product in terms of the reader's own work (the writer shows readers how to carry out tasks, using the product to do their ordinary work).

- The problem-solving model smooths out the process (the writer helps the customer diagnose the problem and arrive at a solution; the situation is significantly different from that portrayed in most manuals in which the writers assume everything is working just fine).

Teaching orientation: I teach people what the hardware or software is and does

Traditionally, we have thought of ourselves and our manuals as "teaching" people what the software or hardware is, what its functions accomplish, and, incidentally, how to use the product. We have taken a narrow view of teaching, seeing it as imparting knowledge from above: We lecture to people; they take notes. We've assumed that we have eager students, ready and interested in learning everything, in reading every page. So, in many cases, we provide textbooks for our "students," who are supposed to study them.

At best this approach works fine for some people or for getting across some ideas, as when an overview puts all the smaller parts in a meaningful context. We empower people by helping them to grasp the big picture. And we satisfy people's need for little details, such as which format they can enter a date in or how many characters they can use in a filename. We describe the product itself.

But few people read a manual the way a medical student studies an anatomy textbook. People most often turn to a manual to answer a question, not to learn the complete skeleton of the product. They do not take notes, they look up facts.

A book that is organized just around the product, with the idea that it should teach the reader everything about the product, ignores the user's real need to apply the product to tasks on the job.

Task orientation: I help people do their work

Trainers set up measurable objectives for their learners to achieve. Those objectives are similar to the concrete tasks the learners will have to perform using the product when they leave the training room and return to work. Only the content is imaginary.

Training often turns the focus onto the tasks the customer must do on the job. Instead of "teaching" the customer to understand the product, trainers show the customers how to do their job, and the product is just a way to do it.

As writers pay more attention to customers, they recognize that after people spend a few days with a product, they don't want to set aside time for learning more about it; they have work they want to do, tasks they want to accomplish. They want to look up how to do specific tasks as they need them in their work.

Following this model, we investigate what users want to do, when they use the product, and then provide step-by-step instructions for each task. Headings in our manuals must echo people's ideas of the tasks so they can look up the procedures quickly. Of course, to follow this model, we must know our audiences and the work they really do. We empower people by speaking the familiar language of their work and their action.

Diagnostic orientation: I solve problems

Because we're human, even writers get into trouble using the products we write about. But instead of ignoring the difficulties that arise or glossing them over with marketing hype, we can make an effort to diagnose the troublesome situation, figure out a solution, and then pass that helpful advice along to customers. That's the diagnostic approach.

We can go further by considering every aspect of a manual from the point of view of a customer in trouble who formulates an idea or a set of questions about the difficulty, then looks in the table of contents or index or headings to find some recognizable representation of the difficulty he or she has encountered. You can add a troubleshooting section that lists the symptoms, offers diagnoses, and provides cures. But taking a diagnostic approach really means considering potential difficulties everywhere they might occur—in the steps of a procedure, in a glossary definition, in a description of the flow of information.

Taking a diagnostic, problem-solving viewpoint sensitizes us to a reader's condition when seeking help. We empower people by making them self-reliant.

Making ourselves useful

Horace said that poems should be sweet and useful. Manuals should be, too.

They're sweet in that they appeal to customers, going beyond friendliness to become truly convivial.

And they're useful because no matter what customers want to accomplish when they turn to the manual, they succeed. When you anticipate and respond to your customers' needs, you make your documentation perform useful work.

Thanks

To Mick Renner, Adam Rochmes, and Linda Urban: your work has helped make this book what it is. Your ideas, comments, and reviews have expanded our views and sharpened our focus, throughout.

To our editor John Carter Shanklin, his assistant Vivian McDougal, and to the Benjamin/Cummings production folks, Megan Rundel and Tony Jonick, for their patient support and encouragement.

To Margot Fuchs Forrest, Meryl Natchez, and Jim Guthrie for their detailed and thoughtful reviews.

To the following writers, editors, artists, and managers, whose ideas have been particularly helpful to us as we created this second edition of the book:

Izumi Aizu, Hiraku Amemiya, Lorraine Anderson, Meg Beeler, Kathleen Bennett, Paula Rae Berger, Stephen Bernhardt, John Bowie, Suzanne Brown, Jon Butah, Geta Carlson, Margaret Cheatham, Steve Chernicoff, Rani Cochran, Carol Cook, Ames Cornish, Rich Coulombre, Martha Cover, Cedric Crocker, Nancy Davis, Jim Dexter, Darcy DiNucci, Susan Dressel, Nancy Dunn, John Dvorak, Art Elser, Ron Erickson, Chris Espinosa, Sue Espinosa, David Farkas, Andy Felong, RuthAnn Fowler, Barbara Gibson, Dirk Gifford, David Gillette, Bill Grout, Joann Hackos, John Hammett, Debbie Hara, David Hathwell, Shuhei Hattori, Seiji Hayakawa, Nancy Hecht, Jeremy Hewes, Judith Hibbard, Leslie Holmes, Peter Honebein, Michiko Horikawa, Bill Horton, John Huber, Dustin Huntington, Francine Hyman, Art Ignacio, Nagatoshi Inagaki, Tina Jalalian, Mimi Jones, Carol Kaehler, Madeleine Kahn, Scot Kamins, Van Kane, Chris Kelly, Koreo Kinosita, Cynthia Kolnick, Joanne Koltnow, Shirley Krestas, Rebecca Kutlin, Laura Lamar, Shana Lavatelli, Dick Leeman, Bob Loftis, Tim Lundeen, Connie Mantis, Taka Masatsugu, Mike McGrath, Joe Meyers, Judy Miller, Sandy Miranda, Lisa Mirski, Marney Morris, Jan Nelson, Cheryl Nemeth, John Noon, Sylvio Orsino, Tom Outler, Yoji Ozato, Su Piercy, Mike Plasterer, Douglas Pundick, Judith Rachel, Carol Ranalli, Roy Rasmussen, Don Reed, Janice Redish, Peggy Redpath, Laurel Rezeau, Dave Roberts, Peter Roche, Marcy Rosenberg, Scott Sanders, Carlene Schnabel, Karen Schriver, Jonathan Seybold, Craig Sheumaker, Bob Silvey, Martha Steffen, Lydia Stough, Rob Swigart, Judith Tarutz, Jon Thompson, Bruce Tognazzini, Molly Tyson, Jan Ulijn, Dirk van Nouhuys, Janet Van Wicklen, Jeff Vasek, Kathi Vian, Allen Watson, Elizabeth Weal, Roy West, Carol Westberg, Doug Wieringa, Ann Wiley, Kathy Williams, Ohiko Yagi, Geri Younggren, and John Zussman.

Contents

PART ONE

Planning

The Project Cycle—What You Do at Each Stage

Our host has filled many notebooks with the sayings of our fathers as they came down to us. This is the way of his people; they put great store upon writing; always there is a paper.

—Four Guns

As part of the project team, you usually write while the product is being created. Your schedule fits in with the larger project schedule, which is sometimes called a project cycle because when you get to the end you often start over. A typical project cycle involves the phases shown in Figure 1-1.

1

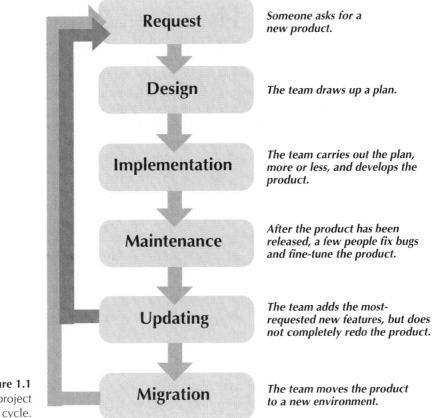

Request	Someone asks for a new product.
Design	The team draws up a plan.
Implementation	The team carries out the plan, more or less, and develops the product.
Maintenance	After the product has been released, a few people fix bugs and fine-tune the product.
Updating	The team adds the most-requested new features, but does not completely redo the product.
Migration	The team moves the product to a new environment.

Figure 1.1
Diagram of the project cycle.

When someone requests a brand-new version of the product or an entirely different product, the cycle begins again. The whole cycle may take anywhere from one to five years, depending on the complexity and challenge, and it may be repeated for as many as twenty years.

Your own work—the documentation cycle—meshes with this overall project schedule. Just where you enter the project and how long you stay depend on what kind of organization you work for. This chapter outlines the most common pattern, but, as the commercials say, your mileage may differ.

Request

Someone asks for a computer program or a piece of hardware, spelling out what it should do. This someone could be a manager who wants to computerize some work, or it could be a marketing person who wants a new product to sell. Perhaps it's a scientist who wants your supercomputer to calculate the change in the weather.

The request—usually a document you can recover from the archives—gives you an idea of the original purpose of the product. By the time you appear on the scene, the product may have been transformed so much that it no longer matches the request, but the request at least reveals the initial inspiration. From it you can gain a deeper, more meaningful understanding of the product in its current incarnation.

Preliminary estimate

If you're an independent contractor or you're doubling as a manager of documentation, the team leader may call you in during the preliminary estimate phase and ask for a rough estimate of your costs. You'll need to prepare a bid or proposal, estimating what documentation will be needed and how much it will cost. The best way to arrive at an estimate that will stand up is to prepare a (very rough) preliminary documentation plan that includes:

- A preliminary evaluation of the audience
- A preliminary description of the product
- A description of the components of the documentation—tutorial, procedures, reference, online help, or training materials
- A preliminary page count upon which you can estimate costs (hours per page times dollars per hour equals estimated cost)

Usually, if your proposal is accepted, you begin a round of negotiations that result in an actual agreement. You are ready to move into the design phase.

Design

An engineering team analyzes what the product will have to do. They come up with a more-or-less detailed plan that specifies the functions people will be able to use and the work needed to make those features possible. In addition to the functional specifications, the team may plan the actual interface—the buttons, commands, or levers a user will push to communicate with the product, and the flashes, beeps, or messages the product will display to communicate with the user.

You may join the design team at this time. If so, you may be assigned to record its progress in a series of minutes summing up decisions at meetings or in monthly reports showing upper management how your team is coming along. Occasionally you get put in charge of updating the specifications. These documents do not directly further the documentation, but they do help you keep on top of the product as it grows.

Subteams may be formed and put in charge of individual modules. If their work diverges, you may be the only person who notices that they are taking different approaches. You may serve in the role Susan Dressel, a manager at Los Alamos Laboratories, calls "rapporteur," bringing the team into rapport by reporting on what they are all doing.

Design is iterative, whether you are designing a car, a program, a disk drive, or a manual. You come up with a plan, create a prototype of some kind, try that out, see what needs changing, and then go back to modify the plan. *Iter* is Latin for *again*, and you'll sometimes feel as if you are going around and around in circles as you develop the product design. But in the process you will be learning a lot from the people you work with, you may help in bringing about agreement among the team members, and in many ways you may be making a contribution to the development of the product itself.

Documentation plan

As the design solidifies, you draw up a documentation plan. You decide who your audience is and prepare an audience profile. You write up what you know about the product, from your point of view, in a product profile. And you decide what documents will best serve the audience, what will be in each document, and when you will create it in the documentation plan and schedule. (You'll learn more about creating a documentation plan in Chapter 5, "Planning the Documentation.")

If you are working as an independent contractor, the plan forms the basis for an informed estimate of the time needed and the costs. (Of course, you may be asked to make an estimate before you make the plan, in which case you should reserve the right to negotiate changes when you complete the documentation plan.)

The documentation plan becomes part of the project's overall plan, and the estimates flow into its budget.

Implementation

Now an even larger team goes to work building the actual product. Implementation takes a year or so for a product the team's familiar with, two years or more for something new. In most organizations you become part of the project after implementation begins, several months before the first milestone (often called an alpha version of the product). If so, your first task is to create the documentation plan and schedule and then, posthaste, to start organizing your material.

You become a member of the team—sometimes sooner, sometimes later, occasionally never. Usually you get to meet weekly with the key engineers. You watch the arguments ebb and flow over key pieces of the interface; you see the team change direction on a major function; you get to complain about a confusing button.

Other members join the team now, too: more marketing people, if this product is designed to be sold; representatives of the user, if the product is for in-house consumption; keepers of the organization's standards (the user interface czar and the quality assurance folks); and maybe even an editor.

The project now acquires a nonfiction schedule, with specific milestones for you and the engineering team. During implementation the team works in several phases, most often called alpha, beta, and final. Usually you must deliver drafts of your documentation at about the same time as the engineering team delivers a version of the product.

Alpha documentation (the first draft)

Formally the team should get an OK on the functional specifications and then, if the product is software, start writing code. (Actually individual programmers have been writing code all along, and when the design has been accepted, they emerge with the first shaky modules of alpha software.) Alpha takes a long time. To qualify as alpha, the product should include all the planned functions and the interface—even if everything doesn't quite work right. The due date for delivery of the alpha product usually gets extended several times. When it is finally delivered, perhaps even accepted by a testing group and blessed with the name "alpha," you must turn in an alpha draft of your manual.

To get started on your alpha draft, you collect everyone's old notes on the design. You may even find some documents titled "Specifications" lying around. Accord this material the respect due an archaeological find: It may not reflect the present version of the product, but it does reflect the dreams of the past.

Start by outlining. Put a lot of effort into developing the structure of your manual, getting agreement from the team on the preliminary table of contents and refining it. Every hour you spend on perfecting the outline means two hours of crises avoided late in your schedule.

Over time you'll see some parts of the product working so you can write about them and record their growth and change. Before you can finish this draft, however, you'll need the alpha version of the product.

As you start writing you consult company standards. You may be handed a template to work in, or a set of writing guidelines. There may be a company book design you have to live with. Essentially you are getting all your tools in order and making sure they are sharp.

Your word processing or desktop publishing software gives you control over the format of every character and the layout of every page. You need to understand your organization's book design, if there is one; if none exists, hire someone to create one or, in the worst case, invent one yourself. As you write, you format. Even your first draft should look like a photocopy from a book. (Later your files may go directly to typeset pages or the film a printer uses to make plates, without anyone else intervening, except perhaps to make sure you have been absolutely consistent in your formatting.) This approach offers you two advantages over the older approach, in which you had to write without knowing what the pages would look like:

- You get to see the page almost the way a reader does. You can adjust what you say to reflect that an illustration appears next to the text, or you can change the format to emphasize an important point.
- You can modify the book design intelligently at an early stage so that everyone who needs to review the changes and OK them gets the opportunity.

Here is what your alpha draft does:

- It describes the alpha product accurately—no mistakes, every keystroke right, no functions left out (although you can flag a few with a note saying, "This function not yet implemented").
- It carries out the ideas you offered in the documentation plan. The material is complete, covers all the functions, deals with every task a customer might want, and has an organization that meets the needs of people who will be learning the program, looking up material, or solving problems. You have included all sections, plus a table of contents, appendices, and maybe a glossary and empty index (without page numbers).
- It includes preliminary drawings or descriptions of all art you intend to put in the manual.
- It meets current standards of usage and format.

The amount of time it takes you to outline and write the alpha draft varies enormously, depending on when you enter the project, how many weeks you are allowed, and how many other projects you've been assigned. At least half of the time available for writing the manual should be devoted to the alpha draft, and most of that should be spent outlining. The cleaner the structure, the faster your beta and final drafts can be produced.

Beta documentation (the second draft)

To move on to the beta draft you need comments from people who reviewed the alpha draft, including, if possible, comments by an editor. You also need each version of the product—the pre-beta, near-beta, almost-beta, and eventually the real-beta versions. When the product finally does reach the status of beta, it should include all the functions that will be included in the final release and exactly the same interface that users will see when they open the box. But beta products do have some bugs: The product crashes occasionally, obscure calculations don't come out right, in certain circumstances you can't perform functions that work at other times. The team should agree that no more changes will be made in the design, or at least that no further changes will be visible to users, so you won't have to document them in the manual.

Your beta draft does all this:

- Reconciles conflicting feedback from reviewers. (If possible, get the reviewers together in one room, and ask them to thrash out their differences.)

- Incorporates all wording changes suggested by reviewers of the alpha draft. Some of these involve technical inaccuracies. Some affect style. Some force you to rethink your organization. Keep the reviewed drafts and mark off the changes as you make them. You must reject pleas from marketing to inject hype and from engineering to turn ordinary English back into jargon. You may even want to write memos to the key reviewers, pointing out which of their suggestions you have and have not accepted.

- Adjusts the structure to reflect your agreement with any editor who reviewed the alpha draft. (From now on you pray you will not have to change the organization of the manual.)

- Documents all changes to the product since the alpha version.

- Includes all screenshots within the files or, if a production team will be taking over, in separate files for them to modify and place in position.

- Provides, usually in attachments, the rough sketches an artist has created for conceptual diagrams.

- Corrects all problems you've noticed in usage, design, grammar, and spelling.

Your beta draft should be so good that you are willing to have it tested by experts who can verify its accuracy, and by typical users who can see if it helps them learn to use the product.

You print out pages that look as if you had photocopied a book. The art may appear in place, or you may leave that to the production team to put in. You have used your word processing software to make your pages look like the final book.

Writing the beta draft does not take nearly as long as outlining and writing the alpha draft did. But you will probably feel as if you are juggling a few too many balls at the same time. You have a lot of little knots to untangle. Timing also depends on how much the product changed, how many comments you got, and how long your alpha draft was. For a 100-page manual you might take three or four weeks to produce the beta draft. Then again, you might have to fix it in a week.

Final documentation

To write the final draft, you need comments from people who have reviewed the beta draft—including detailed notes from an editor if one is available—at least two weeks before the final draft is due. And you need confirmation that all bugs in the product have been fixed and no changes have been made affecting what users see and do.

Here's what the final draft does:

- Incorporates all changes suggested by reviewers of the beta draft and all last-minute enhancements in the program—at least those that affect what the user can see or do.

- Updates all screenshots for areas that have changed.

- Provides beta versions of the conceptual diagrams, either within the file or attached to a paper draft.

- Corrects grammar, spelling, usage, and formatting so that you consider this manual perfect. Well, almost.

To complete the final draft usually takes about as much time as you took on the beta draft.

Once the product has been pronounced final, it goes through heavy testing and fine-tuning to speed it up and make it more efficient. You don't care about that process now, because you may be working with an editor and someone who handles production to comb through your final draft, making sure that you have organized it clearly, written it so the audience can really understand it, obeyed all company conventions, and prepared the file so that it can be handed off to the production team. You just want to know if the engineering team makes any last-minute improvements that would render some paragraphs inaccurate.

You may have to answer hundreds of picky questions, reach a mutually acceptable compromise on some issues, and bow to pressure to meet some standard you had ignored.

Production

Before it's released, the product must pass many tests by people in the quality assurance department. Then an absolutely final, truly perfect version is built. In some software companies that's stored on a disk called the Golden Master—the disk from which all other disks are manufactured. Then someone starts duplicating all those disks, putting labels on them, and fitting the disks into the box with your book. So your book has to be ready in time for shipping.

You or the production staff members see the final draft of your manual through the printing process. Your electronic files form the basis for the material the printer will photograph to make plates for printing. If you are in a startup, you may now have to incorporate all art in your pages, laser print a copy, and give that to the printer as a master. If you work for a larger organization, a production team may add the art for you (retouching little patches here and there, shrinking everything to a standard size), and double-check all your formats, perhaps even switching to a special corporate font you did not have on your computer. In other organizations the production team may drop your word processing files into a desktop publishing system and then place the pictures, choose page breaks, and do some fancy adjustments that your word processor couldn't handle, such as adjusting the spacing between the letters in a heading. Even when a production team takes over, you're involved: You have to answer dozens of questions to keep the work going. And every time a version gets laser-printed, typeset, or turned into film, you have to proof.

During this process you should not tinker with style. Fix typos, yes, but don't take the chance of introducing new errors. You should not write anything new, unless it's absolutely necessary to correct errors that could trash the product, the data, or the user.

The time it takes to finish the proof stages depends on the length of manuscript, the number of absolutely-the-last changes in the product, the number of trial runs, and the quality of the production team. If your company has not really worked out a book design, you're in trouble; you can count on this process keeping you up nights—anywhere from a few days to six weeks. You can get an estimate from the production coordinator if your company has one.

Printing is out of your control and takes from four to eight weeks, even if you aren't printing very many copies for the first release. During printing you don't have much to do. You might get some samples to look over, and if your company does not have a production specialist, you may have to go to the printer and look at the first pages as they come off the press. In most companies you've already been assigned to another project.

The production process includes

- Cleaning up each piece of art, putting it into position on the page, and making sure that it shows what you say it does.

- Adding front matter, such as copyright information, disclaimers, and title pages, and back matter, such as the final index with accurate page numbers.

- Making sure that every page works as a page, without leaving a heading at the bottom of one page or a single word at the top of the next page.

- Proofing the final printout.

- Having the word processing or desktop publishing files typeset or made directly into the film a printer uses to prepare plates.

- Proofing the typeset or film material.

- Pasting any typeset pages onto boards for the printer. If you are using separate photographs or line art, then those may be pasted onto the boards now.

- Proofing the blues (prints made from the first negatives prepared by the printer, before making plates), spotting little splotches, perhaps even the printer's fingerprints.

- Confirming that color is being put in the right spots.

- Printing and checking the pages as they come off the press, adjusting colors, checking solid areas for blotching, confirming that the ink is even across each page, and, oh yes, making sure the pages are in order. (One Bible publisher discovered during a press check that it had left out Genesis.)

- Writing up a project history to pinpoint what worked and what didn't and to leave notes for any other writer who may have to correct, update, or revise the documentation later.

The first bound books go right to the warehouse, where teams pop them into the boxes, shrink-wrap the boxes, and pack them for shipping. In a few weeks you may get to see the actual bound book yourself.

Maintenance

A much smaller team now takes over responsibility for keeping the product running and eliminating any bugs that pop up when the customers start using it. The maintenance team may make some small adjustments to speed some calculations or iron out minor difficulties in the interface, but basically they just keep it running. Maintenance may go on for years. You might think that a product, once released, could just run by itself, but circumstances do change, and that means someone has to make minor adjustments.

Change pages

Occasionally these changes affect what users see or do, and you must rewrite all or part of the manual. In addition you may discover mistakes in your own manual, or customers point them out, so you must send out errata sheets or change pages, postponing the day when you have to update the whole manual.

Updating

Eventually the team may decide it's time to add a passel of new features and improve the user interface. A major housecleaning—a product update—is in order. An update is a new release of the product, but not one that changes so many features and functions that even an experienced user might get confused. An update is supposed to be an improvement of the current release, whereas a new release will look and feel different and offer features never before seen in the product.

Patches

If the original manual seems clear, see if you can patch it. The danger is that you fix one reference but miss another. To minimize the number of plates that have to be changed at the printer, you may be urged to make changes that do not spill over to affect other pages.

If the original manual now looks like a mess, you'll probably need to rewrite it. That's better than trying to apply compresses to the wounded parts. You should start from scratch again, but at least this time you are familiar with the way the product works, and the released version runs without crashing very often, so it won't take as long to learn the new version and go through first, second, and final drafts.

Migration

Sometimes a computer itself becomes outdated. Management, however, doesn't want to waste the money spent developing the product, so they assemble a team to port (as in *transport*) the product onto a new—faster, smarter, smaller, more powerful—machine. The boss announces, "Let's migrate!"

Rewrites

Even though the product will do just about the same work as before, users will probably have to learn a new keyboard or a new set of procedures. The more the interface changes, the more likely you'll have to do a major rewrite. Depending on how much time has passed, you may rewrite the old manual or start a new one. If you're migrating to several platforms (different computer systems), you may want to create one file and write different paragraphs for each system. With some word processing and desktop publishing software, you can make these paragraphs conditional, so that you say at the beginning, "Show me just the paragraphs that apply to the Macintosh," and the software hides, temporarily, the paragraphs that apply to other computers.

Looking back...

When the project team first starts making schedules, their management software shows that you are on the critical path. That means if you don't deliver the manual on time, the whole product release will have to slip. For a while everyone in the team eyeballs you as if you were dragging your feet. Actually the problem is not you but the production and printing time necessary for any book. No one else on the team understands why it should take two months to get a file into print, when they just issue a command and laser-print a memo at the nearest printer.

As the project nears the final product, amazingly hundreds of bugs appear, sometimes thousands. The team no longer regards you as the potential roadblock. They have enough work to do just debugging.

You must get your manual in on time, and you will, in part because it's easier to plan and schedule writing than programming. Eventually you'll be the one going around asking, "So when's the product going to be ready?"

Glancing ahead ...

In the remainder of Part One, you'll learn how to plan for success—gathering the information you need, defining your audience, learning the product, organizing the documentation, setting up and revising your schedule, and getting down to work.

In Part Two you'll learn how to write different kinds of documentation, such as procedures, tutorials, or online help.

And in the last part of the book, you'll find out how to get good feedback, and revise your manual.

Checklist

Here are the major phases in the product cycle. Underneath each you see what documentation work you may have to do during that phase.

Request phase

☐ Preliminary estimate

Design phase

☐ Documentation plan

Implementation phase

☐ Outline

☐ First (alpha) draft

☐ Second (beta) draft

☐ Final draft

☐ Production

Maintenance phase

☐ Change pages

Updating

☐ Patches

Migration

☐ Rewrites

Gathering Information

*Get your facts first, and then you can
distort them as much as you please.*

—Mark Twain

Gathering information about a product is like opening up a giant fish, discovering a dozen smaller fish inside, and cutting those open only to find hundreds more, each with its mouth around two tinier fish. In fact, the process of collecting facts never stops. Even when you've got the manual printed, you'll hear of mistakes to correct in the next edition.

Before you write, as you write, and after you write, you collect information—from the beginning to the end of a project. Learning is essential to this job. At first, when creating your document plan, you're looking for crude approximations—the gist of what you'll have to cover. As you write each draft, you get to know the product better.

Here are three important strategies for collecting the facts:

- Become an energetic and inquisitive reporter.
- Participate with the team, as a full and active member.
- Read everything you can get your hands on.

Become a good reporter

At first you may be almost as inexperienced with the product as a beginner. That's fine. In fact, it's a help because you're in a position to ask exactly the questions beginning users might ask:

- Is this product for me? What does it do?
- What benefits will I get from this product?
- How complicated is it to learn? To use?
- Can I use a small part of it to do real work right from the start, and put off learning the trickier functions?

If the technical terms are buzzing past you like mosquitoes in a swamp and you can't take notes fast enough, or you know that a week later you won't be able to read what you've written, carry a small tape recorder with you and use it. When you're interviewing turn it on, put it down, and leave it alone. Both you and your subject should just forget it's there. Transcribe exactly so you know just what the engineers have said; then attempt your own interpretation, and take that back to the engineers to ask, "Is this accurate?"

Use the product, if you can, to confirm what people tell you. Try out every function, and whenever you think of a question, try to answer it yourself. You want to winnow out the easy questions and focus on the ones you really can't answer yourself.

Beginning writers often stand in awe of experts, with their backpacks full of technical know-how, and approach them apologetically. Some technical people may not value documentation or understand the importance of taking the audience's point of view. As the project schedule slips (and software projects almost always slip), the engineers work under increasing pressure. Time seems short, and so does their patience. Thus the stage is set for encounters that writers often find frustrating, even humiliating.

Perseverance pays off. When you first start asking questions, you may be as inexperienced as a beginning user. But don't let your ignorance embarrass you or hold you back from talking to the experts. Your inexperience is an asset because you can ask exactly the questions members of your audience might ask. Don't accept an answer that you don't really understand just because you think you ought to understand it. Keep asking. Your inability to understand usually indicates that something really is unclear, not that you're stupid. Your naive questions often bring up issues that the experts have not thought through completely and save them a great deal of trouble down the road. Put your questions in different terms, if necessary to get them across, and request answers in different terms, until you really have the information you came for.

Ask questions and talk, talk, talk

Get an overview of the audience and the product as quickly as you can. Interview, question, listen, and talk to develop depth, and then revise your overview. We stress talking as well as listening because by talking you quickly discover whether other people can understand what you think you have learned.

To get at the fine details, make time to have conversations— scheduled and unscheduled—with the programmers, analysts, and marketing team. You're writing for the users of a product, so you're also figuring out how to tailor your manual to their needs. Most writers find these conversations inspiring as well as educational.

Like a good reporter you should be patient, polite, sympathetic, and persistent. You may find the personalities of the engineers you converse with very different from your own. Allen Watson, a writer who has worked closely with both programmers and hardware engineers, asks,

> How do you form an intense relationship with people whose backgrounds are radically different from yours, whose style of expression is different from yours, whose prejudices about the product and the company are radically different from yours, whose work habits are so different from your that you never see them?

> It's almost impossible to describe to programmers or hardware people the narrowness of their view of the product because they have no vocabulary in which you can describe such a thing. From their point of view, they fully understand the product. They designed it, they made it. It is theirs. Unfortunately, their point of view is radically different from the point of view of most people who will be using it.

Today more and more engineers recognize that they do not see things the way customers do; still, they want people to use all of the functions built into the product. These engineers understand that you can help make sure that customers get the most out of the product; your manual may show customers how to use some of those functions the team has just spent so many months preparing. In this sense, you are the engineers' interpreter.

Make sure you understand what you're told

When they talk to one another, programmers and engineers use a verbal shorthand—the jargon peculiar to their area of expertise. Within the culture of a particular company, they also often develop local meanings for otherwise commonly understood words.

Don Reed, who has written manuals for programmers who want to know more about operating systems, says,

> Programmers tend to be more precise about the things that have to be understood perfectly in order to get the program to run correctly. But they are less precise about names—they often call the same thing by different names in different places.

Reed pleads with programmers to write notes. "Sometimes I've had to corner a programmer, and sit down and take dictation at the keyboard. They'll say, 'Well, what you say here isn't quite right,' and I'll say, 'What would you say?' And I type that in."

Keep talking and asking questions until you understand the subject at hand. You may be tempted to fill in a gap in your knowledge by acquiring the right jargon, but don't settle for anything less than understanding the subject in your own terms. You can explain only when you understand and can translate jargon into terms your audience will recognize, and communicating complex ideas with metaphors that would otherwise never occur to you.

Sometimes it helps to take notes as the ideas come to mind, just to get them down.

I can't see any difference between clearing and cutting in this product; neither one puts anything into a buffer for future use. I asked the programmer, Aileen, what the difference was going to be, and she said it was a modal issue. What's that? They act differently, depending on what mode you are in. <u>Which modes</u>? Edit mode vs. Graphic mode. Evidently I have only tested these commands in Edit mode. In Graphic mode, Clear wipes out the selected objects, or if nothing is selected, the whole page. Cut just removes the selected item; if nothing is selected, you cannot choose the command. I now realize we never got back to Edit mode. What will the difference be, when she's got that working right? <u>Check this out next week.</u>

Later you formulate the exact questions you want to ask a team member.

Aileen:

In Edit mode, what will Clear do differently from Cut?

    1) If some text is selected

    2) If no text is selected

Become a member of the team

Many programmers and engineers appreciate your work. They understand that a good manual will encourage people to use the product and cut down the number of calls on the hotline. A few may be hostile or condescending; you'll need to win them over. Educate them about the work you do, the special skills you've developed, and the place and value of your work in the overall scheme of things.

Here are a few ideas on how to work together with the other team members. Not every idea will apply in every situation.

Talk with the team leader first

Ask the team leader to encourage team members to cooperate with you. Make it clear that the manual depends on information from the team. If you're not getting cooperation, point that out, and give the team leader an estimate of how many months this lack of cooperation will add to the schedule.

Say what you're going to do

Let everyone know what you intend to do—and then deliver. When people know that you do what you say you're going to do, they don't feel they're wasting their time talking to you.

Keep everyone informed—even the people you don't think need to know (because they may). When the project begins to miss its deadlines, revise your own schedule and explain the changes so no one expects you to meet the deadlines you set up earlier. When you tell people what you're up to, they don't mind returning the favor and letting you know what they've just done. Stay up to date.

Be prepared

To show respect and courtesy to the rest of your team, be a good scout.

Do your homework. Take an organized list of questions to each meeting. Read every memo from the team. Try out the latest version of the software.

Learn the lingo—fast. As soon as anyone on the team drops a new term, ask what it means. When you do understand it, use it to reassure them that you are following their conversation. (But don't put it in the manual unless you must.)

Don't make people repeat themselves. Once you've learned something, don't make team members repeat it. But if you don't get it, ask again and again until you do.

Recognize that others are creative. Programmers are creators. You actually have more in common with them than either one of you imagines. Show you've really explored the product they're creating.

Advertise

Make it clear why your work will help justify the product, sell it, simplify what users have to do, cut down on hotline calls, and postpone users' demands for drastic overhauls. Remind them that manuals are part of the product and that good manuals sell hardware and software—within your organization and outside it.

Participate in developing the product whenever you can

When Susan Meade joined a team developing a data base, she recalls,

> They were talking about every word that was seen on screen, wondering whether that was the right word. For instance, whether we were going to call the place where you enter a certain type of information a *field*. *Field* is a term that comes from old-fashioned data bases, but we also had a filing product that was supposed to be friendlier, and it used *Category*.
>
> So there were arguments between marketeers who wanted something that would look like the filing product but be bigger, and engineers who wanted their product to be looked at as a real data base, with *fields*, not some fly-by-night little thing with *categories*. It took forever to decide what terminology to use.

You have a lot to offer, even when you don't know programming. Here are some ways to make a contribution:

- **Write down your suggestions.** If you think something in the product should be changed, write down your ideas. Offer well-thought-out reasons for your suggestion; don't rely on emotional appeals.

> Suggestion:
>
> In designing the dialog box for the Units Preference command, I think we need to let the users change the units for the whole grid, and show the effect of the change inside the little box, right away, instead of waiting for them to click Apply. This way they can see what they've chosen before deciding whether to use it or not, and clicking OK. Also, this follows the pattern we've established with the ruler units. When someone changes one of those, we change the imitation ruler inside the dialog box to show what the effect will be. The user can then revise, or OK the change.

- **Study the principles of human interface design.** Often, when you hit a feature that's hard to explain, you're bumping into a violation of the rules. Learning the rules will help you articulate what should be changed and why.
- **Write down any problems you encounter**—with people, the product, or the schedule. As you learn the product, you may be the first person trying to use it in a realistic context, so you become an invaluable source of bug reports.

As the product moves forward you may also find you're at the center of its development, with different technical people working on parts of it and no one really knowing what the others are doing. You can see how the pieces fit together—and make a fuss when they don't. Writer Susan Meade recalls,

> I knew more about how the whole program worked than the individual programmers did, because they never really looked at the other person's stuff until it was time to integrate the programs. I pointed out that the terms one programmer used didn't match what the others were using, that there were three different ways of doing the same thing, and I asked them to settle on one way, throughout.

As you explore, you develop an increasingly sophisticated model of the product, and you can spot inconsistencies, lapses, and gaps before anyone else on the team does.

Read everything

Writing grows from other writing. You won't want to copy more than a phrase or two from a one-foot stack of documents, but you need to absorb the important facts and make sense out of the details.

Collect written materials of all kinds

Cast your net wide to gather documents such as:

- The original request for the product, marketing requirements document, or the proposal for financing. These should outline what it should do and why.

- Flowcharts or diagrams that show how the product works or how information flows through the product. These are very helpful if current.
- Detailed descriptions of the way the product should perform its functions (functional specifications).
- Description of the planned user interface (user interface specification).
- Actual code—computer programs or schematics—if you can read these.
- Memos, reports, proposals, cover letters—anything that might give you an idea what this product is for and how it should work, eventually.
- Electronic mail. Get yourself put on the appropriate E-mail mailing lists. Subscribe to everything at first, and then narrow the list down as you learn who you need to listen to. Print out what you need and add it to your files. Don't forget to search internal bulletin boards and E-mail archives for historical material that might shed light on a current problem.
- Marketing blurbs. These may tell you a lot about your target audience.
- Testing protocols and reports.
- Quality assurance and customer support reports on problems.
- Manuals for similar projects, including internal documentation for the maintenance programmers.

It's a good idea to stamp the date on each piece of documentation as you receive it. You might also mark "New" on a new version of a spec, for instance, and "Out of date" on the old version, so you don't use the wrong one later. This kind of fussiness can prove its worth if you ever need to trace the ups and downs of a product's feature set in order to justify your request for more money.

At times you may feel like a pack rat jammed into a nest stuffed with paper. Most of it can pass through your hands once and be filed or thrown away. To put all this information at your fingertips, try to boil everything down into three working documents that you can use as references and guides during the life of the project:

- Audience profile
- Product profile
- Documentation plan

Curiosity is a job requirement for technical writers. You get a chance to find out how new machines and new programs work, to test your conclusions, and to ask more questions. You're paid to learn.

Checklist

If you have succeeded in collecting the information you need, you have done all or most of the following:

- ☐ Interviewed everyone on the team
- ☐ Asked questions until you understood each fact
- ☐ Double and triple-checked to confirm you understood
- ☐ Participated in the team's work, offering suggestions, pointing out inconsistencies
- ☐ Announced what you intended to do and did it
- ☐ Prepared yourself for further interviews
- ☐ Advertised the importance of a useful manual
- ☐ Contributed to the development of the product
- ☐ Collected every scrap of written material about the product, dated it, and sorted it out for easy access later

Understanding Your Audience and Their Work

I attribute the little I know to my not having been ashamed to ask for information, and to my rule of conversing with all descriptions of men on those topics that form their own peculiar professions and pursuits.

—John Locke

3

When you begin work on a manual, the biggest question you face is, who will be reading what I write? Your answers will suggest an appropriate structure and style for your writing.

The more you know about the groups of people within your audience (usually you write for several groups), the more you can shape your prose so they understand you, and the easier it will be for you to organize your information so they can find what they need. Your understanding of your audience can determine whether your manual succeeds or fails.

Unfortunately many writers begin with only a hazy sketch of their true audience. You may be given a label, which often is just a stereotype, or a dismissive statement such as "Oh, this product's aimed at middle managers."

If you don't know exactly who is listening, you may make your audience angry at your complexity, wary of your oversimplifications, puzzled by your assumptions about what they do, and, ultimately, frustrated in their efforts to find what they need.

Knowing your audience means you can write about what they want to know and what interests them, cut material they find irrelevant, set your viewpoint at their eye level, and set your level-of-detail thermostat to match their comfort zone.

You need to consult with anyone who can tell you about your audience. Then you can prepare an audience profile.

Locate sources of information about your audience

The most relevant experts are the people who will actually use the product you're writing about. They are the best source of information on the tasks involved in their work. Ideally you'd get to know them by talking directly with them and observing them at work. In fact, you're lucky to meet even one.

Despite your best efforts to meet some real users, most of what you learn about your audience comes from the second-best source of information—intermediaries, people who sell the product to customers, or people who help them solve their problems.

Respect the inarticulateness of users

Whenever you can, observe what users do and ask them to describe what they do. People may find it difficult to articulate exactly how they do a task, but they know they do it. It's easier to steer a bike through a curve going down a hill or lob a ball so it reaches the first baseman than it is to tell someone how.

Remember that when you first started learning some task, you probably needed lots of advice, authoritative pronouncements by experts, step-by-step instructions, and hands-on experience. In the next stage you formed a general idea of the proper sequence, but moved slowly and somewhat self-consciously forward through the steps. Finally the behavior became a habit, and you could perform it unconsciously or with minimal attention to the actions (which is why it becomes hard to describe the process for well-learned tasks).

When you are dealing with people who are whizzes at what they do, watch carefully as they zip through a list of giant tasks and then get bogged down in the details of one particularly nasty problem. You'll probably need to stop and digest what you see; then you can go back and ask more questions to clarify the picture.

Talk to those who talk to customers

Customer support staff and tech support engineers spend a lot of time troubleshooting things that don't quite work. They hear about customers' problems, diagnose the symptoms, and decide on the best solutions. As one man said, "These guys are getting their butts chewed up because some customer made a wrong decision somewhere." The manual or the product interface failed. Perhaps the reference manual warned them in small type, but the customer missed that warning or never understood the rationale behind it. Or the customer started using the product for a purpose that was never covered in the current documentation and is looking for details that the last writer never thought to cover.

Talk to trainers and the people who develop the training materials

When someone actually presents software to users in class after class, that person knows a lot about what confuses people and the functions that cause experienced users to blanch. As trainers refine their training materials, they tend to home in on a meaningful sequence of ideas similar to what you may need to present in a tutorial or general overview. Their exercises may provide you with good examples.

Find ways to learn what users think

See what materials the marketing people have lying around—studies of potential customers, demographics, cost justification models. Sign up early to participate in and observe

- Focus groups
- Trade shows
- Visits to potential customers or field trial customers

Perhaps there's a user's group or product newsletter that will give you a clue to the kind of people who really want to use the product.

Become a user yourself

If the product is far enough along in development, use it regularly. For instance, if you're documenting a fax card, install one in your computer and start sending faxes—even if you don't typically do so. Don't use it just for tests—use it for your own work. You'll quickly find what's easy, what's not, what you should always do first. And if there's a current manual, you'll find what's been left out, what questions aren't answered, what's extraneous, and whether the organization is good.

If you're writing about a product that you can't use regularly or don't have a personal need for, be sure to test it thoroughly anyway. You should have a clear enough understanding of your audience to be able to don their hats for periods of time and use the product in ways they will.

Create an audience profile

All the information you gather will end up in your neatly transcribed notes, in the middle of thick, mostly irrelevant reports, and in hasty scrawls on the backs of envelopes. In this form, or formlessness, the information won't be as useful to you as it could be. Take the time to gather everything you've learned into a profile you can use as a tool when you write the actual documentation.

Again and again during the course of writing you'll find yourself faced with some thorny questions—what to write about, what to omit, how to structure a passage—and you'll see that several contradictory answers are possible for each. You can often resolve such questions by reconsidering what you know about your audience. That's when an audience profile will really demonstrate its worth.

What to put into your audience profile

An audience profile describes all the groups in the audience for your documentation. It describes the characteristics of individuals and groups, their work, and their problems. It explains how the documentation should meet the needs of each group, and it points out what concepts about the product will be especially important for these audiences. The profile consists of four broad categories of information:

- **General characteristics of your audience**—who they are, the titles that identify them, their roles in the work context, their level of experience.

- **Key concepts**—subjects that some people in your audience need to know more about in order to make meaningful choices as they use the product. You may need to expand on these topics in your general introduction, emphasize them in your tutorial, and define them in your glossary. These concepts generally revolve around the ideas embedded in the software or hardware. For example, to someone who has used a typewriter and is just learning to do word processing, wordwrap and automatic formatting are key concepts.

- **Tasks**—the jobs people do, easy or difficult, frequent or infrequent. The structured list of tasks you compile will translate more or less directly into the procedures—that is, the step-by-step instructions for accomplishing those tasks.

- **Problems**—the ones people face in using the product in their work, including the questions they ask in order to solve them. The troubles you uncover and resolve can go directly into a troubleshooting section and, in a broader context, help you take a diagnostic approach, steering people out of trouble at key moments.

Describe the characteristics of your audience

Your audience includes a wide range of individuals performing differing sets of tasks and doing their work in differing social contexts. That means you must understand the needs and resources of particular individuals and the place of the individual in a wider social context.

In general you'll be writing for people who want to get a job done using a computer. These people see the computer and your particular product as a tool or appliance, not an opportunity for 18 compellingly interesting hours of tinkering, troubleshooting, and debugging.

Their backgrounds and contexts

The characteristics of your audience will become clearer and better defined as you develop answers to questions like these.

- **How educated are your users?** Most of the people you'll be writing for know a lot—about their own work and the world. They are not naive. You can figure that some read private newsletters, professional and trade journals, *Business Week, Fortune, Time,* the *Wall Street Journal.*
- **What role does the product play in their work?** What impact will a software product have on the way people get together, schmooze, trade gossip? Some software isolates people, automates their tasks so intensely that they feel stupid and have to rush just to keep up with the demanding computer. Other software makes a job so much easier that people whoop with

pleasure. You need to find out how the product is really going to affect people on the job. Will it motivate them to learn, or will it undermine their willingness to use the documentation?

- **Did they make the decision to purchase?** If not, will they accept the introduction of the product willingly, or is it being forced on them? As the cognitive psychologist Don Norman says, "When we put a new machine into an office, the entire sociological structure of the office will change."

- **Are some people afraid of the computer?** Or are they resistant to the new product? If so, you'll need to offer more handholding and include more metaphors based on their real-world experience, as when the software represents directories as folders, and individual files appear as icons of a sheet of paper.

- **Are different cultural groups represented in your audience?** What percentage of your audience reads English easily? Should you be considering a simplified vocabulary? How do people in these other cultures normally expect to learn? What ideas give them difficulty? How do they expect a book to be organized? What do they consider a problem, and how do they describe such problems?

Levels and types of expertise

People come to a product with different experiences. A person may be a beginner or novice, an intermediate, or an expert in any of these areas:

- Their work, the job they do
- Doing a particular task
- Using computers
- Using the kind of product you're writing about
- Using the particular product you're writing about

You can pinpoint what each segment of your audience needs by locating the level and type of experience in a matrix such as the one in Figure 3-1, which was designed for users of computer products.

If you think someone's a novice, find the Novice row and scan to the right to find the area in which the person might be called a novice. For instance, someone might understand the task domain but be unfamiliar with computers. In that case, what material should you include in the manual? That's what appears in the cell at the intersection of Novice and Using Computers.

Audience/experience matrix .

	Task domain	Using computers	Using this type of product	Using this product
Novice	Explain the basic work flow; show how tasks fit into an overall process; introduce tasks they have never imagined.	Include material about ordinary computer tasks; reasons why (why save?); show basic work flow, standard techniques and settings.	Connect this product to what they already know; make it easy to look up procedures.	Sum up ways in which this product takes off from or improves on earlier or competitive products they already know.
Intermediate	Provide quick access to procedures showing them how to do tasks they already have done before, or have never done but know about.	Point out unusual parts of the interface, modes, work habits for this particular product, how to do tasks. Provide details about each command, such as optional settings.	Compare this product with products in the same application area; give details about commands; index procedures in terms people may know from another product.	Show how to leverage knowledge of similar products and earlier versions of this product; give shortcut reminders; provide details about commands; show how to do rare or advanced tasks.
Advanced	Explain how this product defines the tasks they already know well; show how this product carries them out.	Give tricks and tips for efficiency and extra functionality; give background and details on commands; show how to do advanced tasks; give power settings.	Summarize ways in which this product is similar to and different from other products in the same application area; show how to do a task; give details on commands.	Show how to leverage knowledge of similar products and earlier versions of this product; provide fast lookup of advanced details

Here's an example of the way you might prepare a matrix for your audience profile, if you were documenting an electronic order entry system that you think will be new, in various ways, to all three main groups: data-entry clerks, service technicians, and sales representatives.

A completed sample matrix.

	For those new to order entry	**For those new to using computers**	**For those new to using this type of product**	**For those new to using this product**
Data-entry clerk	We explain the basic work flow and show how their tasks fit into each overall process; they need to see the importance of their work, their contribution.	We will prepare job aids for all ordinary computer tasks; make up a set of step-by-step procedures for basic work flow.	In the introduction we must reassure them that if they've used ABC before, they already know how to do X, Y, and Z.	In a separate section for experienced users of the earlier version, we'll list ways in which this product takes off from or improves on the versions they already know.
Service tech	We'll devote a part of the book to their needs; make all examples relate to service and repair; include all procedures with longish introductory paragraphs, setting the context.	We'll point out differences between this keyboard and a typewriter keyboard; explain telecommunications in the overview.	We'll use the overview to show how this product goes beyond paper-based systems; stress the benefits of an electronic approach.	We'll use many of the terms they learned in Order-All to help them transfer skills; give reminders of shortcuts.
Sales rep	We'll give them their own section and explain how this product saves time and gives them control over work they may not have done before—why this program will help them become better sales reps.	We will point out differences between this keyboard and a typewriter keyboard; explain telecommunications in the overview. (Same as for service techs, but in the sales rep's section.)	We'll list the main benefits of using the electronic form of order entry.	We'll devote a special section to people who have already used Order-All or other competing products, so these folks can leverage their knowledge when learning this one.

Here's what people with varying levels and types of experience tend to need or look for in documentation.

Novice (beginning) users. Beginners need help constructing a workable mental model that connects the task domain with the product. Left to their own devices, they tend to construct overly complex models based upon superstition and ritual. Such models reach dead-ends in practice and become difficult to replace with more accurate representations of the system. Beginners need to understand the sequence of major tasks, and they need to recognize where their job fits in. Beginners don't know how to accomplish the particular little tasks along the way. They do not know how various features or modes fit together; they feel shaky on each step. Many beginners miss out on training, but they need a way to learn key concepts and basic tasks.

Occasional users. These people need the product to do some real work, but they don't use it very often so they tend to forget commands, sequences, tricks. They do not want to know much about the software; they just want to be able to look up a particular task and do it.

Intermediate users. Intermediate users want to look up step-by-step procedures that they haven't become familiar with. They tend to flip through the tutorial as an introduction to this particular product and then use documentation for quick look-ups. They like conceptual overviews as a way of understanding how various parts of the program interact. Another kind of intermediate user is the person who has used the competition's product, knows it well, and comes with suspicion or hope to see how your product performs similar work. They yearn for a section comparing your product with the competition in terms of tasks.

Advanced users. Experts sometimes want to be able to look up step-by-step procedures on tasks they haven't done recently or have never done; they want a quick reference card as a reminder of specific steps or parameters. They like neat tricks and advanced advice.

Decide what key concepts your audience needs to understand

Think through what it is that someone needs to know to make the best use of the product. Note the ideas, the new ways of working, that you should present to your audience.

First, what can a user accomplish with the product? What's it good for? Think through an answer for each identifiable group in your audience as you answer this question. For instance, with a high-end word processor, users can create memos, letters, reports, fliers, form letters, and newsletters—from simple to complex.

Next, are there ways to use the product that make a user's job easier, more productive? For example, without a word processor, revisions to documents are tedious and time consuming. With one they become easy, so the user can stay focused on what he or she wants to say.

Finally, think through the features of the product. Which ones are central or deserve special note? You can't list every feature or idea you may need to explain, but you can point to the large areas. Similarly you may want to alert the team that you do not intend to go into certain topics because they are of no interest or use to your audience. For instance, in a user manual on telecommunications, you might rule out explaining the different lines and services available from the phone company.

Here's a table in which the writer shows which group needs to know something about which topic.

A completed audience/topic matrix.

Group	Printing	Telecom	Price changes
Data-entry clerks	✔		
Service techs	✔	✔	
Sales reps	✔	✔	✔

Later, when the writer is developing separate books for each group, this table answers the question: Should I put this subject into this book?

List tasks your audience must do

Your audience has real work to do—tasks people would have to do even if they didn't use your product. They have bought the product, or been handed it, to get those tasks done faster, better, more efficiently. They still care more about their work than your product, so they want you to organize a major part of your documentation around the tasks they see in front of them. "Tell me how to use your product to do my work."

You need to understand these tasks from the point of view of the customers, as part of their job rather than as examples of "use of the product." Such tasks may include extremely broad and complex jobs as writing a report, or such finely focused jobs as checking the spelling of one word. The more you understand these tasks—as the customer sees them—the more easily you can explain how to use your product to accomplish work, rather than how to exercise various neat features.

Of course, once they begin using your product, people may face additional tasks—chores they have to carry out to get the most out of the product (such as customizing or preparing for first use). But these housecleaning jobs are secondary and incidental, maybe even annoying.

Record every task you can discover

At first be indiscriminate. Compile a list including everything that occurs to you or your informants. If you begin winnowing too soon, you may judge an important task irrelevant because you don't know your customers' work or your product well enough yet.

You may have to include some housekeeping tasks for the product, such as saving, setting preferences, changing the pointer icon, or reformatting the disk directory. But do not just list product features, as if they were tasks someone really wanted to do (for example, using the negative button).

Recognize that software may offer a chance to do something few people did before—reach new goals and accomplish new tasks. For instance, using a style to format a paragraph rather than erasing the paragraph, choosing a new margin, and retyping. In turn, these abilities lead to the development of many styles and the opportunity to import a stylesheet that gives consistency across a series of documents. Include these in the task list. They're tasks your audience will want to do once they know about them.

Analyze the tough tasks

Every once in a while you encounter a task that's hard to understand and difficult for a user to explain. Even engineers get tangled up in jargon when they describe what they think users will do. Then it's time for you to do a task analysis. For example, when each member of the team explains a color calibration feature with difficult-to-pin-down metaphors, and the two lead programmers use very different mathematical expressions, "just to clarify," you know it's time for you to do a task analysis.

(Normally, a systems analyst performs task analyses while developing the functional specifications for the software. If you can, get a copy of the analyst's breakdown of the troubling tasks. If none is available, you may need to carry out a rudimentary version of analysis.)

When you're not sure about the nature of a task, analyze these aspects:

- **Situation**—when people decide they need to perform a certain task. For instance, is it during editing? Or during the initial work? Or as part of the final cleanup? Also, who usually does this task?
- **Name**—what the customer called the task.
- **Decision**—the thinking that goes on beforehand (decision and terms). You want to know the scale of the task, the frequency with which it is performed, its part in a sequence or stage.
- **Objects**—what is being handled: a complete sentence, perhaps, or a circle, or one packet of information.
- **Characteristics**—those relevant to the objects; for instance, the sentence begins with a capital letter and ends with a period, or the packet has no stop bits.
- **Steps**—first you do this, then you do that.
- **Result**—Has the task been successfully carried out?

When you need to, turn your notes into a more formal task analysis.

Notes in narrative form.

In revising I want to take this sentence, which is out of place down here, and move it to the beginning of the paragraph. I could wipe it out here and type it there. But there must be a way to grab it and drag it up there, or something like that. Maybe to move it. So I will select it and then look for a Move command. Here it is. Now it says to click where I want the text to go. Click. OK, it moved!

You begin analyzing the narrative.

In revising **(the initial situation)** I want to take this sentence **(the object)**, which is out of place down here **(characteristic)**, and move it to the beginning of the paragraph **(another object)**. I could wipe it out here and type it there. But there must be a way to grab it and drag it up there, or something like that. Maybe to move it **(decision)**. So I will select it and then look for a Move command. Here it is. Now it says to click where I want the text to go. Click **(steps)**. OK, it moved! **(result)**

The final task analysis .

Situation: revision or edit stage

Name of the task: moving a sentence.

Decision: to move the sentence within the paragraph.

Objects: complete sentence, as a unit and the paragraph.

Characteristic: location of sentence within paragraph.

Steps: selecting the sentence, issuing some command, pinpointing the new location, indicating that this is where the sentence should go.

Result: sentence appears in the new location, and the paragraph reassembles itself around the sentence.

Don't plan to analyze every task. You don't have time, and in most cases you don't need to. Focus instead on the tasks you find yourself struggling to describe.

Group the tasks according to their scale

As you work with the list of tasks, you begin to see that dozens of tasks (changing a font, changing the size of a character, saving in a different file format) can be grouped into major task areas such as editing or file handling. And between the small-scale tasks and the large-scale tasks fall groupings for mid-scale tasks, such as editing text or editing graphics. Often the general tasks a user is trying to accomplish become the large- or middle-scale tasks, under which smaller-scale tasks can be organized.

Depending on the size of the manual, you may devote a chapter or part to a large-scale task, a chapter or subsection within a chapter to a mid-scale task, and a step-by-step procedure to each small-scale task.

Sometimes you discover that what you thought was just a step in a task is actually another task, or what you expected to be a major chapter resolves itself to a single mid-scale task, taking up a few pages in some other chapter. Organizing means reorganizing as you learn.

Use an outliner to make your arranging and rearranging easy. You'll usually alternate between grouping and ordering as you work with your list.

Here's a partial list of tasks for a flat-file database program, an example of arranging tasks by scale.

Large-scale tasks	Mid-scale tasks	Small-scale tasks
Creating a Database	Creating fields	Creating a field Creating a Calculation field Creating a Summary field
	Automating data entry	Choosing entry options Getting information from another file Checking accuracy
Displaying Information in Forms	Creating forms	Creating a single-page form Creating a multiple-page form Creating a label form Creating an envelope form

Arrange tasks in a meaningful sequence

The best sequence in which to present tasks is in the order customers feel most familiar with or can recognize quickly. In general, people do one task and then another, so start by organizing chronologically.

Chronological order. Arrange tasks in the sequences in which they are usually done. Many mid-scale tasks contain a number of subtasks you have to do first, several optional tasks you can do at any time after the beginning, and then several that tend to cluster toward the end of the work session. Other mid-scale tasks fall naturally into a set of tasks on creating, another on modifying, and a final set on erasing, destroying, and deleting.

Chronological order of tasks.

Working with jog points

    Inserting jog points
    Highlighting or modifying jog points
    Changing jogs for sets of wires
    Changing jogs for individual wires
    Deleting jog points

Familiar order. Another way to organize is to go from the known to the unknown. Arrange tasks starting with the most common and familiar and move to the most unusual and foreign. You might want to use this type of ordering when the tasks can be done in any sequence.

Simple to complex. Start with as simple an instance as the product or the real-world work situation permits, and then move on to more complicated tasks. If there are any variations, separate and subordinate them clearly.

Simple-to-complex order of tasks.

Drawing objects

    Drawing lines
    Drawing rectangles
    Drawing circles
    Drawing polygons

One to many. A variation on ordering based on degree of complexity. When you think people will find all the tasks unfamiliar, and time sequence isn't relevant, you might order tasks in a sequence that's likely to represent an increase in complexity.

One-to-many order of tasks.

Selecting

    Selecting a single object
    Deselecting a single object
    Selecting objects by area
    Deselecting objects by area
    Selecting all objects
    Deselecting all objects
    Selecting all but a few objects

Similar objects. Group tasks that deal with the same object or the same type of object. Usually you'll want to combine this ordering technique with another method, such as chronological. In a series of tasks dealing with objects, follow the same set of objects over and over.

Ordering tasks by similar objects.

Adding wires

    Placing the power wire
    Placing the ground wire
    Connecting to power
    Connecting to ground

Adding contacts

    Placing the power contact
    Placing the ground contact
    Placing output contacts

Adding pins

    Placing power pins
    Placing ground pins
    Placing input pins
    Placing output pins

Discuss the task list with your team

You should deliver the task list as part of your audience profile so your team can go over it early in the project, adding and subtracting, changing names, suggesting new sequences. In this way you reach agreement with the team about exactly what user tasks you should cover.

With some revision your task list may form the basis for the table of contents for a section on procedures. But in the early phases of a project, the task list helps make clear to your team that you intend to serve the user by describing how to do ordinary tasks with the software, rather than just describing the software and leaving its use to the customer. According to ancient engineering traditions, documentation should just tell customers what will happen if they issue a particular command. But true procedures tell people how to do a particular piece of work, even if it happens to involve using several different commands. You may have to make a strong case for providing users with step-by-step procedures.

If you anticipate that you may need to change some attitudes, you'll get the issue out in the open early with a task list, and the list will show how much information people need beyond mere reference.

Consider potential problems and solutions

To write helpfully, you need to be able to steer people away from trouble. For instance, many people do not know how to place paper in a printer tray, so you would want to tell them clearly and carefully how to get the paper in the tray before you tell them to perform a step that could cause a jam. Of course, if you never ask about problems or take note of them when you run into them yourself, you'll leave that kind of information out of your manual and let customers handle it themselves, swearing.

As you develop your audience profile, ask users, marketers, and engineers, What problems have people encountered while using an earlier version of this product, or a similar or competitive version? Talk to the hotline and support staff, and if possible listen in on calls from users. You should come up with a damning list of problems. Of course, the answer may have existed in the old manual, but what's important is that the customer couldn't find it and instead called for help.

If you see problems clustering around a particular function, you may want to analyze what customers have been saying. Then you can write a heading that represents their view of the problem, a description of the real symptoms, and a clear set of steps for solving the problem. Here are some questions to use in anatomizing customer queries:

- What is the customer's stated objective?
- Do customers know where to begin?
- Have they made a move the software considers an error?
- Is the structure of the software unclear to them?
- Can they tell what to do next?
- Can they tell how to stop?

Note the way customers formulate their problems and wishes. You should echo their terms in your table of contents, troubleshooting sections, index, and menus for online help.

In presenting a list of problems to the project team, you face a diplomatic issue: you don't want to seem critical of their product or the earlier product of the same kind, but you do need to make clear to everyone what you've discovered about where customers had trouble. You want the team to understand why you are taking a diagnostic approach in your manual. First assure team members that you expect no one will have any problems with the new software. (Try not to laugh while typing that.) Then point out ways that the new interface might avoid these problems and any ways you see to improve it. Finally, state concretely how you are going to steer people out of trouble, and then, if they do get into trouble anyway, how you are going to get them out.

Draw some conclusions

Too many descriptions of audiences peter out at the end, with no conclusions, or with conclusions that do not seem to be based on much thought. So what's the point? After all this analysis, show what difference your study makes.

Here's an obviously inadequate, but nonetheless typical, audience profile:

Audience Profile

This manual is aimed at all 1200 of our supermarket managers. They know a lot about supermarkets, but nothing much about computers, so we'll have to tell them a lot about the interface, processing, input, and output to bring them up to speed. We expect they will need three four-inch ring binders for the documentation.

In this paragraph, we hear two broad generalizations about the audience (they know a lot about supermarkets but not about computers), and based on that slender analysis we get a decision about the four major parts of the documentation. You get the feeling that the writer is just confirming a plan that was made long before anyone thought to ask who would be reading the books.

But how different the analysis and the conclusions that you can draw, when you really interview people! Here's an audience profile for the next version of the same product:

Audience Profile

In developing this audience profile, we have had the privilege of talking to 10 managers who gave us a good cross section of the larger audience. In addition, we have talked at length with the experienced installation team, and with the people who train checkout clerks.

Overview

This manual is aimed at the 1200 managers of supermarkets in our chain. We envision a hundred-page binder with tabs to signal each part—the Overview, the Tasks, and Troubleshooting.

Background and Experience of Our Audience

They know supermarkets inside and out. They know their customers, who are impatient to check out quickly. They all speak English fluently, and they score high on IQ tests. They are all high school graduates, but only 34% have completed college, although almost 90% have taken some college-level courses. They have little interest in computers, except as tools to do their job. Not one has a degree in computer science. They have received on-the-job training on what they have to do to maintain the satellite link, and they will receive a day of training on this new scanning system during installation at their store. To sum up their experience, they are professionals at supermarketing, are intermediate users on computers, and have a good deal of experience on similar systems they've used in the past.

Impact on Documentation

We cannot assume any interest in what goes on behind the scenes. In taking off from the old manual, we should drop all the material about processing. We should focus on what they see, and what they do. In a visual overview, we can introduce the few network concepts they need to know.

Continued

Continued

Key Concepts

We must teach them a few basic concepts. They need to understand the way information flows from one checkout stand to the next, back to the office, out through the satellite dish, and via satellite back to the home office. They need to understand the way information comes back, updated, from the home office, gets stored on their mini computer, and then pours out, as needed, to the individual checkout stands on their little network.

We should not attempt to teach processing. These people do not need to know the details of the multiple data-bases, the way transactions get recorded real time, or the techniques of compression for satellite transmission.

Tasks

These managers must do or supervise the following large-scale tasks (each of which deserves its own chapter):

- Schedule and plan the installation with local construction crews and our installation team; schedule training for all checkout clerks
- Receive the initial transmission to set up the price list on the in-store mini-computer
- Modify the prices of items delivered directly to that store, such as flowers and bread
- Bring up the local network that includes all checkout stands
- Run end-of-day consolidation of all sales, producing day's totals, and transmitting those to the home office.
- Prepare the mini-computer for routine reception of the late-night satellite transmission from the home office

You'll see a list of the medium and small-scale tasks within each of these chapters, in the attached Task List.

Problem-Solving

We must provide a set of questions like those a doctor asks a patient, to help the manager diagnose what's gone wrong. We start with a list of all the possible symptoms someone could see, helping to identify the major problems a manager might face:

- One checkout stand is down.
- Several neighboring checkout stands are down.
- Several checkout stands are down, but they are not next to each other.
- Every checkout stand is down.
- You are getting the wrong price on an item and need to change it.
- An item does not appear with a price.
- One or more items display the message, "Not Found."

If a manager recognizes one of these, we ask further questions, narrowing down the source of the problem. When we think the manager has identified the problem, we state the solution. Attached to this document you will find a list of all the problems identified by the 10 store managers we talked to, and the members of the Installation Team.

Show your team that your audience analysis is really shaping the documentation.

Revise your audience profile

You've included a lot of information in your audience profile: the general characteristics of the audience, a summary of the ideas they need to learn when using the product for the first time, a list of the tasks they'll use the product for, and a list of potential problems they'll encounter, plus a summary of the way in which you'll shape your documentation for these groups.

Your first draft of the audience profile probably will not include full details in any of these areas, but hand it in quickly, anyway. You need the comments and suggestions of the team to proceed. As you take their ideas into account and revise the audience profile, you are, in a real way, developing your manual. You are not just writing a throw-away document, something that gets in the way of the real work. The more you know about each aspect of your audience, the better you'll be able to organize and write introductions and overviews, reference sections, procedures, and troubleshooting material. And by circulating this profile to your team, you are also giving them a preview of the kind of manual you intend to create. That should make for fewer disagreements, surprises, hurt feelings, and revisions later.

Checklist

Your completed audience profile should include these sections:

Characteristics

☐ Background and education

☐ Job title

☐ Role of the product in their work (impact on their work, loss of control, fears)

☐ Purchaser of the product

☐ Levels and types of expertise (a novice in one area may be an expert in another)

Key concepts

☐ What users can accomplish with the product

☐ How the product makes work easier, better

☐ Features needing emphasis, advertising

Task list

☐ Grouped by scale

☐ Arranged in a meaningful sequence

Problems and solutions

☐ Problems with earlier versions of the product

☐ Suggestions for improvements

Conclusions

☐ How this analysis will affect the documentation

Learning About
the Product

I am a camera with its shutter open, quite passive, recording, not thinking.

—Christopher Isherwood

4

When you're in a hurry, you may be tempted to write on the fly, drafting parts of the manual as you learn about the various features of the product. But giving in to that temptation may lead you into many false starts, and you could end up with a manual that's as poorly organized as a first-timer's quilt.

You have to learn the product yourself. You can't just copy notes from engineers. You must understand what the product does, what its parts are, and how they fit together. First understand, then outline and write. It's odd how many times writers, pursued by the Deadline Devil, skip understanding and go right to writing. They end up revising technical notes or marketing, and often make the incoherent original worse by introducing errors. Under pressure we all tend to seek the familiar and avoid the unfamiliar.

When you write from your own understanding, however, you are working on solid ground. You know what mistakes you made as you explored some part of the product, and you can help users avoid those. You can invent metaphors and explanations that would never have occurred to you if you had just paraphrased someone else's memo or the specs.

You put the most effort into learning a product at the beginning—while you're also learning about the audience and planning the documentation. From then on you'll need to spend five or six hours every week just to stay current, tracking developments as features get implemented, changed, dropped, or added.

When you're learning about a product, you travel along five more or less parallel routes:

- Keeping track of the product in a product profile—a document that helps you record and organize what you learn
- Using the software yourself to gain first-hand experience
- Getting familiar with the technology through background research
- Dissecting the written specs for details
- Interviewing experts on the team

If you're pressed for time, you'll still need to follow these routes; you just may not be able to go as far.

Keep track of what you learn in a product profile

Often you acquire your first knowledge of a product before a working version has been constructed. Your first information about the product comes from talking with the project manager or another member of the team, or from seeing a demo of a prototype. Perhaps you're handed a stack of existing documentation and asked to familiarize yourself with it. Before your notes pile up into an unmanageable mountain of disconnected details, take a few minutes to begin organizing what you know into a product profile—a tool for transforming raw information into concepts you feel at home with.

To start a product profile, put all the information you acquire into an outline. Make a giant list of all the features, parts, and commands, and describe them in your own terms rather than those of the functional specification—or the manual you will write. This profile is mainly for you—not the engineers and not the users. It helps you make sure you've firmed up your own understanding before you begin trying to organize the information from the point of view of your audience.

The product profile differs from the outline of the manual. In the profile you structure information in order to analyze; when you create an outline for your manual, you will structure information in order to inform an audience. Usually the product profile isn't even a deliverable. Like your notes, it's a tool strictly for your own use.

Use the product profile to

- Make sure you understand the product **before** you begin organizing subjects from a reader's point of view.
- Confirm with the team that the features you're tracking are indeed the features planned.
- Confirm that you have not left anything out.

Your profile may be especially useful on projects where functional specs are nonexistent, incomplete, or confusing. But even on a project with good functional specs, the different point of view provided by your product profile ensures you will not take anything for granted or get stuck in an engineering perspective.

Here's an example of the first-level headings in a product profile for Rainbow, a hardware and software product that turns a high-end copy machine into a PC printer.

The subject categories point toward the information the writer needs to understand the product.

Rainbow Product Profile

Hardware

Software

Setting Up

Printing

Networking

Rainbow Scan

PostScript Commands

Downloading fonts

Other Applications

Troubleshooting & Maintenance

Testing

In the manual the sequence of subjects partially follows the product profile but is not identical to it.

The manual's setup instructions precede information about using the software, concerns about networking are diminished, and other applications have been eliminated.

Rainbow User Guide Outline

About This Manual

Introducing the Rainbow ColorController

Setting Up the Rainbow ColorController

Unpacking Rainbow

Connecting Rainbow to the Copier

Connecting Rainbow to the Network

Using the Rainbow ColorController

Downloading Printer Fonts

Maintenance

Troubleshooting

Specifications

Index

By the way: use dedicated outlining software for your product profile because such software gives you the most flexibility in structuring and restructuring information. You can move items around easily and quickly view the structure at any level. (You can find more information about using outlining software in Chapter 7.)

List and describe the product's features

Whenever you learn a fact about the product, record it in the product profile. When profiling a hardware product, for instance, include all the components, with descriptions of their functions. List the hardware's inputs and outputs, all its controls and what they do. Record information about maintenance, calibration, and troubleshooting. List safety considerations and warnings. Describe what you learn about the way the product will be unpacked, installed, and set up.

The hardware section of the Rainbow product profile lists each piece of equipment expected to ship with the final product. The Rainbow unit has not yet been designed, nor the monitor selected, but anticipated features and questions about the equipment are noted.

Hardware

1. Rainbow Unit

- On/Off switch is rocker switch in lower left corner.
- Floppy drive is in lower left corner.
- Reset button

2. Monitor

- Does monitor need turning on? Or is turning on Rainbow sufficient? <u>JP to inquire and confirm.</u>
- "Monitor" not "console" (marketing idea: from LL).
- Monitor cables permanently attached to monitor.
- Power cord.
- Video cable.

3. Keyboard

- Keyboard cable is permanently attached to keyboard.

4. Cables

- Which cables are permanently attached to which pieces of equipment?
- Do monitor and keyboard need connecting? <u>HK to inquire and confirm.</u>

5. Rainbow may be shipped with "furniture."

What is "furniture"? <u>HK to inquire and confirm.</u>

6. Resident fonts

7. Shipping

- 4 boxes
- CPU, keyboard, monitor, cabinet (probably disassembled)

When profiling software list all of its features and functions, the various modules, and every command. Describe the software's other controls: all icons, buttons, or tools. List dialog boxes and the software's various windows or screens. Include information about installation, setup, and troubleshooting. List the formats in which information can be input, saved, and output.

For any product keep track of system requirements, such as computer memory requirements, and other constraints.

As you become familiar with the product, you will come across terms that describe concepts associated with the product's use, or technical terms for the product's parts and workings. For example, a drawing program might include terms such as *layer, bezier tool, or cross-section*—all part of the domain in which the software is used. Begin compiling and maintaining a list of terms and their definitions as part of the product profile.

Through casual familiarity with a technical vocabulary, members of a project team often slide into using terms ambiguously or inconsistently, without ever realizing it. For example, on a project for a product that created interactive presentations, the word *link* appeared as a noun (meaning the connection between two parts of a presentation), a verb (meaning to branch or connect), a software feature (the user's ability to connect two nonsequential parts of a presentation), a menu command or tool (used to create the connection), a part of the presentation file (the pointer that tells the presentation to branch to a different location), and an element of the user interface (the icon that indicates a connection has been created). The product profile glossed each use of the term, and by grouping all these definitions, made the distinctions clearer. Use the product profile to confirm that you understand what terms really mean. If you don't understand them, your readers surely won't.

You can circulate the list from time to time to make sure you've reached agreement with other team members about the meaning of each term. As the experienced hardware writer Adam Rochmes says,

> Your list can help the whole team agree on usage and develop the product along consistent lines. Later, the list can help you determine which terms to define in the manual's text, which to include in a glossary, and which ideas need special emphasis.

As you become familiar with the product, you usually learn methods for using it productively and efficiently. The product profile is the place for recording this information. Later it may evolve into procedures for the user guide or tips that you can scatter through the manual.

Organize and reorganize until you are confident of your understanding

Divide the product profile into sections for tracking information about different subjects. Then, within each section, organize the information in a way that makes sense to you. Revise the product profile repeatedly, not only to add to it, but also to experiment with different ways of organizing the information. Revision and reorganization makes you think about the product, and that clarifies your understanding.

For example, you issue a command to a pen-based notebook computer by writing on the screen with an electronic pen. You can begin by organizing a list of commands by name as you hear about them, and then, as you gain familiarity, you can organize them by function.

Use the profile as a basis for questions you submit to other members of the team. If you're using outlining software, scanning the subheads at a given level very quickly locates the gaps in your knowledge and shows you what to ask about. As the profile evolves, you can test the description of the product and the way you organize it on other people to see if you are making sense.

Keep the profile up to date

Plans for computer products are rarely fixed. Particularly when a startup company is developing its first product, plans can exfoliate like an overwatered weed. Developers may want to plug in every idea they've ever had, and venture capitalists may want the product to be all things to all people. The feature list grows and grows.

Tight schedules force the developers to become more realistic. The feature list shrinks as the team has to prioritize, dropping features that are more difficult to implement, postponing others until a future version of the product. T-shirts appear with slogans like "Put it off to Version 2.0."

Organized by name, each writing action issues one command. When you organize the list by function, some commands are part of larger groupings and appear under more than one heading.

Writing actions, by name

bracket, left/right

> Writing a bracket selects a word to its left or right; writing a second bracket selects all the words between the pair of brackets.

caret

> Writing a caret inserts text.

circle

> Writing a circle over a word selects it.

cross-out

> Writing a cross-out or X over a selection deletes it.

question mark

> writing a question mark opens the help facility.

Writing actions, by function

Select

> To select a range of words—brackets (open bracket on first word, close bracket on last word)

> To select a word—circle

Insert

> To insert text—caret

Delete

> To delete a word—circle

> To delete a word or object—cross-out

> To delete a range of words—brackets, then cross-out

Open Help

> To open the help facility—question mark

Revise the profile as features are added or dropped, or when the way they work changes. Reorganize it as the emphasis of the product changes.

Maintain a section in the product profile for features that have been dropped, because you can never tell when a feature will be resurrected. You can easily move its description back into place instead of writing about it all over again, and when the time comes to start work on the upgraded version, your list of postponed features will come in handy.

The user interface for a computer product—the set of rules and conventions by which a person communicates with the computer system—usually undergoes revision as the product grows up. Options move from one menu to another or from a menu into a dialog box, and the appearance of the dialog box changes. The names and graphic representations of icons, tools, and other onscreen objects change. Sometimes usability testing reveals that customers can't understand or operate the product, so the team undertakes a wholesale revision of the interface. The interface metaphor, which helps users associate an unfamiliar electronic environment with familiar objects, may be scrapped and replaced with another. For example, on one project the metaphor for a document management tool started as a collection of lists, briefly used the metaphor of a library, complete with icons representing check-in and check-out desks, and finally ended up as an onscreen office filing system.

Excerpt from the product profile in June.

Preferences Dialog Box Items

Data Format option offers a pop-up list allowing you to pick one of four date formats as the standard to be used whenever you tell the program to insert today's date automatically.

- 10/19/92
- October 19, 1992
- 19/10/1992
- Monday, October 10, 1992

Drawing Start Points option offers a pop-up list that lets you set the starting point (for drawing any object, such as a circle, rectangle, polygon: ask what else?) to be one of the following:

- Top-left
- Center
- Bottom-right

Ruler Grid Units option offers a pop-up list letting you choose one of four preset measurements for the grid and ruler

- 12/inch
- 8/inch
- 4/inch
- 1/inch
  (Will they allow customization?)

Excerpt from the product profile in July.

Format Menu Items

Note: The following three new commands used to be options within the Preference dialog box, and there is still a lot of support for that placement (Al, Sue, and Billy).

Data Format command offers dialog box allowing you to pick one of four date formats as the standard to be used whenever you tell the program to insert today's date automatically.

- 10/19/92
- October 19, 1992
- 19/10/1992
- Monday, October 10, 1992

Drawing Start Points command offers a dialog box that lets you set the starting point (for drawing any object, such as a circle, rectangle, polygon, in fact, any preset object that appears on the tools palette) to be one of the following:

- Top-left
- Center
- Bottom-right

Ruler Grid Units command offers a dialog box letting you choose one of four preset measurements for the grid and ruler

- 12/inch
- 8/inch
- 4/inch
- 1/inch
- Custom: There will be some mechanism, probably a field into which the users can type, showing how many units per inch they want. Lower limit: 64, upper limit 1, no fractions please. There will be some kind of message warning people off of the unacceptable custom units.

You can expect major interface changes up to the release of the beta version of the product. At that point the interface *should* be frozen in its final form because the documentation needs to be finalized so it can be sent to production in time for bound books to show up at the warehouse, on the day the company starts packing boxes. In real life, however, small changes frequently occur up to the release version of the product, making parts of your manual inaccurate before the first customer opens it.

As the product approaches completion, your manual usually supersedes the product profile as a resource for guiding your understanding of the product. But don't abandon the profile too soon. It may be the only complete and up-to-date description of the product in existence.

Use the product yourself

The best way to become familiar with a product is by using it— learning by doing. You gain first-hand experience with the things you need to describe to users, and by putting yourself in their shoes you'll be in a better position to write from their point of view.

Explore the product

If working software or prototype hardware is available, you can learn to use it as a new user might. Dip into the features, a bit at a time. Use it to accomplish some real tasks. As you explore the product, keep notes on everything you discover. Your goal is to explore every nook and cranny, every feature, command, tool, window, and dialog box, and record what you learn in the product profile.

Note your entry points. The features you decided to try first may turn out to be the ones your future readers ought to start with.

Record your first impressions. You may not know exactly why you like a particular feature or why another makes you uncomfortable, but don't ignore these impressions, and do make a note of them. Over time you can refine your perceptions. If a feature is bothersome enough to warrant changing, you can bring it up with the team to see if improvements can be made. If not, you'll know you need to make a special effort to talk readers through that feature. Remember your early experience, so that as you become more familiar with the product you can always touch base with the point of view of a new user.

Note what you wish were available to help you learn. Would you like to watch someone else use the product? Would you like to be guided through the basics until you're comfortable enough to work on your own? Do you wish there were a way to remember steps that you have to do over and over? Your wish list can help you assess the types of documentation the product needs—perhaps a video tour, a tutorial, or a quick reference card.

Find real uses for the product in your own life and make using it part of your everyday routine—if you happen to fall within the potential audience for the product. You'll be able to document the product as an audience insider and may accumulate a wealth of practical tips and troubleshooting suggestions to pass on to readers.

Note the sticky points. What features were difficult to understand or use? Keep track of your ideas for interface improvements so you can bring them up in team meetings. Record problems—features that should work but don't, and fill out bug reports to inform the programmers.

Here the writer mulls over what she knows about a file that seems to be misnamed.

> The database file:
>
> This seems to be a complete catch-all. My impression is that programmers who don't know where the key facts will be just say, "Go look in the database file."
>
> This file is not a database. It is just one long ASCII file. It does not have records. It just contains a string of commands, in no particular order.
>
> In one sense it is data. But again, who thinks of commands as data? These are, mostly, various settings. For instance, what color do you want your background on the screen? What file contains the actual data for your current schematic? What is the main library of routines to be used by everyone in the company, including the current user? But even these "facts" occur inside command strings ("For Main Library, follow this path").
>
> For all these messy reasons, then, I think that the term "database file" is junk. Perhaps "settings file" would mean more to users. ACTION: Bring this up at next week's team meeting, and press them to hand it over to the Terminology Squad.

If you can't use the product yourself...

Circumstances may prevent you from learning by doing:

- No working prototype may be available. Sometimes, when you enter a project at an early point, the product exists only on paper.
- The task domain may be unfamiliar and very complex, requiring special expertise, such as software that engineers use to design integrated circuits.

- The product may be usable only in the actual setting, such as an acquisition/catalog/circulation system for a library.

If not even a prototype is available, you're limited to absorbing the current documentation and trying out comparable products (more about both of these subjects later).

If some version of the product is in use at a test site or customer installation, arrange to observe experts to see what's possible and neophytes to see how they approach learning and how they get into trouble. If your presence on site is welcome, hang around as much as you can. Look for ways in which you can make yourself useful. You may find that some of the users reciprocate by acting as willing teachers.

Many companies marketing a highly complex or technical product maintain training programs or on-site support for their customers. If you're stuck in your attempts to learn the product, get training. A company training program may provide a thorough introduction and indicate which aspects of the product the company emphasizes. Trainers are responsive to customer feedback, and may present the product from their customers' point of view.

Get familiar with the technology

Any product, even a radically innovative one, is developed within a technological context that includes a task domain and competing products. A laser printer, for example, has a historical place in the task domain of creating documents that goes back to typing, handwriting, and even marking on clay tablets. It encompasses technologies such as software controllers, laser beams, and powdered toner. It's marketed in the context of alternatives such as other laser printers, printers that employ different technologies (inkjets, thermal printers, impact printers), and professional printing methods.

Your audience deals with the technological context when doing their daily tasks and when choosing a product. You don't need to learn the technology in as much detail as you need to learn the product. You also don't need to know it as well as your audience: you don't have to become an architect or engineer, for example, to document CAD software. But becoming familiar with the technology provides more common ground from which to address your audience and helps you to collaborate more closely with members of the project team.

Get to know the basic ideas

In addition to learning how the product works, learn the concepts that your audience works with when they use the product. For example, when documenting a telecommunications product, learn about modems, communications protocols, networks, file compression, and encryption. When documenting color image processing software, learn how the human eye processes color, how a video monitor produces color images, how color printing works. Become familiar with terms like *hue*, *brightness*, and *saturation*.

Do some background research. Make a trip to the public library or the library of a local university. Spend some time in your client's corporate library, if there is one. Start with basic books on the subject, and then move on to trade or professional journals. Take a whirl through a trade show, and pick up all the marketing literature to see what's in, and what's not, and, if possible, get a sense of what the latest buzzwords mean, if anything.

Here are one writer's notes on a broad marketing concept.

Groupware: Thanks to the Expo, I've concluded that if a group can use a product, marketing is going to call it groupware, at least for another six months. There are at least four kinds of programs calling themselves groupware:

workflow managers (and task managers)

information sharers

schedulers

electronic mail, networking, and conferencers

Our product falls into the first two categories, in that we help people manage the various versions of a document that many people can work on at once. We depend on the fourth (networks), and we must learn to get along with the third (schedulers). Ask Peggy about interfaces with schedulers. Is this going to be important?

Create a section in the product profile for background information and use it to summarize and organize what you learn.

Get to know the lingo

Familiarizing yourself with terminology is crucial if you want to coordinate your work with that of other project team members, participate in team meetings, and understand what other people are talking about. In addition to terms from the product's task domain, you may find it helpful to learn some lingo of programmers, marketing, and production people. Don't hesitate to ask questions when you hear people using odd or unfamiliar terms. Folks like explaining their own work—at least once.

For easy sorting, reporting, and updating, use database software to maintain a glossary of product terminology. The glossary, which you can continually update with definitions gleaned from experts, periodicals, and manuals, will prove invaluable on project after project. When you need accurate definitions for manuals, you no longer need to hammer out the same wheel again.

Compare other products

If you know about products similar to the one you're documenting, try to obtain and use them. Comparing products helps keep your product's features and interface in perspective. Beg or borrow the competitor's products from someone in marketing—the person who just wrote the analysis of the competition, struggling to establish a marketing position for your product.

You may find features in another product that you haven't noticed in yours. Did you overlook them, or does your product simply not have them? Better check. You may find features unique to your product that make it particularly versatile or easy to use; you may want to emphasize them in the manual to promote the product. You may find another product works in a way that sheds new light on your product's function: For example, what you thought of as fax modem software, you begin conceiving as a document-management system.

When you compare several products with similar functionality, you begin to distinguish between the basic features shared by every product, functions that are essential for the tasks users want to do, and the unnecessary bells and ornamental whistles that developers glue on, hoping to distinguish a product from its competition.

Dissect the specs

Specifications are the team's record of the product. Projects vary enormously in how complete the written specifications are and how frequently they're updated. On a large, well-staffed project, keeping detailed specs up to date may be one team member's assigned task. Other projects forge ahead with little or no written engineering documentation.

Members of the team will expect you to be familiar with the specs. When you join a project already under development, reading the specs may be the quickest way to get up to speed. If the specs turn out to be haphazard or incomplete, keeping your product profile up to date may become crucial for you and the team.

Hardware and software products are similar, but the specification documents may not be. Software usually has a user interface spec; many hardware products do not. The following sections describe the most important written specifications and the use you can make of them.

See the customer's viewpoint in the marketing requirements document

A marketing requirements document, sometimes simply titled "Requirements," appears when the company begins thinking about developing a product. Like an in-house request for a product, this document describes what the product will mean to its audience, lists the main features and related benefits of the new product, and compares it to the current competition.

Because the marketing requirements document provides an early description of the product from what marketing thinks is the customer's point of view, reading it can lead you to a first approximation of the audience's point of view.

You can begin learning how the features of the product correspond to the tasks of the audience, what features are especially important, and what will demand space, time, and emphasis in the user documentation. You may also find the names of similar products to try out.

Part of a marketing requirements document, spelling out what features the marketing group wants in the product, along with the supposed benefits for a customer

Features and benefits, Part 15: Kerning and Tracking

We must offer the abilities to turn on or off automatic pair kerning, and to kern a pair by hand. Even better, we should offer the ability to kern a selection (anywhere from two characters to a full paragraph). And we should be able to offer several tracks, from loose to tight, for any length of text or a paragraph.

Tracking

Features	Benefits
3 kinds of tracking: loose, medium, tight	Easy to change the overall color or look of a paragraph, without having to set numeric values yourself or do individual kerning.
Preset tracks for 24 standard fonts	Better tracking because it's based on the particular fonts.
Custom tracking	Lets you adjust tracking for a new font, set your own values, or adjust the default ones; means greater control.
PostScript output	Your PS file says it all; no need for extra adjustments or files when you send your document to a service bureau for typesetting.
Display tracking values as numbers or graphs	Lets you see the difference between one track and another, adjust them numerically or visually.

Learn how the product should work, with functional specs

Functional specifications describe in detail what the product should do and how. Complete and detailed functional specs may provide the same information as your product profile, but the product is described from the point of view of engineering. You'll often get the sense that you are reading notes from a meeting. Many sentences begin "If the user clicks button A" and then tell what would happen. Features are sometimes grouped around the technique engineering will use to make them work. This makes sense for engineering, but not for your understanding or that of your audience.

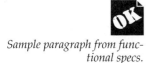

Sample paragraph from functional specs.

Tracking values can be specified with a precision of up to 1/500 of an em in the Character Spacing dialog box. Tracking must be based on point size. One em equals the point size. Tracking can be turned on and off, separate from kerning. The user can turn kerning off and still use tracking. If tracking has been turned off, we default to the font's own track. Whenever a font is chosen, and tracking is on, we look to see if we already have defined tracks for that font; if so, we use the Medium, and allow users to switch to the other two. If not, we apply the Standard. Users can then customize the Standard, using the Custom input field. To create the Custom track, users must select a specific increment, in 1/500ths of an em to be deleted from the space between characters or added to it. The user must type the value into the field and confirm with OK.

You might expect specifications to serve as a set of working plans for the construction of something. The specs for a building, for example, list all the materials, hardware, and fixtures the contractor needs to buy, and where they belong in the finished structure. In contrast, software specs often change as the testing of prototypes reveals weaknesses or missing features. In this case the specs sometimes serve as a record of what's been done so far, and sometimes as a plan for what will be done next. They aren't necessarily a blueprint for the final product.

If the project is strapped for time or money, the specs may not be kept up to date. Even on the most thorough and well-funded project, development goes on continuously, while the specs freeze a moment in time. By the time you receive a spec, it's often at least mildly out of date. Use the functional specs to develop a complete list of product features, but take your list and the descriptions in the specs with a grain of salt. Keep testing the information in the specs for accuracy and consistency.

Look in the specs for priorities, too. If development slips behind schedule, some features may be postponed until future releases. In that case you don't want to have just spent a month documenting them.

Read the User Interface specification to learn how tough your job will be

Software user interface specs describe in detail the rules and conventions by which the program will communicate with the person using it. Complete specs detail everything users will see, and every means by which they can manipulate the program.

Along with working prototypes the User Interface specs enable you to approximate the step-by-step procedures that you'll document in a user guide. An understandable, consistent, and intuitively operated interface means you'll have an easier time documenting the product. There's less to explain, less to rationalize or excuse. A confusing, inconsistent, or difficult interface, on the other hand, suggests you've got tough hardpan to hoe. Making the product usable will be up to you, and you'll have to make up for its deficiencies by organizing information clearly and writing expressively.

Here's part of the User Interface spec.

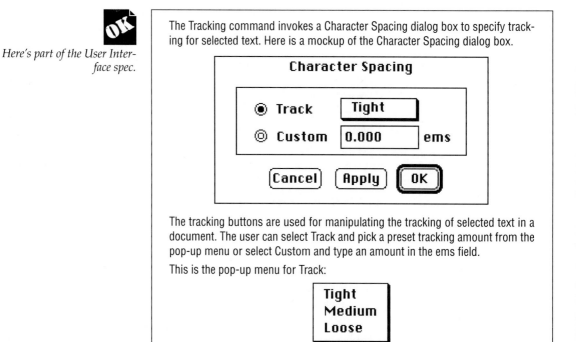

The Tracking command invokes a Character Spacing dialog box to specify tracking for selected text. Here is a mockup of the Character Spacing dialog box.

Character Spacing

⦿ **Track**   Tight

◎ **Custom**   0.000   ems

Cancel   Apply   OK

The tracking buttons are used for manipulating the tracking of selected text in a document. The user can select Track and pick a preset tracking amount from the pop-up menu or select Custom and type an amount in the ems field.

This is the pop-up menu for Track:

Tight
Medium
Loose

Often, User Interface specs are not updated as frequently as functional specs. Because the user interface changes in response to testing prototypes, the specs you receive may be inaccurate. Be sure to check the spec against the actual software, and when you find discrepancies, ask which way the product is intended to work.

Interview the team's experts

Organize your questions to the experts so that you deal with one subject fully before moving on to the next. Sequence your questions within each subject to lead from general issues to specific details. Try not to go back and forth, bouncing from subject to subject or from small detail to broad overview. That's frustrating for the person you're interviewing, because he or she can't assess what you're looking for in order to help you find it.

Your evolving product profile should reveal the gaps in your knowledge. It can help you develop a list of questions to bring to meetings.

Interview programmers and engineers to learn about the product's workings

The product's programmers or engineers can help answer questions on functionality—what's working and not working now—and describe how particular features work, from the point of view of engineering. As the experienced writer Linda Urban says, "If you're using early versions of a software product, you need to know which features and functions will crash the software so you can avoid them." Staying on top of what's currently working can save you lots of time and trouble.

Ask about the inner workings of the product. You probably won't need to tell your readers, but the information will make what you do say more accurate.

Here are some other questions to ask programmers or engineers, after you have tried to figure things out reading the specs and testing the product:

- Exactly what equipment will be required in order to use the final product?
- What steps will users go through to install the product and set it up? (The way users will install the product may be entirely different from the kludges you have to go through when you install it during development.)
- What features have been implemented, and what problems can be expected when using them in the current version of the product?

- What do they anticipate that users want in a certain function, and why did the team build it the way they did?
- What commands are available in the current version, and how do they work?
- What information can users enter and in what format—in dialog boxes or in response to requests from the product?
- What's optional and what's required in particular fields or dialog boxes?
- What might go wrong and how can users recover (and when will these disasters go away)?
- What goes on behind the scenes, unseen by users, during a particular operation?

Talk to marketing people about how to present the product

Marketing people can provide the big picture, helping you capture the essence of the product in a few choice words or in a metaphor familiar to your audience. You'll want to talk to them to find out how they plan to present the product and position it with regard to competing products, and which features or functions they plan to emphasize. (A feature is a particular command or tool; a function is something you can do with the product, and may involve several features.) Their input can be especially helpful in planning overviews and introductions.

Ask marketing people these questions:

- What's unique about the product?
- Why will people buy it (what will they really use it for)?
- How does the marketing department conceive it?
- What promotional material describing the product is available—marketing plans, advertising brochures, sales material?

Interview customer support people to acquire a diagnostic approach

When you're documenting a product already on the market, the customer support staff can be your best source of troubleshooting information. Support staffers are on the phone day in and day out with customers who can't figure out how to perform a task or how to outrun a bug or limitation of the product. In helping get customers out of trouble, support people often become experts with the product.

By the way: Having to devote a lot of people to customer support should indicate to management that the current documentation is inadequate; such costs provide the initial incentive for revising it, but management rarely spots this equation. You should point it out.

Ask customer support people these questions:

- What do customers use the product for? (This is helpful for illustrations)
- Where do customers have trouble?
- What are some techniques for getting out of trouble?
- What undocumented features, customer tasks, and work methods have they come up with?
- Do they have any tips to pass on to help customers stay out of trouble?

Interview trainers to learn their approach

Trainers show new customers how to use the product to accomplish some of the tasks they face on the job every day. Along the way, trainers may also teach key concepts, and provide people with an understanding of the way work flows through the system.

As an ex-trainer, writer Mick Renner says, "In a trainer, you're likely to find an ally, someone who's thought about the learning process and is familiar with both the product and the customer's point of view." Forging a working relationship with training people can be of mutual benefit. In many companies, however, the training department and documentation department often work in relative isolation, so your request to meet may seem outside the norm.

Ask them these questions:

- How do they teach people concepts or train them in specific tasks?
- Which features are essential for a beginner?
- Which key features require special emphasis in the documentation?
- Which features seem to confuse novices the most?

- What training materials—handouts, workbooks, manuals—are available?

Interview various testers to learn about life in the trenches

Companies use testers in various ways. To locate weaknesses and bugs, quality assurance testers may follow a rigorous protocol that pushes the product to its limits in an attempt to make it fail. The idea is the equivalent of slamming a car door 10,000 times, lugging the transmission repeatedly, or crushing cinder blocks in a hydraulic press.

Other testers, called usability testers, monitor subjects as they use the product to identify its strengths and weaknesses as a useful tool. Usability testers typically observe people who have a particular level of experience with the product—beginners, intermediate, or advanced—and then interview them.

If you can talk to usability testers, or, better still, watch them at work, you can supplement your own experience of learning the product. You'll learn the strengths and weaknesses of the user interface and get an idea of topics you must take extra pains to explain in the documentation. Look for

- What's awkward about the interface
- What works smoothly
- What people find hard to understand

Checklist

When profiling hardware, describe the product and the system in which it is designed to operate. Be sure to include

- ☐ System requirements and constraints
- ☐ Components, with descriptions of their function
- ☐ Inputs and outputs
- ☐ Controls
- ☐ Unpacking, installation, setup
- ☐ Maintenance, calibration, troubleshooting
- ☐ Safety considerations, warnings

- ☐ Tips
- ☐ Terminology

When profiling software, make sure you have included

- ☐ Features/functions
- ☐ Modules
- ☐ Commands
- ☐ Controls: icons, buttons, tools
- ☐ Dialog boxes
- ☐ Windows/screens
- ☐ Installation/setup
- ☐ Troubleshooting
- ☐ Tips
- ☐ Terminology

Planning the Documentation

Many things difficult to design prove easy to perform.

—Samuel Johnson

You've started analyzing your audience and you've begun a profile of the product. With a sense of the people whom you're writing for and what you're writing about, you can begin roughing out a plan for creating the various documents. You can save yourself a lot of rewriting later by making some smart decisions now:

- Define the goals you hope to achieve with the documentation.
- Decide what documents will best serve the needs of your audience.
- Outline the contents of each document.
- Describe the book design.
- Determine who will do what when.

The entire documentation cycle looks something like Figure 5-1.

5

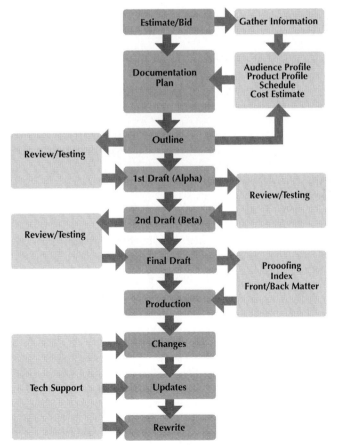

Figure 5.1
The documentation cycle.

Make a written documentation plan

You're sketching out your idea of the documentation. Like an artist's rough drawings, the plan blocks out the major elements of the picture, hints at the style, and lets other people envision the final product. Your plan, then, helps you figure out where you are going and then confirm those ideas with your team.

Think of the documentation plan as the place you record your inspirations, note your assumptions, and come to decisions. A documentation plan doesn't have to be elaborate. You might develop a page or two for a 40-page manual and 10 or 20 pages for an entire suite of materials. But the purpose remains the same: to set your goals and then organize the documentation so it will meet those goals.

Good planning pays off

You may be itching to leap right into writing, especially if you're excited about a new project and brimming with ideas or if you're on a tight schedule. But you'll find it's worth the time and effort to plan first. You'll see these benefits:

- You make decisions up front, rather than as you write. Once you start writing, you'll have a sharper focus, a better sense of the relationship of parts, and a clear idea of where things belong. You won't have to stop midway to determine the book's design, structure, or style.

- As you add more detail to the plan, you bring problems to the surface before they get built into the draft. You can then change the plan before you write.

- You can use the plan to get agreement from the team on what you intend to do. Afterward, if people object to the approach you've taken, the documentation plan shows that you've done what was agreed on.

- On a large project the plan becomes a resource for all the writers and other team members, helping to answer questions such as what goes in what manual and what approach or style to use.

Ironically the time to do planning is often left out of preliminary schedules. Yet to set a project squarely on course, you may need to devote as much as 20% to 25% of the time to planning and preparing the documentation plan, the audience and product profiles, and the schedule.

If those figures seem incredibly high, keep in mind that when you plan thoroughly up front, you're actually performing tasks that you may be used to leaving until later—like considering the structure of a book, its page design, and its production.

Define the goals of the documentation

First figure out what you—and the team—think the documentation should do for the customer. Then define the constraints you have to live with, including drop-dead dates and fixed page limits. Perhaps they will force you to leave out something or treat some subjects rather lightly. If you're considering an unusual approach or one your organization hasn't used, you need to spell that out, too, and show how it grows out of the goals and constraints you've defined.

What the documentation should accomplish

The purpose of paper and onscreen documentation may be to introduce beginners to the product, to help users get up to speed quickly, to present the product as a hot new item in the computer field, or as a simpler alternative to its cumbersome competition.

Ask questions like these to help define the goals:

- Is the purpose of the documents to train beginners in elementary tasks, instruct in key features, provide quick look-up of step-by-step procedures or facts about the product itself, or support hands-on classes that the user will take?
- Is the documentation meant to be comprehensive or to be used with other materials?
- Is a major purpose of the documentation to provide answers to questions that plague users and solutions to common problems?
- Are there particular ideas you want to emphasize?
- Should the bulk of the documentation address the needs of beginners? Or are most users already familiar with the product?

- What is the appropriate tone to use when addressing the audiences for this documentation?

- How should the product be positioned in relation to the competition and earlier versions of the same product? Can the user perform tasks in a new way with this product? Does the product introduce a new way of working or speed up existing methods?

Here's a goal section from a documentation plan.

Goals of the Documentation

- Introduce EverFax as the first product available for use on this platform for receiving and distributing images and other files using the combined technology of the PC and fax.

  - Help users see how easy it is to distribute, file, and retrieve information electronically with EverFax.

  - Show users how to create distribution lists, filing instructions, and other forms that tell EverFax what to do.

  - Teach users how they can best manage the storage of images on their personal computers, using the file management tools provided with EverFax.

  - Provide the answers to any questions people may have about EverFax.

Include the scope of the writing project

Are you providing complete documentation for a new release, rewriting an existing manual, updating a manual for a new product release, or editing a draft? The scope will affect your goals. For example, if you're rewriting a manual when no new version of the software is planned, be sure to include the purpose and intent of the rewrite. If your documentation is for a new version of the product, what will the new version provide that the old one didn't?

Specify any limits

Limitations may also shape the documentation. Are there cost, size, space, or schedule limitations? If you're limited to 75 pages or must plan, write, and produce a document in eight weeks, your direction will be very different than if you can use as many pages as are required and have six, nine, or twelve months to complete the job.

Describe any departures from standard practice

Are there special goals or requirements that dictate a special approach to the documentation? Must you keep documentation to a minimum? Would an approach that relies on graphics serve the product and the audience best? Does the presentation need a style the company has never used?

If you're planning a new approach, think it through early and describe it in your plan as best you can. You want the team to agree to it, and you may need to show them samples of other documentation that takes a similar approach.

The minimalist approach. You might decide to keep paper documentation to a minimum for a variety of reasons:

- Your users can't carry heavy manuals with them to the locations in which they will use the product, so the team wants you to document only what is absolutely necessary—not every detail.
- You must drastically reduce the page count to meet the budget or schedule.
- You decide to put more information online, and less on paper.
- You are writing tutorials or training materials, and you feel that your users would appreciate getting to explore more on their own, with less hand-holding than usual.

The expression "minimalist approach" has been picked up by some managers to suggest that writers should spend less time writing and turn out fewer pages, and they believe that, as a result, the documentation will be simpler and easier to use. This is poor reasoning. To make fewer pages just as useful, you have to spend more time condensing, rewriting, and editing than you would if you could just ramble on.

The main point of the minimalist approach is not just to reduce the page count; it is to get out of the way of the learner—to clear away the apparatus that seems to get in people's way, such as long overviews, unneeded introductions, and padded explanations.

You'll need to decide explicitly what can be left out—and get approval from the rest of the team. You may not be able to do this all at once, because your view of what can be omitted will change over time. Don't throw troubleshooting, screenshots, or the index overboard.

Because you are going to omit some details, it's crucial that you set aside time to test the documents—and test again, and again—as part of designing the document. What works? Don't wait to test just to confirm accuracy at the end of the project. You will need to make repeated adjustments to what you include and exclude.

A visual approach. You may decide to put graphics first and add text just to explain or illuminate—the opposite of the way most of us work, writing first and then adding art for illustration's sake. For a product with a great graphic user interface, starting with illustrations can help you communicate how people should move around, use various tools, and carry out a lot of tasks, without giving people the feeling that you are loading them down with information. They can see most of what they need to know in the art; the text just confirms what they've noticed or adds a detail.

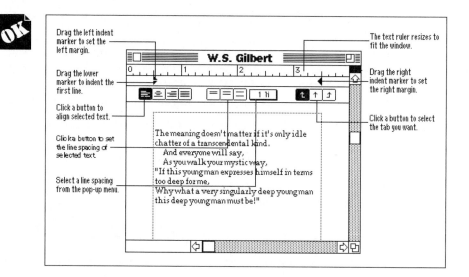

If you're working for a company or a department accustomed to seeing densely packed characters stretch from edge to edge of the page, you may have to prepare sample pages and provide examples from other documents to educate the team about the advantages of a visual approach. Also, choosing a more visual approach can affect page count, page layout, tools for screen capture, and use of artists, so deal with these impacts in your planning.

A new style. Often there's a half-articulated corporate style, and you're expected to lay it on with a trowel. For instance, if the company describes the corporate style as "practical," you may discover that means "Use the passive voice wherever you can, and include lots of jargon." Or, on the other hand, you may hear that your company wants a really user-friendly approach but no jokes, so you are supposed to talk like an extremely sincere steward.

If you're going to try some variations, you'll have to make a case for the change. For instance: "This is the first time this product has included a tutorial, and because this tutorial is aimed at absolute beginners, some of whom have never even heard of a baud rate, we will go against company policy—just in the tutorial—and offer brief definitions of each new concept when it first appears."

Decide which documents best serve the needs of your audience

Now what exactly are you going to write? In putting together the whole set—the documentation suite—consider which document types might form part of your suite. Each type serves a particular purpose, such as teaching basic procedures to beginners or diagnosing and solving problems; and each type tends to have its own book design and style.

Consider the possible types

Here's a list of some of the typical types of documentation. Don't worry at this point whether a single piece will be a whole book, a part, or a chapter. Just figure out which pieces you are going to put together. You may decide to write one or two—or all—of the following:

- **Quick Start**—provides fairly experienced users with only the briefest explanations of key concepts, and abbreviated steps for fundamental tasks such as installing a piece of hardware.
- **Tour**—takes beginners by the hand and shows them what the product can do, with plugs for its most dramatic features (intermediate and experienced users rarely have the patience

for this). A tour gives people a good sense of the interface, so it seems familiar when they start using the product.

- **Tutorial**—shows beginners exactly how to do basic tasks with your product while learning their way around the program and gaining confidence. (A tutorial does not cover every feature; no one needs that much training.) For complex products, you may need a series of fifteen- to twenty-minute lessons. Users with different needs and different levels of expertise can use them to learn specific tasks when they're ready to, without having to do each one consecutively.

- **Computer-based training**—provides interactive training that gives you more control over the user's actions than a paper tutorial can. You can catch many of the beginner's mistakes and offer immediate suggestions to correct them.

- **Procedures**—provide step-by-step instructions on how to use the product, addressing the full range of tasks a customer might want to do.

- **Command reference**—lists all the commands, along with their dialog boxes, choices, options, and little idiosyncrasies, with full explanations.

- **Onscreen help**—puts useful information such as procedures, command reference, and keyboard shortcuts on the screen so a user can see it while working with the software.

- **Quick reference card**—reminds users how to carry out the key steps of procedures or, at the very least, a map showing all the possible menus and commands.

With a large and sophisticated product, you might want to use most or all of these elements as separate books in your documentation suite. On a smaller project, you might turn several of them into chapters in a user guide.

Consider how to meet the needs of each type of user

Make sure you plan a document or a section of a document for each level of experience and each audience type. You may want to make up a table in your notes or in your plan to ensure that you have, in fact, met all the needs of your users.

Audience/document-type matrix.

	New to computers	New to this product	Experienced users	Occasional users	Expert users
Table of Contents		✔		✔	
Visual Introduction	✔				
Tutorial	✔				
Task-Oriented Procedures		✔	✔	✔	
Advanced Procedures					✔
Command Reference		✔			✔
Troubleshooting			✔	✔	
Keyboard Shortcuts		✔	✔		
Index		✔		✔	✔
Online Help		✔	✔	✔	
Quick Reference Card		✔	✔	✔	✔

Responding to the needs of different groups in your audience will likely result in different books (for example, a tutorial and a reference) or different sections within a book. It will also determine what you include in introductions and explanations.

Define each piece and its purpose

Having defined your goals and decided which types of document will best meet the audience's needs, provide a list of each document or section you will create and briefly define its purpose and audience. These are the pieces of your documentation suite—the books that tumble out of the box when a customer starts unpacking.

Here's an example of the definition of pieces for a simple set of utilities.

The Tapestry documentation suite should include:

- A short (12- to-16 page) booklet, How to Set Up, showing how to install and start the Tapestry software. Experienced users can follow the steps, but beginners will want to read the lengthy explanations, as well.
- A User Guide (100 pages), including a 20-minute tutorial for beginners, a detailed set of step-by-step procedures for all users, and a very short command reference, consisting mainly of functional definitions for the curious, followed by a glossary.
- A Tapestry How-To Card, with a condensed version of every procedure from the User Guide, on a six-panel laminated card folded accordion style, for intermediate and expert users who want to be able to look up a small detail.

Describe the relationships between the parts

For each group in the audience, decide what material they should read first, second, and third. Orchestrate their experiences so they can move without confusion or redundancy from some form of introduction, say, to a tutorial if they are beginners, or perhaps to procedures if they are experts. Whatever their needs, state explicitly what trail they should take. That way, if you happen to end up writing the second book in a series, you'll know what the first book covered and you won't bore people with the same explanations.

Audience Tracks:

Here's how we expect users to move through our documentation.

An intermediate or expert user will skip the overview in the User Guide, use the Quick-Install sheet to get up and running, and turn directly to the procedures for sending and receiving (reading only the boldface instructions). On the road this user will carry the Quick Reference and perhaps consult it once or twice, just to make sure.

A beginner or inexperienced user will use the installation chapter in the User Guide because of its in-depth explanations, then turn to the Visual Overview to understand how the product works, and then turn to the procedures section for the first few sends and receives (reading every word, including all explanations). These users will probably also turn to the Glossary and the troubleshooting sections during the early weeks of use. They are likely to carry the entire User Guide

Continued

Continued

> with them on the road for the first few weeks; after they feel familiar with the product, they will leave it back in the office and take the Quick Reference with them.
>
> Our Read Me First sheet will provide a visual map showing each group of users what trail to take.

In addition to planning the sequences people will follow, you need to make explicit the relationship between similar pieces, such as a tutorial and computer-based training. Is there really a need for both? Will they cover different subjects? Serve different audiences? Accomplish different purposes?

Often, the team wonders why you want to include topics in online help when you have already planned to include them in the paper manual. Here's one writer's rationale:

Here's one writer's rationale for including topics in online help when you have already planned to include them in the paper manual.

> The online help should include **at least as much** information as the manuals. That way, if people look up a hard question in the help, they'll find the answer; that encourages them to come back the next time, and the next. On the other hand, if the information's not there, few people return for a fourth or fifth try. In effect, hundreds of thousands of dollars of work on the help has been thrown away.
>
> Also, people turn to online help when they are in the middle of their work to get a quick answer and then go back to work. The situation in which they turn to the manual is different. Often people look up a new task in the manual **before they start,** when they have the leisure to leaf through the chapter, flip back and forth, get all the facts. People hate using manuals when they are in the middle of work and anxious to get back to it; that's when online help, if it provides the answer, makes people feel as if the software itself is answering the question. When online help works, people do not identify what has occurred as "a problem." If they do, then they turn to the book.

Some redundancy may be appropriate when you think people will turn to one of the two pieces in different circumstances, or for different reasons. But make clear to your team, up front, what you intend to cover twice, and why.

If you believe that two elements (such as online help and a book of procedures) serve two different functions, or help people who find themselves in different situations, then it's OK to discuss the same topics in each. If not, one must go.

*Here's one writer's rationale
for cutting the paper version
of a command reference.*

What Information Goes Where

In our product we have only 25 commands and 5 dialog boxes. The context-sensitive part of the online help will pop up a definition of each command and each option in the dialog boxes. In addition, the table of contents for online help advertises a chapter on commands and dialog boxes, so users can look them up there. Is there any reason to repeat all this in our book? I think not. Let's save ourselves the 40 pages. That will cut our printing costs by 20% on this book and reduce the weight of the box by 10%.

Make tradeoffs, if you must

Budget. Time. When there's not enough of either, you must choose a subset from all the document types you want to create.

If you can create only one document, do a set of procedures. The introduction can provide an overview and key concepts, and users can then find what they need to complete their work. They'll have to pick up information about the product itself (the answers to the questions that begin, "What is...?) as they go.

If you have a bit more time, add one or both of these:

- A brief tutorial that steps people through the basics, so they can do some work on their own and turn to the procedures only when they need to

- A glossary instead of the fully detailed command reference section that details every option of every command

And if you have a little more time? Van R. Kane, a writer who has had to produce a half dozen manuals, each within a few weeks, recommends making sure you add these to your documentation suite:

- Overviews and summaries. These paragraphs help readers get oriented—even if what follows is a bit hectic.

- A good index. You can make up somewhat for the disorganization brought about by haste if you include an accurate index.

- A table of contents with lots of headings. These help readers browse and skim when they're looking something up.

Outline the contents of each document

Your documentation plan should include a preliminary outline of the contents for each document—paper and onscreen. You can attach the preliminary table of contents to the document plan as a separate document if you need to emphasize it.

Go into the details

Include enough detail to show where all main topics will be covered, but go no deeper than two or three levels. (Just indicate the structure—it's not time to start writing yet.) Here are some elements to include in the content outline:

For a section of procedures, include the chapters, main sections, and names of the specific procedures covered in each chapter.

For a command reference, detail the chapters, main topics, and commands included.

For a tutorial, include the chapters, procedures users will follow, and a summary of the features or functions exercised in each procedure.

Here's an example of the way a writer takes the general plan, and starts an outline for one of the pieces.

Overview of the Documentation

Here's what we'll put into the EverFax documentation:

- **For experienced fax users,** we provide a Quick Installation sheet, so they can get up and running without being slowed down by elaborate explanations.

- **For the more anxious or inexperienced,** we include in the User Guide a chapter on installation, with detailed instructions, lots of illustrations, and explanations.

- **For people unaccustomed to using fax or telecommunications,** we will include a visual overview at the beginning of the User Guide.

- **For users of all levels when they are on the road,** away from their own computer, we will include a Quick Reference—brief instructions for using EverFax from the field.

- **For users of all levels in their own office,** we provide complete instructions for using EverFax on the PC. For the impatient intermediate or expert user, boldfaced instructions will stand out, letting readers skip explanations; but for beginners we provide detailed

Continued

Continued

Here's an example of the way a writer takes the general plan, and starts an outline for one of the pieces. (Continued)

explanations in indented plain text paragraphs. These procedures will be in the middle of the User Guide.

- **For anyone who gets in trouble,** we provide a troubleshooting section at the back of the User Guide.
- **Particularly for beginners**, and anyone who wants to know what a particular term means, we include a glossary.

We are not developing related documentation, such as documentation of the platform and script language for VARs. We understand that manuals are being developed separately.

Here's the top level outline of the contents of the User Guide.

Contents of the User Guide

The User Guide will be approximately 130 pages and will include these sections of information:

- A visual introduction to the product
- Step-by-step instructions for installing EverFax under Macrosilt Windows, with extensive explanations
- Step-by-step procedures for using EverFax, with instructions in boldface for intermediate or expert users to skim through, and explanations in plain text for less experienced people to read
- A brief troubleshooting section
- Glossary
- Index

Here is the detailed outline of the contents of the procedures section

Contents of the Procedures Section of the EverFax User Guide

Preparing your files

    Identifying files you want to be able to transmit

    Putting filenames onto your form

Sending a file by fax

    Selecting the file to send

    Faxing

Calling into your personal computer

    Filling out the form with your requests

Continued

Continued

Here is the detailed outline of the contents of the procedures section
(continued)

Faxing the form

If you have difficulty

Asking the PC to show you a directory

Instructing your PC to send multiple faxes

Sending instructions from a fax out on the road

Giving instructions to the PC using EverFax

Setting up your PC to receive and send faxes

Setting the PC up before you leave the office

Turning the PC on from a remote fax

Creating new forms

Starting a new form

Including the glyphs that EverFax will read

Adding text and graphics

Saving in EverFax format

Create headings that make sense

The headings you include in this outline are your first pass at headings for your eventual table of contents. They may change a lot or a little as the project evolves. Draft them with your audience in mind, even though they may change. That way you'll have an accurate picture of the documents. Avoid the urge to use technical jargon in this outline. If you give headings technical names at this stage, you'll slip toward organizing the documents from the product's point of view. And don't just settle for naming the topic; write a heading that will mean something to the ordinary user.

Now's the time to polish the structure—not after you have written a few drafts. An experienced manager and writer, Edmond Weiss, says, "It is wrong to believe that usability can be substantially enhanced after the draft is complete; the most resistant and elusive usability flaws in a publication are built into a draft and are not likely to be ameliorated by after-the-fact testing."

Outliners are great tools to use for ironing out the wrinkles. They make it easy to rearrange topics and to change a chapter into a topic in another chapter, or to promote a subheading to a chapter of its own. You'll find more about outlining in Chapter 7.

Describe the book design

If you're working for an organization with an established book design, don't describe it in your documentation plan, just acknowledge it. But if you have a new design in mind, you need to describe what you want it to do and how it will differ from the current one.

Book designers take raw text, consider the purpose of every sentence, and create a certain look for each purpose. A designer might read, "Issue the Init command," and think, "This is an instruction, something a reader must notice, so it's got to stand out. It's more important than the next sentence, so I need to separate it from that and elevate it somehow. I wonder what boldfacing, numbering, and outdenting will do?"

In developing a design of your own or discussing an evolving design with a designer, you should go through these phases:

1. Choose a page size.

2. Design a page layout for each type of document and each section of a document (such as a chapter opener or index page)

3. Create samples.

4. Get critiques from a wide range of people, and revise.

5. Describe the design and show samples as part of the documentation plan.

You go through a similar process developing screen designs for online help or computer-based training.

When you plan a book design up front, you can keep it in mind as you write. Better yet, if you can use a word processor that lets you write in that form, your writing will fit into the design better.

Choose the page size

The size of the page determines how much information can fit on one page, and what combinations of art and text you can use. What fits on an 8 1/2- by-11-inch page is very different from what fits on a 5-by-7-inch page. An average book page size is 7 inches by 9 inches.

Most often, you'll find your choice of page size constrained by packaging dimensions and company standards.

Design each type of page

The design may be up to you, or you may work with a designer. Either way, be sure you've considered the layout for each type of page in your book, including

- Preface
- Table of contents
- Introduction to the book
- Chapter opening
- General chapter page
- Two-page spreads that work as a unit
- Step-by-step procedures
- Command reference
- Summary tables
- Glossary
- Index

Figure out the purpose of each element on the pages, too. If you have three levels of headings, define up front what the difference is. What should go in a level three head? What's the purpose of the element you call a note, and how is it different from a caution or an ordinary paragraph of text?

In defining the purpose of each element, you prepare yourself to talk with a designer, explaining what you hope each element will do, while leaving to the designer the decisions about exact typeface, size, slant, and position.

Create sample pages

Plan to mock up the major page types. Format everything, place art, add callouts. It's better to know early if ideas you've had for the page layout just don't work, when there's still time to make changes.

If you're working with a separate production group, provide them with text and art and ask them to prepare it as they would a final. Doing a trial run will help them, too. They'll know what to expect and can plan and schedule for the work.

Show the design around

People on the development team may not really understand what you tell them about creating user-oriented tasks, 20-minute tutorials, or a visual approach. Showing them real pages can get the ideas across much more fully. What sounded simpleminded when described in words may come across as forceful and concise when you show samples.

Listen to the team's objections, but don't rush to revise in the way they suggest. Their solutions may derive from their fondness for an earlier design, or they may be overemphasizing one aspect. Focus instead on the fact that something disturbs them, and reach your own conclusions about redesigning.

For onscreen help, create a screen design

Don't leave out onscreen materials when you design pages. If the help interface isn't solid yet, mock up screens to show the placement of text and art. As with a book, work through a series of screens, so you are aware of the details that will affect how you write and how you "chunk" information.

Create a layout for each type of screen:

- Table of contents or menu and submenu
- Introductory screen
- Command information
- Cross reference (link to related information)
- Procedure
- Diagnostic
- Definition (pop-up or glossary)
- Map of the help facility, if any
- Index

Describe the design and its purposes

Build the book design into the documentation plan to get early agreement on it. Everyone on the team will have an opinion, and you want to take their views into account while making sure you have enough time to maintain the overall coherence of the design.

Put some of the sample pages into your documentation plan. Make sure you explain each element of the design, and say why you're formatting it that way. You may also want to show an older design first as a point of comparison.

You may not get a final version of the book design until much farther along in the project, but include any prototypes you have. Just explain that they aren't final. The point is to avoid an emotional explosion late in the project when someone discovers that you are using Helvetica, not Optima, for notes!

A comparison of the old and new book designs, aimed at explaining the purpose of the new design to the team.

Here is a sample of our old book design.

It's hard for users to figure out what to do because the instructions have been folded in with the explanations. Also, when people turn away from the page for a moment to do a step, they often lose their place because there's no separation between steps.

```
Issue the Init command. You may issue the command
from the Device menu or from your Design Flow. The
Initialization form now appears. Enter the purpose
of your device in the Function field. You may already
have defined the purpose of the device when you cre-
ated an instance of it; if so, that purpose appears
in the field. Select the physical type from the
scrolling list in the Type field. Click OK. The soft-
ware now initializes the instance.
```

Here's a sample of our new book design.

We make instructions stand out by boldfacing them, outdenting them, and adding white space after each one. That way users can spot each instruction, and experienced users can skip all explanations. The explanations have their own format now, indented, in plain text, so all users recognize that the explanations are subordinate to the steps.

1. **Issue the Init command.**

    You may issue the command from the Device menu, or from your Design Flow.

    The Initialization form now appears.

    (Art)

2. **Enter the purpose of your device in the Function field.**

    You may already have defined the purpose of the device when you created an instance of it; if so, that purpose appears in the field.

3. **Select the physical type from the scrolling list in the Type field.**

4. **Click OK.**

    The software now initializes the instance.

Describe who does what, and when

Your documentation plan acts as a contract between you and the rest of the team, committing you to deliver this, that, and the other thing by certain dates, and committing them to give you the information you need to review your drafts and test, and in some cases take over the manuscript and see it through production.

Determine whom you will rely on for information, and how you'll get it

Specify in writing how you expect to get news from the team. Maybe you'll have a primary contact on the development team. Or you may attend regular staff meetings and work with all the developers. Whatever your situation, put your expectations on paper.

Spell out the materials you need:

- Regular updates
- Current software or hardware
- Changes to specifications
- Timely reviews

Say how you expect to get what you need, too:

- If you're in a different location, will you stop by and pick up the latest information, receive files in the mail or by modem?
- How often should you expect updates?

If you're contracting, it's a good idea to agree on one main contact who will keep you in mind, update you on a timely basis, and answer your questions. (That doesn't mean you never see the rest of the team.) And when several reviewers disagree about a passage, you have one person to turn to as the arbiter.

Summarize how you will review and test

Reviews and user tests of your manual keep you from working in a vacuum. Decide at what points you'll get reviews and from whom:

- **Marketing.** Have them review most steps—at least the documentation plan, the outline, and the final draft.

- **Product manager.** Probably, this person will decide who else on the development team will review, and when. Ask for one key reviewer who will take responsibility for reading everything to ensure accuracy.
- **Product engineers.** Make sure the engineers go over the documentation plan, first draft, and second draft, for technical accuracy. Don't wait until the final draft or you'll discover you've misrepresented or left out key tidbits. Get quality assurance to review the final to make sure every sentence is true.
- **Developmental editor.** After the outline and the first draft, this editor can give you suggestions about large issues of structure and style.
- **Copy editor.** Just before the final draft, if possible, the copy editor should actually get a "pre-final" draft. You roll in the copyedits and comments and then submit the final for everyone's blessing. (More traditionally, you receive a copyedit as part of the production process.)

Plan to do some testing, too. Product development schedules usually allow for user testing of the product, but the documentation is often overlooked. When documentation testing is planned up front, odds are much greater it will happen.

If documentation testing isn't in the overall schedule, fit some less formal testing into yours. Users from the real audience are your best bet, if you can get them. If not, ask a coworker or friend to work through your material.

Summarize production plans

Whether you're in charge of production or will hand it off to a separate group, think through the production process and include it in your documentation plan. You should know

- Who will produce the books, video disks, floppy disks, job aids, and assorted paraphernalia in your documentation suite
- What method and software will be used to produce the pages or screens
- What is required to prepare your text and art files for use with the production software
- Approximately how many illustrations you expect to use, and what tools will be used to create them (for each book)

- The size of the book—both trim size, and rough page count (for onscreen documents, the size of the screen and how many screens)
- How the book will be bound; for instance, stapled, spiral, three-hole binder, or perfect-bound
- How many colors will be used on the pages
- Any special problems you expect to come up during production; for instance, if you'll be printing four-color on two sides, you'll need thicker paper than usual
- Who will assemble the books with the product and when

If there's anything unique about the way in which customers will receive the product and the documentation, mention that, too. For instance, are paper documents provided in a disk file that the customer prints? Is a beginner guide shipped with the product, and the main user guide sent out after the company receives the registration card?

List and describe your deliverables in each phase of production

Break your work into phases and spell out what documents you will hand in at each phase. Here's a summary of common phases:

- **Planning phase.** You create your documentation plan, including or accompanied by a preliminary outline, audience profile, and schedule.
- **First-draft phase (alpha).** This is a complete draft of each document, in writing, with descriptions of conceptual art that's needed and locations for specific screen art in the text. When the product is in flux or very complex, this draft may take the form of a detailed outline down to, say, the level of numbered steps in a procedure. An outline draft lets you reorganize efficiently and usually ensures timely and complete second and final drafts.
- **Second-draft phase (beta).** Another complete draft that incorporates edits and review commands. Includes all introductions, explanations, the glossary text, and any preface material and screenshots. Be sure to include a table of contents. (Emphasize to all reviewers that this is the last chance for major changes.)

- **Final-draft phase.** This is it—a final, technically accurate draft of every document. You should send the final draft to a copyeditor to check for consistency of style, proper grammar and punctuation, and accurate references. Once copyediting is done, the development team should have a final peek, but they can only request short wording changes.

- **Production phase.** At this stage you have a version of every document that should be ready to be typeset, or almost. After this no substantive changes should be made. You want the text and the art to be final. Do plan to work with the production crew. You want to make sure art and callouts are placed in the right position, headings are kept at their appropriate level, pages balance. And you'll create your index.

Here's an example of a set of deliverables by phase on a project with no time for a second draft:

Planning Phase

    First draft of audience profile

    First draft of documentation plan

    Preliminary schedule

    Final audience profile

    Final documentation plan

    Schedule

First Draft

    First draft of Bonanza tutorial

    First draft of Bonanza manual (including procedures and command reference)

    First draft of Bonanza online help

Final Draft

    Final draft of Bonanza tutorial

    Final draft of Bonanza manual

    Final draft of Bonanza online help

    First draft of Bonanza quick reference card

Production Phase

    Production (camera-ready art) copy of Bonanza tutorial, with all art in place

    Production copy of Bonanza manual

    Production copy of Bonanza online help

    Production copy of Bonanza quick reference card

Of course, one phase sometimes bleeds into another. Technical details have to be added after you thought you were long finished, and some hidden reviewer pops up during the final draft phase with great ideas for topics or tasks you hadn't planned on. But spelling out the phases can help keep those events to a minimum.

Include a schedule, even if it is fictional

Scheduling is a creative art in its own right. When you start a project, you may have only the team's hoped-for ship date and your starting date. Yet you need to fill in interim dates at the beginning, even though you know they'll change. Once you begin to block out how many weeks you really need to plan, outline, write, rewrite, and receive reviews, your plans may appear in quite a different perspective.

We talk about scheduling in detail in Chapter 6.

Review the plan

You will probably need to do a few drafts of the documentation plan, collecting comments and news as you go.

- When you've developed your plan and put it on paper, have the development and marketing teams review it in depth.
- Get the team's approval. You want to be sure you all agree that you're taking the proper direction before you're deep into drafting text.
- Revisit the plan at key points throughout the development. Once you're into the details of writing, you may lose sight of the overall picture. Revisiting the plan at key points will remind you of your early decisions, and point out what's worked and what hasn't.
- Revise the plan when appropriate.

In many organizations you'll need to get an official OK or signoff before proceeding. In other companies you have to plunge ahead, assuming approval will be forthcoming. But remember that the plan functions as an informal agreement between you, your manager, and your project team. That's why you need to hammer out disagreements and record them in another draft.

Sometimes a project plunges into such slippery ground that you seem to be pointing north, south, east, and west, swirling around from week to week. In such confusion you can turn to your documentation plan to get back on track.

Remember, your plan is a tool—for yourself and for others on the team.

Checklist

A complete documentation plan is one that
Defines the goals you want to achieve with the documentation

- ☐ Establishes the broad scope of the documentation
- ☐ Specifies constraints and limits
- ☐ Describes (and justifies) any departures from standard practice

Specifies the pieces that will make up your documentation suite

- ☐ Shows how you propose to meet the needs of each group of users
- ☐ Indicates what sequence each group of users should follow
- ☐ Explains the different purposes of each piece

Contains a preliminary outline of the contents of each document

- ☐ Includes detail
- ☐ Uses headings that will make sense to users
- ☐ Organizes topics in a way that will be familiar to users

Describes the book design

- ☐ Specifies the page size
- ☐ Shows sample pages with a design for each purpose
- ☐ Describes the purpose of each element of the design

Describes who does what when

- ☐ Spells out who you'll get information from, and how
- ☐ Summarizes the plan for reviews and testing
- ☐ Summarizes production plans
- ☐ Lists the documents you'll deliver in each phase
- ☐ Includes a preliminary schedule

Developing a Schedule and Estimating Costs

What do you want me to do? Stop now—
and release it as The Five Commandments?

—Cecil B. De Mille

People sometimes think of writers as lying around, sprawled out for an inspirational nap; staring into space. Occasionally scribbling a line or two before turning back to lunch; living a wonderful, happy-go-lucky, unplanned existence. Instead, scheduling keeps us up at night calculating, imagining, having bad dreams, because on many projects the schedule is our greatest work of fiction.

Developing a realistic schedule can help keep you sane—and ensure the success of the documentation you're planning. You'd think scheduling should be simple. Just figure out how many hours you'll need to write the manuals and then try to find those hours in your calendar. But then reality intrudes. Factors change—product development slips, the team adopts a new approach to the user interface, or the manuals get redesigned—and you begin the continuing process of revising and updating the schedule to reflect the current status.

Making your schedule—step by step

You should be able to provide a fairly accurate schedule after you've created a document plan and you've seen an alpha version of the product. However, the schedule's accuracy depends on the team you're working with and the product under development. If you know the team, you know something about their work and scheduling styles. You know if you can count on early estimates to be accurate or if they're likely to be way off the mark. If you're not familiar with the team, hope for the best and plan for the worst.

By the way: Schedules for hardware products are often more accurate than for software, at least in our experience. Perhaps the hardware world has had a few more years to develop strategies for solving problems and overcoming surprises.

Here are the main steps you need to take as you schedule (and reschedule):

1. Estimate the number of pages and writing hours.
2. Refine your estimate by thinking through the process.
3. Allocate hours to each phase and put your milestones on the calendar.
4. Reach agreement with the team.
5. Estimate costs, if that's appropriate.

6. Revise the whole thing.

Now we'll look at these steps in detail.

Estimate page count and writing hours

A long book usually takes longer to write than a short one. From that truism writers have concluded that the best way to estimate time is figuring out how many pages you're going to write and multiplying that by how long, on average, you'll need to develop an individual page from scratch to press. Of course, some chapters will zip along while others slow to a crawl, but in general you shoot for maintaining your average.

Guesstimate the number of pages

For the purpose of estimating length, you need an approximate idea of the page size and contents. If you have no corporate model, pick a book that seems similar to what you have in mind. Use your outline to determine how many procedures, commands, and general topics you'll document and, based on the standard page you have in mind, how many pages they'll require.

Procedures. How much space does a single procedure occupy in your model book or standard book design? One page? Half a page? Two? Multiply your rough count of procedures by the amount of space they'll take up to get a page count for that section of your manual.

Command Reference. Consider how many fields, arguments, or options are available for most commands. Decide whether to plan for several commands per page or one or more pages per command.

Overviews. If you think you'll be writing lots of general overviews, look at each subtopic and add up all the potential paragraphs to get a rough page count.

Add more pages for other kinds of chapters, appendices, front matter (yes, you take credit for the title page in these totals), and back matter (including glossary and index). You want the grand total number of pages the final book will contain (not just the number of draft pages).

Online help. For an online help facility, make a list of subjects you'll cover and estimate the number of screens needed. For context-sensitive help, list all the interface objects that you'll define, and figure a sentence or two per object (you might end up with 30 to 50 single-spaced pages for a complex consumer application).

Guesstimate the number of writing hours

Now that you have a rough page count, multiply that total by the average number of hours you think you'll need to write each page. If you aren't sure, consider that industry averages range from three to six hours a page, depending on the complexity of the subject. That includes every minute spent on that mythic average page—taking notes, going to brainstorming sessions, writing, revising, holding review meetings, conferring with the editor, revising the format, preparing the manuscript for production. For a 200-page manual, then, you might need between 600 and 1200 hours. For online help there are no dependable averages yet, but gossip reports three to six hours per screen when the screens have been extracted from a manual, four to seven hours if done from scratch.

Refine your estimate by thinking through the process

Make a list of all the things you expect to do as you write the manual; doing this will help you decide if you should edge toward the low or high range of the hours-per-page estimate. Think out loud and imagine how long each task is likely to take, depending on the people involved, the situation, your other chores, and your stamina.

Here's what I'll do on the StarMaker documentation:

- Create a full documentation plan, including the audience profile and a product profile. I have the audience profile from the last version; and the specs are pretty good, so the product profile won't take too long, at least for the first version.
- Gathering information—should go pretty easily; the engineers are friendly and talkative, and the product manager is effervescent.
- Attending meetings. I'll attend regular team meetings (about two hours a week)
- Developing an outline (about three weeks, I think)
- Writing the first draft (may take about two months, more if the software slips)
- Describing or sketching conceptual art (shouldn't take long; I think I can use the art from the older manual)
- Receiving review comments and incorporating them (about two weeks on the first draft)
- Receiving edits and incorporating them (another few days on the first draft)
- Writing the second draft (about a month)
- Rolling in another set of review comments (two weeks)
- Capturing screens (a solid week)
- Writing the final draft (another week or so)
- Rolling in tweaks and changes after final (agh, another two weeks, off and on, not full time)
- Incorporating copyedits (three days)
- Creating an index (two days, minimum)
- Proofing pages (three days)

Based on your reassessment of the project, reestimate the hours you need.

Add a little stretch time if you face obstacles

As the manager of more than a thousand technical writing projects, Joann Hackos points out that if you really want to schedule realistically, you must take into account the obstacles you may encounter along the way. For example, if you're entirely new to the subject you're writing about, add about 10% to your estimate. Of course, if

Here's an estimate based on six hours per page in a 200-page manual.

Estimate of Hours	
Documentation plan	100
Meetings	90
Perfecting outline	300
Writing first draft	200
Dealing with reviews (all drafts)	80
Dealing with editor (all drafts)	80
Writing second draft	130
Writing final draft	80
Capturing screens, describing art	40
Incorporating copyedits in final	30
Index	40
Proofing	30
Total	**1200**

you know the subject well, you may be able to subtract 10%. Here are a few typical obstacles to watch out for:

- The engineers are close-lipped.
- You have a very unstable product, and it's very likely that the feature set will change dramatically.
- You face uncooperative reviewers who disagree with one another.
- You're one of a team of writers, and most of them are entry level.
- You're writing for a very sophisticated audience and know very little about them.

Allocate hours to each phase

Writers often spend half the available hours creating the documentation plan, outline, and first draft. The second draft often takes about one third of the total hours, leaving under 20% for the final draft. If you don't add additional hours for proofing during production, be sure to reserve some time for that task.

To do a thorough job with fewer revisions, however, you must put half your time into planning and outlining. You will get the manual so well organized that you can afford to drop a draft afterward. You'll find the number of changes you have to make later also drop dramatically, allowing you to catch up on your hours late in the project.

Rough out a schedule by phase

To make sure you're allocating enough time to each draft, take the list of tasks you created and group them into phases.

Hours By Phase	
(200-page manual, 6 hours/page)	
Product & audience profiles, & documentation plan	100
Outline and 1st draft	590
2nd draft	210
Final draft	160
Production (Art, copyedits, proof, index)	140
Total	**1200**

Consider how many hours per week you'll spend on this project, or if you're planning the project with more than one writer, consider how much time each writer has for this manual. If you're figuring full time, it's better not to plan a full 40 hours per week. Figure 30 or so, instead. That allows for some down time, regular staff meetings, training sessions, vacation, and illness.

Several large companies report that writers get to spend only a quarter of their time writing. The rest of their hours get eaten up by the flu, meetings, vacations, inaccessibility of the software, crashed computers, earthquakes, and the general slow pace of communication within the team.

OK

	Number of Weeks		
	(200-page manual, 6 hours/page, 30 hours a week available)		
	# Hours	# Wks (1 writer)	# Wks (2 writers)
Doc plan	100	3.3	1.7
Outline	390	13.0	6.5
1st draft	200	6.7	3.4
2nd draft	210	7.0	3.5
Final draft	160	5.7	2.9
Art	40	1.3	0.7
Copyedits	30	1.0	0.5
Index	40	1.3	0.7
Proofing	30	1.0	0.5
Total	**1200**	**40.3**	**20.4**

Caution: Doubling up the writers does not really cut the time in half. After all you have to spend some time exchanging tips, gossips, and strategies; and you can't just divide a manual up in the middle—one person's going to do a little more, the other a little less.

When you're ready to fit your hours to a calendar, you need to know the key dates for the whole project cycle. Your drafts will be dependent on having updated versions of the product and key decisions made by the engineers and implementation team. You can work forward from today or backward from the projected ship date to see how the schedules mesh.

Here's a sample schedule you might develop. You start out knowing project development dates for alpha and beta versions of the product but not much more. We're assuming a 200-page manual, with two writers who can work full time. This company uses a printer who requires four weeks—pretty standard. Notice that we include columns for revised and actual dates from the start.

Event	Original Date	Revised Date	Actual Date
Preliminary Documentation Plan Phase			
Receive software, specs, product materials	1/15	2/1	2/1
Submit Final Document Plan	2/26	3/5	3/6
First Draft Phase			
Receive alpha software	4/10	4/15	
Second Draft Phase			
Receive beta software (interface frozen)	5/15		
Final Draft Phase			
Receive release version of software	6/15		
Production Services Phase			
All files to printer	8/1		
Printed books to packager, to product ship	9/1		

That's how you start. Now let's fill in the gaps.

The preliminary phase

You're working intensively on the outline now, developing an excellent understanding of the product and the audience. You test out everything you learn about the product, try out whatever version you have, change your outline, and check with the other writers.

Allow time for two versions of the documentation plan: an early one, roughing out audience information and approach, and another one, after you've gotten some feedback from the team and become more familiar with the product.

The first-draft phase

The first draft is sometimes called the alpha draft, because it is often linked to the availability of an alpha version of the product. You start your first draft when you've received approval of the approach presented in the documentation plan and at least a few weeks before the alpha version of the product appears.

Preliminary Phase (Documentation Plan)	
Event	**Original Date**
Receive preliminary software, specs, product materials	2/1
Submit 1st draft documentation plan to product team	2/15
Receive review comments	2/22
Submit 2nd draft documentation plan (including preliminary outline and sample page design) to product team	3/1
Receive review comments	3/6
Submit final documentation plan	3/30

First-Draft Phase (Alpha Draft)	
Event	**Original Date**
Receive approval for document plan	4/2
Receive alpha software	4/15
Submit 1st draft to product team	4/27
Submit 1st draft for developmental edit	4/27
Submit description of conceptual art to production or graphic artist	4/27

By the way: If you're starting very early in a project, this draft will take much longer. For example, if you're asked to start when the programmers start, you could spend two years writing a series of incomplete drafts as the product design evolves and changes. You may get to try out several approaches to the documentation, and you'll definitely need more hours.

The second-draft phase

Writing the second draft shouldn't take nearly as long as writing the first draft did. But you will probably feel as if you are juggling a few thousand balls at the same time. Timing depends on how much the product changed, how many comments you got, what editing suggestions were made, and how long your first draft was. For a 100-page manual, you might take three or four weeks to produce the second draft. Then again you might have to fix it in a week or 10 days.

Start your second draft when you receive comments and developmental edits on the first draft, and when you have a new version of the product—preferably a beta version.

Allow for review periods. Most reviewers have many other duties in addition to reviewing your work so you need to allow at least seven to ten days for the review, and possibly as much as two weeks. Noting this clearly in the schedule will help engineers, programmers, and marketing staff plan some extra time for reviewing.

Allow for edits. Ideally you'll receive a developmental edit on the first draft and not the second. (A developmental edit checks your structure and approach at a high level—no grammar or style critiques.) Not all companies provide a developmental edit. Take it if you can get it. You'll learn a lot and receive comments while you still have time to make major changes.

You may have to answer hundreds of questions from your reviewers, reach a mutually acceptable compromise on some issues, and bow to pressure to meet some standard you had ignored. The time all this takes depends on the length of manuscript and the amount of editing done during first- and second-draft stages. For a 200-page manuscript, not seen before, an editor might need several weeks.

Some companies have no official edit. If this is the case, ask another writer for an edit while your manual is out for review, so you can at least get the benefit of another pair of eyes.

Second-Draft Phase (Beta Draft)	
Event	**Original Date**
Receive review comments on 1st draft	5/7
Receive developmental edits (structural)	5/14
Receive beta software (interface frozen)	5/15
Receive test comments on 1st draft	5/15
Submit 2nd draft to product team	5/25
Receive preliminary version of conceptual art from production or graphic artist	5/30
Submit comments and changes to art	6/5

The final-draft phase

When you've collected all the comments on your second draft, you can start your final. Your reviewers should restrain their comments to errors in your description of the way the product works. It's too late for changes to the organization or suggestions on new ways to approach the subject material. You'll also receive comments from testers that let you know not only if what you've written is accurate, but also whether you've left out anything and whether the information is clear.

The schedule we show here includes a copyedit as part of the development of the final draft. If the second draft is complete enough, you can also send it to the copy editor, saving some time on this last draft.

OK

Final Draft Phase	
Event	**Original Date**
Receive release version of software	6/1
Receive test comments on 2nd draft	6/1
Receive review comments on 2nd draft	6/1
Submit final draft to copy editor	6/15
Receive copyedited manuscript	6/22
Submit draft to production, with copyedits incorporated	6/29
Deliver screenshots with art list	6/29

Here the preliminary schedule follows the announced dates for the product: The team has confidently announced that beta testing will take only two weeks. You can rest assured that their estimate is stupendously overoptimistic. It will probably be more like two months or, in rough cases, six months. But for the moment, you have to fit your schedule into theirs, even though you're certain you'll have a breather after beta.

Production phase

With a sigh of relief, you hand off your final draft into the nether-land of production. This may be an in-house production group making minor formatting changes, a page layout group pouring your text into new files, adding screens and other art, and adjusting the spacing and positioning on each page, or your text may go off to a typesetter.

If you're creating online help, your text and screens may go to a group who add codes to make the information appear where it should.

At some point, from one to three or even four weeks later, you'll receive page proofs. This production draft is the first complete version of the manual as it will look when printed. You have two jobs at this point: to correct all the errors you can find and to create an index. At this early stage in scheduling, you can leave these dates blank because they depend so heavily on the production team.

Production Services Phase	
Event	**Original Date**
Receive camera-ready art	
Submit proofed camera-ready art to production	
Receive production draft	
Return proofed production	
Submit Index to production	
All files to printer	8/1
Bound books to warehouse	9/1

Reach agreement with the team

Because your writing must fit in with the overall development of the product, it's common to begin planning your time, reviews, and edits around the product development schedule. Often there are too few weeks in which to cram all your work. What can you do besides tearing your hair?

Negotiate around predetermined dates

A schedule always emerges from a complex form of give and take. You figure how much time you need; you get pressured into planning for less; you adjust the length and complexity of the manual to match the time available; and finally you agree to a series of deadlines, which will probably change as the project evolves. Sometimes negotiating a schedule can be as simple as accompanying your new schedule with a memo; sometimes it involves a week of informal discussions.

If you're lucky, you need only tweak the dates so they fit the product development schedule. If you think the manual will take six months to write, and the team expects to ship the product in four, you're facing a common problem. You may add more writers, determine with the product manager that the schedule must slip, or reduce the work by eliminating some of the documentation or by writing fewer drafts.

Talk with the team to get a sense of when the product will be functioning well enough to describe it. Maybe you can begin writing before the alpha version is available. If you do, make sure you have at least a week's time with the product in its alpha, beta, and final versions before releasing your first, second, and final drafts. You can make educated guesses about the product before it's delivered, but you must see the actual thing to be sure you've described it accurately.

When the product is on schedule, and you must eke out some extra time somewhere, there are three key areas to try adjusting:

Shorten reviews. If you're really on a scrunched schedule, ask reviewers to stop everything and turn the review around in one, two, or three days. Coordinate this with the product manager. Maybe you can narrow the review team down to two or three key people, instead of the whole team.

Speed up production. Talk to the production coordinator to find out what would speed up their job. Is there formatting you can do that will make their lives easier? Can they add an extra person to the job?

Speed up printing. Four to six weeks is a fairly common length of time for a manual to be at the printers, but you may be able to negotiate a shorter time, or find another printer who's faster. This will have other consequences, though. You may be able to get a rush job done, but for twice the cost.

Taking other projects into account

Don't forget to consider other projects on your desk. You and your supervisor or your colleagues should agree on a plan for your work over the next few months, and count on revising it every week or so as the situation changes. Having a long-range schedule in hand will help you determine when you can take on another project and when there's no way.

If you have several projects at any given time, be sure you estimate the hours and weeks for each of them to see if they add up to more hours than you have available. If they do, talk to your supervisor. If you're a contractor, make sure you're not biting off more than you can chew.

Circulate the schedule and make an agreement with the team

A schedule is a kind of contract. It has a two-fold purpose—planning and recording when you need to complete each milestone and letting others on the team in on your plan. If you're a contractor, you'll probably submit the schedule to a project manager or marketing manager—your main contact on the job. When you circulate the schedule, introduce it with a cover memo highlighting the dates you expect to get information from key people. Make clear that the schedule depends on them as well as you.

Give the team a sense of what you'll complete at each milestone on the schedule by making sure they see the documentation plan and, in particular, the section describing what will be included in each draft. If you think you need to explain the whole process to them so they see why you depend on them to meet the schedule, use a chart showing the relationship between software and documentation development. That makes it clear that you can't test your beta draft before you receive beta software—despite the fact that some people wish you could.

By spelling out what you need up front, you make sure everyone knows what's required to produce the manual. You also lay the groundwork for revising the schedule.

This chart makes clear how the user guide follows the development of the software.

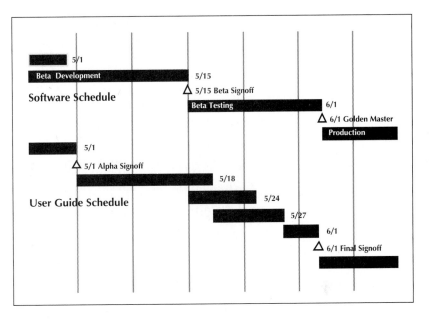

Estimate costs, if that's appropriate

If you are a contractor, whether or not you get a job depends largely on the cost you quote to the project manager. Costs depend upon time, so your ability to estimate how long a project will take assumes a new dimension of importance.

You want the work, but you also want to be paid for it adequately. Hourly rates vary according to your level of experience and to the part of the country you live in. Get a sense of the going rate by comparing fees with other writers and checking with local organizations, such as the Society for Technical Communicators.

If you're an employee, contract rates may seem high, but remember, a contractor's rates include overhead for the writer's business—everything from equipment, to office space, to insurance, to marketing time.

When you give your clients an estimate, you may want to base it on hours, billed once or twice a month, with a "not to exceed" amount, or you can give them a fixed bid—a promise to deliver the manual for a set amount of money, paid in several installments throughout the project.

Here's how you might estimate the cost to write a manual:

200 pages x 6 hours = 1200 hours

1200 hours x $50 an hour = $60,000

Whether you provide an hourly estimate or a fixed bid, be sure to include in your proposal any circumstances under which you'll have to adjust the cost, such as

- Major changes to the product
- Requests for a different slant to the manuals after your documentation plan has previously been approved
- A request for an additional draft, such as an extra version to be distributed for press reviews
- Substantial changes to the interface after beta
- Slips of more than two months in the schedule

If any of these events occur, you should say you will dispatch a change notice, letting management and the team know how these new circumstances will affect the schedule and cost of the documentation.

Revise...when the schedule dissolves

Inevitably schedules change. Expect to update yours and distribute it whenever a major change occurs. This keeps everyone informed about the status of the documentation and reminds them that their actions affect your schedule.

For all your planning, priorities will shift on high and you won't see anything close to beta software for two more months. It's tempting to stop work on the project and wait for news. "The worst aspect of all this," Dirk van Nouhuys says, "is that you don't do the work you should do. For instance, when a project begins to slip, you tend to jump to another crash project." Then when you come back to the original project, you don't have time to do more than a quick fix. "So you have six consecutive quick fixes, instead of one or two fundamental changes."

Delays don't usually come from last-minute additions of excellence. Often they stem from the very people who complain the most bitterly about the schedule: marketing people with a must-have design change late in the project; engineers who tinker long after the agreed-upon day for the product to be finalized; important users who think of new functions after seeing the final software. **Every** time a slip occurs in the project, reevaluate your original schedule and let everyone know about changes immediately.

Your schedule affects other people

Half a dozen other schedules probably interlink with yours. Editors have a schedule showing when your manual will hit their desk. The production team anticipates your manual coming in at meteoric speed, unless you warn them about a delay. Marketing may also have its own list of products, with release dates. And the operations team has another list showing when they have to get the product up and running. If your company sells the product, then manufacturing wants to know when they'll get every part of the final box, including your manual.

If you decide you've got to make changes, here are a few things you should do:

Talk with your supervisor. Ask for help in carrying the message to the other team members involved. Show your scheduling chart to anyone who complains about the manual's slipping. Explain why publication takes time. Talk about what you've done to speed things up.

Write a change notice or memo to the entire team. If you don't speak up, everyone may just assume you can meet the original schedule. Say what the new schedule is and why you have to revise it. Give them new dates when you expect them to provide you with a functioning product and the dates when you will deliver drafts. Change notices get the problem out on the table and force managers to accept your suggested changes in schedule or negotiate with you and the rest of the team. If you're working on a contract, such a memo also justifies changes to your bid. Notify the client of changes as soon as you become aware a change will be required. Don't wait until you've been paid the total originally agreed on and still have another draft to write.

Negotiate. Offer alternative possibilities and identify tasks you could accomplish while waiting for slipped software or hardware. Maybe you can provide only two drafts instead of three. Or perhaps the chapter on applying the software to specialized needs should be omitted in this version.

Checklist

Your final schedule should take the following into account:

☐ Estimated number of pages

☐ Estimated number of hours (page count times hours per page)

☐ All the tasks involved, to see if the estimate should be increased or decreased

- Creating a documentation plan, including an audience profile and a product profile.
- Gathering information—testing the product, talking to engineers, reading specs and other documents. Is information hard or easy to come by?
- Attending meetings. Will you attend regular staff meetings? How many other meetings can you expect to attend?
- Developing an outline.
- Writing the first draft.
- Describing or sketching conceptual art.
- Receiving review comments and incorporating them.
- Receiving edits and incorporating them.
- Writing the second draft.
- Rolling in another set of review comments.
- Capturing screens.
- Working with an editor on various drafts.
- Writing the final draft.
- Rolling in final tweaks and changes.
- Incorporating copyedits.
- Creating an index.
- Proofing pages.

☐ A little stretch time if you face obstacles

☐ Hours allocated to each phase

☐ Dates for what you deliver and receive in each phase

☐ All announced project dates, included or negotiated around

☐ Other documentation you may have to write

☐ Estimated costs (by multiplying total hours times cost per hour)

☐ Announced reasons why you might have to issue change notices when forced to adjust schedules or costs

As You Write—
Working Methods

It is only well with me when I have a chisel in my hand.

—Michaelangelo

7

The results of your work will get better over the years if you pay attention to the way you work. By evaluating your work practices you can discard old habits in favor of newer, more constructive methods. You can learn strategies and ideas by watching the way people work in other professions: how an architect designs an office building, how a builder constructs a house, how a psychotherapist interviews a client, how a graphic artist composes a page and picks a typeface, how a reporter writes a story, how a musician plays an instrument.

Here are five strategies we recommend you think about before you write, so you can apply them as you work:

- Collaborate with other writers and team members.
- Develop your own sense of design.
- Focus on structure, early and often.
- Polish your drafts before handing them in.
- Use the tools available for increasing your productivity.

Some of these practices have been brandished as ideals by many people and then ignored as impractical or too difficult. Today's hardware and software makes them all easier and more practical. So make the most of your computer—it's not just an expensive typewriter.

Collaborate

Collaboration isn't simply getting along with others, improving the product, or learning from team members, although it should include all of these. Collaboration is a practice that makes "the whole greater than the sum of the parts." The more complex the technology we document and the greater the number of people involved in its creation, the more collaboration becomes necessary.

Cultivate a collaborative attitude

You can collaborate with other writers, editors, reviewers, engineers, marketing people, and quality assurance testers. What's most important is attitude. Collaborative teams function well when each person regards her or his work as being constructively and creatively shaped by the work of other team members, no matter how divergent their areas of expertise.

The collaborative attitude transcends cooperation, in which different people create independent parts that fit together to make a whole, or when different people contribute sequentially to shaping the product on its linear route toward completion. In a collaboration, the parts are continually reshaped and redefined by each person's contribution, so the product evolves without any one person owning it, or even part of it.

Here are some hints on how to collaborate.

Agree to agree. Don't plan to compromise, go along, acquiesce. You have to be willing to stick around as long as necessary to work out important conflicts and reach a real consensus—not just a vote—before moving on to the next stage. But planning to agree does not mean wearing a smiley face.

Speak up the moment you sense disagreement. If you're uncomfortable with a decision, note that discomfort and address it as soon as you can. Don't hold secret reservations, object inwardly, or wait cagily until the team has gone down the wrong trail and gotten caught in the tar.

Plunge in with the almost-right. You can't wait until you've got the perfect phrase. Try for something close. Be prepared to have your idea picked up, kicked around, revised, and perhaps adopted.

Stick to your position. Don't give up your ideas until you genuinely change your view. You need to be convinced. Unlike cooperation, collaboration demands that you stick to your guns until you really do change your mind—or everyone else does.

Take turns leading and following the other person's lead. No one is the boss; no one is an employee. If someone is inspired, encourage that person to go on; if there's a pause and you have an idea, charge ahead.

Include everyone in the information loop. Don't let secret alliances develop; don't hog news; don't wait to be asked. Speak up as soon as you can.

Focus on structure. Collaboration pays its biggest benefits when you focus on questions of organization. The best organization expresses what you mean at every level, but that takes hard work, hammering away at every ambiguity, repetition, and inelegant sequence. You have to agree on what's more important, and less.

Consider the emerging documentation to be mutually owned. The more you collaborate, the less you can point to any one idea or phrase as "mine" or "yours." The whole product becomes "ours." You need to be willing to be paid, graded, and evaluated on the collective results. No one owns a specialization or a medium.

Stimulate collaboration via computer

There are four situations in which you can use your computer to invoke and support collaboration.

Same time, same place. You gather around the computer hearth to synthesize designs for a project and its parts and to solve problems when they arise. Currently that means one person acts as recorder/facilitator for the group as you talk and try out your ideas. Here's where a first-class outliner makes an enormous difference in letting you construct what-if scenarios until you reach consensus.

Same time, different place. For most writers this means conferencing from two or three locations via telephone, with a computer active in each location. If you're working in larger corporate settings, you may have the necessary equipment to video conference and use interactive software to work on a shared file at the same time on each of your screens.

Different time, same place. You share documents in progress by circulating files over a bulletin board, an in-house network, or by sneaker net (carrying them down the hall). After you arrive at a design working face-to-face, the parts can be developed simultaneously by each of you. As you work you annotate the file with comments, explanations of the reasoning behind otherwise obscure decisions, questions, and suggestions for additions. You agree to work with software—an outliner, a word processor, and page layout and publishing software—that lets you hide annotations onscreen and choose to print or not print them on paper. Unresolved questions remain with the file throughout its development until they get resolved.

Different time, different place. Sometimes you send files directly to each other over the phone lines. Or you post your work on a bulletin board or on a commercial service such as AppleLink, CompuServe or MCI Mail, and have the other person download the files from there. Then you work separately on your own time.

In any of these situations, keep the size of the group limited so that no more than five or six people are working on the same document. Once a group gets much larger, the time spent on coordinating everyone's work begins to eat into the time you could spend doing the work.

The benefits of collaboration

When team members collaborate, customers get better documentation, with fewer ambiguities, tangles, and omissions. The structure is clearer, more accessible, stands up to more intense questioning. Because several minds have worked on every inch of the document at once, more perspectives get included, so more customers can connect to the work.

Management gets relief: Fewer crises late in the project (like land mines, they've all been exploded much earlier); faster delivery of late drafts; a cleaner product overall.

And you may enjoy yourself more, working closely, quickly, with someone else. You learn a lot about your own biases and habitual tendencies, because other people bump right into them, sand them off, point them out.

Develop your design sense

As writers, we tend to be prejudiced in favor of our own medium— words. We usually think of words first, pictures second, and the layout of a page third, if ever. We sometimes even describe pictures as "illustrations"—meaning that they show what we are talking about as a kind of example, and many of us resent having to include any pictures at all. In the rare moments when we think about book design, we usually show an intense attachment to one particular design solution, which we've used over and over because we are familiar with it and can, basically, ignore it. We rarely begin by considering art and proceeding to add text as annotations.

We need to develop our own design sense for the sake of our users. Users—notice that we don't call them readers here—learn far more from good book design and art than most writers recognize. Users appreciate—and explore—good design.

We also have more responsibility for the nonverbal aspects of our communication than ever before. We now have tools that give us the ability to draw pictures and create page designs, and although we may not be the final artist or designer, our early use of these tools to do preliminary page designs or rough sketches of images can heavily influence the final designs. On most teams we work side by side with professional artists and book designers. The way we communicate with them can mean the difference between a lively, visually expressive book and a boring, text-laden book no one wants to open.

Think like a designer

Learn to express your ideas in terms that make sense to artists and book designers. Understand what they can—and can't—bring to a project.

Think first about your media. A book, for instance, involves at least two: paper and ink. Those can be manipulated to put art and words on the page. Similarly, online help and computer-based training begin with dots on a screen.

Careers have grown up around the extensions of these media—writing, book design, art, and user interface design. In a sense, we are each designers in our chosen media.

Here's how you go about designing your text, at the same time the book designer and artist are designing their contributions.

Plan your effects

Figure out what you want to do for or to your audience. What result do you want to achieve? How will you know if you've been successful? Usually all three of you—writer, book designer, and artist—can agree on the main purpose of a section of your book or help; for instance: "We want to show users how to draw names and addresses from a database, and combine those with a standard letter created in a word processor, in order to send out form letters."

Employ your medium to influence your audience

Design involves planning and creating a series of experiences for your target audiences. If your design is successful, the audiences will notice something like what you want them to notice, feel something like what you want them to feel, think something like what you want them to think. In that case you've **communicated** (more or less). If not, you've just provided another meaningless experience in a culture full of them.

There's a purpose behind almost every move you make. The cumulative effect of all these small decisions should be to achieve the main goal you have agreed on, as a team.

It is at this point that writer, book designer, and artist diverge, because they use different media. For example, here are the kinds of decisions you make about language and the corresponding decisions a book designer or artist might make.

Language. Directly address the audience in the imperative voice, in simple sentences ("Hey, you!"). In a procedure deliver a series of experiences that add up to a reader's mastering of the product for his or her own ends (rather than just fitting into its clutches). Do this by pointing out where we are going, introducing the subject, making the first step clear, showing the results of an action, confirming progress, and giving closure to the experience to solidify long-term learning.

Book design. Select Franklin Gothic as a headline font, Palatino for text, 14-point type for headlines, 10-point for running text. Make the steps in a procedure stand out by boldfacing and outdenting them, and separating one from another with extra white space between steps.

Drawing. Draft very fine irregular lines, indicating this picture is drawn by hand, not by machine. Indicate a diagram or conceptual drawing by using squiggly lines, with no border; place the elements clearly in separate areas by using a 3x3 grid; emphasize the resulting form letters by using an arrangement that shows data flowing from top-left to join with letters coming from about three quarters of the way up and three quarters of the way to the right, to form a big explosion of papers in the bottom right quadrant of the drawing.

Work with a book designer so the page design reflects your intentions

Page design communicates the relative importance of different elements (first- and second-level heads, rule lines, running text, numbered steps, footnotes, and so forth) and thereby suggests the relationship (this heading goes with this introductory text, which leads to this step, and so on).

To communicate with a book designer, you have to be able to articulate the purpose of each element on the page so you can evaluate the designer's solutions and say whether or not the book design seems to be carrying out the function you intended. For instance, is the 10-point boldface type large enough, and visible enough, for the instructions in the procedure? Will some people have to squint? You want to make sure nobody misses this information in a situation where people are looking back and forth between the screen, the keyboard, the mouse, and the book.

You shouldn't insist on a particular solution ("It must be New Century Schoolbook or else!"), because you aren't facing the job of harmonizing the look of procedural pages, reference pages, tables of contents, and indexes. Do, however, point out when, for you, the design is not performing its intended function.

Back in the days when all a writer had was a typewriter or a character-based screen with 24 lines of 80 monospaced characters each, you had few ways to differentiate one element from another. Here, the writer has used position, spacing, and styling to show that some elements are more important than others, that the reader is to take a pause between elements, that a new thought is beginning.

Underlining the main title indicates it is more important than the headings that follow.

Adding a blank line sets off the main heading even more, emphasizing that this must be a really important idea.

The indentation indicates the beginning of a new paragraph.

Centering the title sets it off from the rest of the text, and indicates that it sums up what is to come. But because it is not set off by a blank line, we are to understand that it is less important than the heading above and is tied more closely to the text immediately following. It does not, we interpret, predict the content of more than a few paragraphs.

Using Electronic Mail

When you want to send and receive messages to and from one or more people, use the electronic post office on the HotLinks BBS. HotLinks operates in the background so you can read other messages or work in other programs while you send or receive messages.

To send a message

You can send a message to an individual or to a conference. You can send the message by itself, or you can attach one or more files to send with it.

1. Choose New from the Message menu to open a form.

Your name as sender is already filled in.

2. Type a brief description of the subject and press Tab.

3. Type the name of the person or conference you want to send to.

You can also type the first few letters of the name and press Return. HotLinks fills in the rest or displays a list of possibilities to pick from. Double-click the name you want.

4. Click in the message area and type your message.

Continued

(continued)

Continued

To attach a file to your message, choose Attach File from the Message menu, navigate to find your file, select the filename, and click Attach. Repeat to attach more than one file.

5. When your message is ready (and any files are attached), choose Send from the Message menu.

HotLinks sends your message and puts a copy in your mailbox.

Here's the same page laid out by a book designer, taking advantage of the tools available in desktop publishing software.

Different fonts help the eye distinguish between headings and text.

Placing the heading here makes clear that you are starting a major new section.

The margins and font size used for this introduction suggest that it applies to all that follows, not just the very next section.

Smaller size, different style, and different location indicate that this heading is less important than the first one.

Here the margins indicate that this introduction belongs only to the secondary heading.

Boldfacing, numbering, and white space make this instruction stand out, so an expert user can zip past the explanations.

A third set of margins shows that the explanatory paragraph is even less important than the step.

Using Electronic Mail

When you want to send and receive messages to and from one or more people, use the electronic post office on the HotLinks BBS. HotLinks operates in the background so you can read other messages or work in other programs while you send or receive messages.

To send a message

You can send a message to an individual or to a conference. You can send the message by itself, or you can attach one or more files to send with it.

1. **Choose New from the Message menu to open a form.**

   Your name as sender is already filled in.

2. **Type a brief description of the subject and press Tab.**

3. **Type the name of the person or conference you want to send to.**

   You can also type the first few letters of the name and press Return. HotLinks fills in the rest or displays a list of possibilities to pick from. Double-click the name you want.

4. **Click in the message area and type your message.**

   To attach a file to your message, choose Attach File from the Message menu, navigate to find your file, select the filename, and click Attach. Repeat to attach more than one file.

5. **When your message is ready (and any files are attached), choose Send from the Message menu.**

   HotLinks sends your message and puts a copy in your mail box.

Work with production specialists to make sure the page design is carried out consistently

Most of the documents you create will employ captions, call-outs, leader lines, boxes, several levels of heading, numbered and bulleted lists, and dozens of other typographical devices that were anticipated in the book design and specified in a long document that reads like a typesetter's nightmare ("Sixth-level headings will be 12-point Extended Bold Helvetica Light Italic, 12-point indent," and so on…).

As you head into print, you often get the assistance of a production team, whose job is to make sure you have applied the book design throughout, with consistency and rigor. The production team may include

- A production supervisor who coordinates all the aspects of getting your manuscript into print.

- A book designer who is responsible for the overall appearance of the finished document. Often the designer creates a template using desktop publishing software and answers questions about the best way to format unplanned elements.

- A formatter who takes your manuscript and puts it into a template.

- A paste-up person, who, even in this day of desktop publishing, may have to paste art into slots on the master pages.

Collaborating with production specialists always saves you time and effort. Find out in advance exactly what kind of manuscript files, specifications, and art files they like to work with, and what constraints they must work under. Deviating from the book design here and there, inventing your own new formats, adding unexpected elements, and half-heartedly applying the formats will almost always result in long, grim, painstaking, bleary-eyed sessions in front of the computer screen.

And face it, even in the best of circumstances, a few errors are bound to creep in. You'll always discover a few leader lines that point to the wrong item. Make sure you review the artwork carefully. You may be the only person who can correct this type of mistake, because only you know what you intended.

Work with an artist to communicate more

To collaborate well with a graphic artist, you must have a good idea of what pictures can communicate that words can't.

Words	Images
Use names to point to things	Represent the thing itself
Tell about objects	Show objects
Present ideas sequentially	Represent the whole idea, all at once
Represent size, quantity, and duration with numbers	Portray size, quantity, and duration directly or by changing the scale of objects

Images can represent objects you want identified with certainty. Picturing the overall appearance of something provides a meaningful frame of reference for writing about it—you show what you mean in context. For instance, when we look at the front or back of a computer console, left and right are reversed. Correctly locating a control button or a socket on a piece of equipment with no more than a written description for guidance may prove difficult for some readers, nearly impossible for many dyslexics.

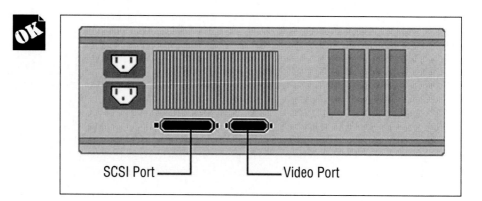

Images can represent ideas, complex processes, and organization, making them more accessible.

This drawing explains the relationships between disks, directories, subdirectories, and files.

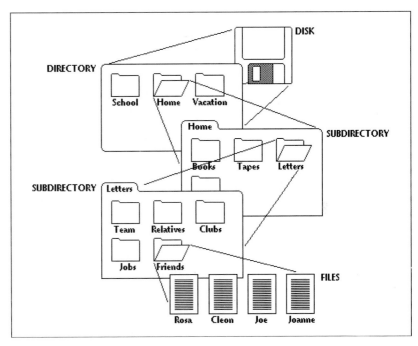

Formatting a floppy disk is like laying out dividing lines in a parking lot.

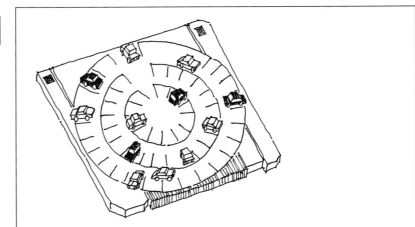

Ask for art when your book needs to

- Explain the purpose of various unlabeled icons, buttons, and tools in a piece of software, or in the control panel of a machine.
- Emphasize important features, buttons, or switches.
- Show users exactly where to attach a cable. Is it on the right or left, front or back?
- Help users distinguish between objects that have very similar names, but different functions. For instance, a window in a drawing program may have a close box, a zoom window, a resize box, and zoom control box.
- Get across an idea in a glance.
- Make clear the main steps in a large, complex process. If there are branches, spread them out across the page so viewers can see how one branch grows out of another.
- Indicate the relative duration of tasks by showing them in scale.
- Distinguish between actions and the results of those actions.

When you are planning your document, start by asking yourself, What can I best express through art, using words only as labels or captions? When the product you are describing has a rich graphic user interface, you may find that you can provide a visual overview—a chapter introducing users to the major screens, tools, icons, and buttons.

Work face-to-face with the artist as you plan and execute artwork

There's no substitute for a few face-to-face sessions. You sketch, the illustrator sketches, you both make overlays that incrementally improve the idea under development. And you can leapfrog one another's ideas in a brainstorming session.

Explain your intentions to your illustrator colleague as clearly as you can. Focus on what you want to communicate to your audience. If you have an image in mind, sketch it, no matter how crudely. An artist's first attempts at representing an idea may not be any more sophisticated in appearance than yours. Accompany your sketch with a written description that mentions details you couldn't draw or that you want emphasized. If you can't clearly conceptualize an image or it is too difficult for you to sketch, provide a written description, even a list of associated words, so that the illustrator can translate your idea into a visual metaphor.

In any case, whether up close or at long distance, develop a good working relationship with the illustrator. Solicit suggestions and pay attention to criticism. Remember that illustrators put as much time and care into learning to invent and implement ideas in visual images as you have put into learning to represent ideas with words.

In working with an artist, as with a book designer and the production team, you are giving up your primal attachment to words—not to get rid of them, but to fit them into a book so your ideas will leap off the page, with the words reenforced by the art and both supported by the book design.

Learn what makes an image attractive

To expand your sense of the possible, examine the drawings and photographs in your favorite magazines, looking not at their content but at their function; go to the museum; visit galleries; take a course in design, or better yet, drawing. Keep asking yourself, how could this art be done better, communicate more? What works, or does not work, in this painting?

Enjoy the interplay of purely visual elements such as color, line, shape, scale, and texture; recognize how these contribute an extra dimension of pleasure to a reader's experience of a document. Imagine a grid behind a drawing; ask yourself whether the picture is balanced visually, or, more likely, tilted to give it more movement.

Taking a life-drawing class or two is the best way for anyone to enter the world of visual representation, because you are actively practicing. A good instructor will pass on time-tested techniques for developing your visual acuity and provide you with personal direction that lets you make the best of your strengths and balance your weaknesses.

Unless you uncover a hidden talent for drawing, you won't become a fine artist, but you will change forever your appreciation of the relationships between objects in three-dimensional space and their representation on the two dimensions of a page. As an added bonus you'll almost certainly become more confident and proficient at sketching your ideas for an artist to flesh out.

Learn what makes images meaningful

You should also become skilled at inventing images that convey the subject appropriately and memorably. You need to be able to distill your thoughts so you know just what you want to communicate; to put together half a dozen half-formed ideas and synthesize them in one drawing; and then to redraw and redraw until you get the idea just right. The more you draw, the more meaning you'll be able to compact into a drawing.

Collect examples of graphs, charts, and diagrams that grab your attention and help you understand the ideas they represent. Paste them in a scrapbook or file them in categories. Take the time to go beyond your first impressions. Evaluate each addition to your collection and make some notes about why you found this particular example effective.

Develop your document's structure

In the nineteenth century the structural template for architects was the Greek temple; you could put a courthouse in it, a bank in it, or a railroad station in it, but it was still a Greek temple. Then a new idea caught on: Perhaps architects ought to find out what people need to do with a building and design around those activities. Architects began to create new structures for new functions.

Structure communicates more than style. When your main point appears in a heading, people spot it and keep it in mind as they scan subsequent paragraphs. When your structure is not visible, or looks like a crazy-quilt, people have a hard time looking things up, and if they do find anything, they have difficulty understanding you because unimportant items distract them from really important ideas. Most writers pay too little attention to organization and too much attention to the style of individual sentences.

You can keep yourself focused on the structure of your book by using a good outliner. Begin using it early—when you set down your first thoughts—and continue using it to rough out a structure for your project and then to amplify and refine that structure.

Of the total time available for your project, spend almost half your time researching and developing your outline as you conduct your research into the audience and product. Think of an outline as a blueprint directing the construction of a building.

A good outliner helps you develop structure in several ways:

- Expanding and contracting the outline to see many or few levels helps you develop a well-rounded conception of the project.

- Contracting the outline to a few of the higher levels lets you take in the whole at a glance so you can assess large-scale structure, making sure that all headings at a level are consistent and develop logically.

- Expanding the outline to see more of the lower levels lets you check for consistency, glaring omissions of subjects, and balance between parts.

It's true you can, with effort, do these things using a word processor or desktop publishing program. But using an outliner you can test alternate structures and develop your chosen structure in a balanced manner. With a word processor you laboriously cut and paste to get the same effect that you can achieve in an outliner by dragging a topic from one position to another. Word processors usually have outlining facilities, but they are clumsy compared to dedicated outliners, because they come trailing all the appurtenances of word processing. When really focusing on structure, you need to subordinate writing and formatting to outlining.

Think of the outliner as a writing spreadsheet that lets you perform what-if investigations of alternative information structures. Don't get stuck on one idea too early in a project. Instead, rough out several approaches and evaluate the merits of each. Play with groups of subheads as if they were building blocks. Move them around, create a sequence of chapters, group the chapters in parts, promote and demote topics, rearrange everything. Compare different information structures to see which one best gets across what you mean. In this way the outliner lets you do on paper—quickly and visibly—what you used to do in your mind as you pondered what material to include in a chapter or part.

Of course, for most writers a bad odor clings to outlining because of our experience in high school, where we all wrote our papers, and then wrote the outlines. But our teachers had the right idea: We ought to plan our structure carefully before writing. It's just that back then, with a pen and paper, we had terrible tools for making an outline.

Like any good tool, your outliner should fit your work style. A well-balanced hammer is a pleasure to use, as well as being more accurate and safer than a clumsily balanced throwaway. If your outliner bangs your mental thumbs, get a different one. Here are some of the tasks an outliner should help you accomplish, whether you use a separate outlining program or an outliner built into word processing or page layout software.

Move a heading, with all its subheadings, to any place in the outline simply and quickly. You should be able to move the heading faster than if you were to cut and paste, and you want to bring along all the associated subheadings. Speed here makes organizing, experimenting, and reorganizing practical.

This is your first pass at arranging a set of topics.

Installing the Toner Cartridge
Loading the Paper
Checking the Power Supply
Turning the Power On

Then you discover that the power has to be on in order to move the paper tray.

Installing the Toner Cartridge
Checking the Power Supply
Turning the Power On
Loading the Paper

Format each level of heading differently. When you start outlining you can begin approximating typefaces, sizes, styles, and layout for the finished book. As you develop your outline, you also refine your approach to the way your words will appear on the page. Roughing out the page in this way helps you track the page count and stay on schedule and on budget. Basically, you want the software to change the format whenever you change a heading's level, so that all first-level headings, say, are automatically formatted the same way.

The format reveals the level at a glance.

Preparing the Printer

Installing the Toner Cartridge

Checking the Power Supply

Turning the Power On

    Locating the Switch

    Powering On

Show the top two levels of heading, say, without any of the others. You need to see if all the headings at one level fit together, form some progression, have the same weight. If one seems out of place, you investigate by opening it up and looking at the third- and fourth-level headings within it.

In general, you should struggle to reduce the number of levels in your outline. Too many levels, even in a well-developed outline, usually means you need to think through the subject matter more carefully, because you may grind your details so fine that they no longer have any of the flavor of the main theme.

Attach different kinds of labels to headings. Most projects have a structural logic you can help make explicit by the labels you choose, such as a Harvard or legal numbering system or several styles of bullets. Their purpose is to help you track the levels of structure while you work; they usually don't appear in the actual manual. Labels also provide a way to refer to passages when you're conversing on the telephone or preparing a list of questions.

Changing the labels reminds the reader that these are parts of the startup checklist.

Preparing the Printer

    ☐ **Installing the Toner Cartridge**

    ☐ **Checking the Power Supply**

    ☐ **Turning the Power On**

    ☐ **Loading the Paper**

Print flexibly. You should have the ability to print as few or as many levels of headings as you need. For instance, you may want to distribute only the top three levels of headings and subheads as an approximation of a table of contents so that managers get the big picture. At the same point in the project, you may also want to distribute all or part of the outline in detail to engineers for a thorough review for accuracy.

A good outline will guide your writing so that it goes swiftly and smoothly, decreasing the likelihood that you'll need to reorganize drastically later on when revisions take a lot more time and effort. Try, then, to resist plunging into writing a draft in running paragraph form until you've developed the outline to the level of the numbered steps in a procedure.

If you've learned to write your text first and then summarize it in an outline as a grim chore engaged in to satisfy the powers that be, you'll need to try real outlining a few times until you get the hang of it.

Here are some other suggestions for keeping the focus on your structure.

Make each draft complete

Complete means that you develop each part of the document to the same level of detail. For example, when you are outlining, don't develop your outline so that Chapter One has eight levels of subheads and Chapter Five has only two. We tend to flesh out what we know most about when we're arm wrestling with a new subject. Don't get lost in details at the expense of the whole. Keep developing your documentation in outline form, adding detail evenly throughout the outline, level by level.

Sometimes you just have to get the details about a subject out of your system so you can stop thinking about them. Go ahead. Just don't write your whole outline this way. Your final draft will probably be lumpy and uneven, some subjects covered thoroughly and others skimpily.

When you discover that part of your project is underdeveloped in comparison with the remainder, you need to find out more about that subject or rethink your approach to writing about it. Discovering this early helps you focus your efforts on needed work and helps prevent last-minute crunches.

Ideally you create a complete draft for each milestone of the document—outline, first draft, second draft, and final draft. As product development time shortens to satisfy the demands of heated competition, you may need to get your manual into the production pipeline in installments. In this circumstance the completeness of your outline is crucial to creating a well-balanced book.

Annotate your drafts as you work

Make notes directly in your computer file as you work so you have handy reminders that you can't misplace. Writer Adam Rochmes says, "The notes I record about the steps of a procedure often contain just the kind of nit-picky details—such as constraints on a command—that can get lost if I don't keep careful track of them from early on." Keep these comments in the outline, and don't remove them until you draft the text in paragraphs. Your annotations can include

- Notes about what you need to do
- Questions to yourself or to reviewers
- Problems you encounter, but cannot solve yourself
- Items that you cut
- Comments from reviewers

Remember to add dates to material you cut or to questions that arise. Later you may need to reconstruct the history of your thoughts.

Whenever you can, use software that lets you view or hide the notes onscreen, print or not print them; that way you can see what the text looks like, uninterrupted, or go through the notes one by one. Apply an "invisible" formatting style to your text if your program has that feature. If not, reserve a particular text style or color for notes. Or enclose notes in special characters such as brackets [note] or chevrons «note» and put them in separate paragraphs. If your software lets you append separate blocks of text to a heading, use those for your notes, or reserve a level of the outline instead. In some software you can set up conditional text: You can make this text visible or not, depending on what you want to look at, so you can print the notes for reviewers but turn them off when printing for a beta tester.

Polish your drafts before delivery

When possible, write in a format that's like the one your words and art will appear in when printed. You may not have the font that will appear in the printed book, but you can use one with the same x height and width so you can approximate the line breaks and page breaks. Ideally you should be able to see that layout on screen as you work and in printouts. Keep adjusting your style to match the length that's appropriate for the design. For instance, in a layout built around art, most callouts should be no more than a sentence long; but if you ignore the layout, you may be tempted to write a whole paragraph, only to have it cut in production.

Apply formatting consistently

If you're going from a word processor to page layout, you'll need to know, fairly early, what formats to use. You may be handed departmental templates. Use them.

If your word processor files will be reformatted in a desktop publishing (DTP) program, you may need to use a consistent set of codes or styles that the DTP program can read. Your printouts won't look exactly like the final book, but they will be usable.

If the production folks are going to strip your files down to raw, unformatted text and rebuild them from there, format in a way that approximates the final book design, but don't worry about minor variations. Then, just before turning your files in, remove all formatting for the production people.

Clean up each draft

Writers often think that writing is all they should have to do and that their words alone will get their point across. But people stumble over an accumulation of little problems, such as typos, strange spacing, inconsistent or unconventional punctuation. And it's not just end-users, it's editors and reviewers who should be able to ignore such chaff.

Before you hand a draft over for review or production spend some time putting it in order. The ideas and skills you're writing about can be lost in the welter of little things readers stumble over.

Check the spelling. At least use a spelling checker. You won't catch homonyms such as *bore* and *boar*, but you'll catch typos, most of which aren't in the dictionary. If you have the time and aren't bleary-eyed in a last-minute dash to completion, proofread the draft.

Check punctuation. Proofreading is the only way. Use a search-and-replace facility to catch and repair the hard-to-see typos, such as space before a comma and extra spaces after a period.

Yes, you should search for empty space. People are used to first-rate typography in books and slick magazines, and in many manuals. They may not know why, but they draw back from a page that has a sprinkling of unnecessary space characters before periods.

Take advantage of productivity tools

Your group may have a set of tools to increase your productivity. In some departments you're handed a template you can write from; in others, you receive preset styles to use in your word processing program.

One of the most overlooked tools is the department style guide. Many have been badly designed, so it's hard to look things up in them; but do not shove them back on the shelf just because they're difficult. Used together with the macros (preset styles or electronic stylesheets for your word processor), these humble books can help you leap past many of the most thorny questions a writer faces.

Follow—or create—a style guide

Most of us have used the word *style* in two different contexts with a different meaning in each. The first usage refers to the acceptable mechanics of the language in which we write—how we use and spell words, how we punctuate sentences, how we apply grammar. The second sense applies to how we use our language to express ideas—formally and academically or informally and conversationally—how writing sounds to us. A style guide is a document that records and sets standards in each of these areas. The style guide reminds you of decisions you and your team have made.

A style guide might provide guidelines for all or some of the following areas:

- Abbreviations and acronyms
- Formatting conventions
- Grammar
- Tone and voice
- Readability level
- Usage of technical words and terms
- Spelling
- Capitalization
- Punctuation

As Meryl Natchez, manager of TechProse, says, "A good style guide lets you build on what has gone before, refining and improving, rather than continually reinventing."

Sometimes you are handed a style guide, and told, "Follow this." Other times you make up your own. In fact, on almost any large document, you have to create your own supplement to the style guide for all the special cases that come up.

Usually you can collect the beginnings of your own style guide from parts of the documentation plan—from statements about the goals of the documentation, from evaluations of the needs and expectations of the audience, from prose descriptions of the documents themselves. Then collect notes about phrases, terms, and approaches you're considering or using. If you can have several documents open at once while you work, keep your style guide open and add your ideas as you write. Don't put it off until later, only to be forgotten. Even when the style guide is someone else's job, keep a record of style issues for discussion with the team.

You'll probably want to adopt a general style manual as an authority so you don't have to decide commonplace issues of grammar, punctuation, and idiom. You might rely on *The Chicago Manual of Style* and *The Elements of Style*, plus your favorite dictionary. Those books can take care of common problems, while leaving issues special to your company or product for resolution in your style guide.

Here's part of a corporate style guide.

acronym Always say what it stands for when you first use the acronym. When forming the plural of an acronym without periods, do not add an apostrophe before the *s*. For examples, see *ANSI, ASCII, BASIC, EBCDIC, IEEE, ISO*.

addresses Abbreviate avenue (Ave.), building (Bldg.), boulevard (Blvd.), place (Pl.) and street (St.) when used in a particular address. Use U.S. Postal Service abbreviations for states (no periods). Separate the state abbreviation and the ZIP Code with two spaces.

address, memory Use memory address or memory location. Only use address or location for brevity.

affect, effect Affect, as a verb, means to influence, as in, "Failure to discharge static electricity may affect your computer's ability to function." Affect, as a noun, refers to evidence of emotion, as in, "She had a pronounced lack of affect." Effect as a verb means to cause, as in, "We shall effect these changes in the next few months." Don't use this form: it's affected. Effect as a noun is more common and means result.

afterward Not afterwards.

allow Use instead of enable, except when referring to circuitry. Hardware enables; programs allow.

all right Not alright. If possible, avoid altogether, as too colloquial.

alphabetic Not alphabetical.

ANSI Acronym for American National Standards Institute, an industry standards organization.

Use macros (style sheets) to automate repetitive tasks.

All current outlining, word processing, or page layout programs let you completely format a character, word, or paragraph with a few keystrokes or mouse clicks. Most programs collect the formatting rules in a list of named styles, usually called a style sheet. Some programs go further and provide a macro facility that lets you condense a series of commands for pasting words, paragraphs, whole pages, and graphics into one command. Or you can use separate macro software that lets you automate almost anything you do on your computer. In addition, in many word processors, you can store long, complex phrases in a glossary and, by pressing one or two keys, have the software type the whole thing for you.

Bullet #1	Heading #1
Bullet # 2	Heading #2
Caption	Heading #3
Callout	Heading #4
Caution	Label
Chapter title	Note to Production
Chapter introduction	Running Text
Computer Voice	Table #1
Example	Table #2
Footer	Table #3
Header	

Part of a list of styles for a user guide.

Running Text: Font: Special Serif 12 Point, Indent: Left 1.5 in Flush left, Line Spacing: at least 14 Point, Space Before 4 Point

Here are the details of the style called Running Text.

Macros, glossaries, and style sheets make it easy for you to apply elements of the style guide. They can ensure correct spelling of technical terms. They can consistently format every instance of every part of a manual so that its appearance is standardized— onscreen and eventually on paper. But don't expect someone else to be happy about learning, all at once, the 400 macros you developed over three years' work. If you create too many macros, or use them inappropriately, they can slow down the writing.

Create your own database tools

Get familiar with a database and a spreadsheet program—familiar enough to craft your own tools. If you are a contractor, your business success will depend on tools such as timesheets, estimating, and billing files.

Databases let you pull together groups of records for the purpose of the moment and prepare a variety of reports. Spreadsheets are better when you want to massage and refine your numbers.

Timesheets. Create a timesheet database that suits your work style. Begin with the minimum—set up fields for the date, the job, and the hours. Then add any other fields you need for your situation: document type, for example, or phase of development, or a description of work done. If you're responsible for a group or reporting to one, you'll need to assemble your data into reports such as time spent on all jobs, broken down by job, or the details of how much time has been spent in each phase for one job.

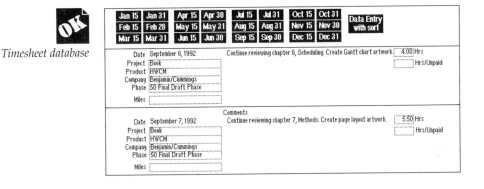

Timesheet database

Keeping reasonably accurate timesheets is a chore that's well worth the effort because you can develop better estimates. After a while you'll have your own figures for how much time you or members of your team need to get a particular job done.

Estimating and billing. Which is better to use for these, spreadsheet or databases? Estimates fit nicely into a spreadsheet format because typically they consist of a matrix of repetitive calculations, such as page count times hours and time allocated versus time spent. Billing goes better in a database, because you'll need to collect and sort all the bills for one job or client or pull out all the unpaid bills.

Glossary. Why not just use an outliner or a word processor for your glossary? With a glossary database you can organize and reorganize as many subsets of terms as you need, for as many jobs as you have. You can define fields that let you collect and sort by the date you created the entry, the source of your definition, and the jobs for which you've used an entry. And you can search your definition fields to find all the terms with a particular word in their definition.

Bibliography. Make your own with a database or use dedicated bibliographic software. The dedicated software is initially easier to use, doesn't require designing, and often has sophisticated formatting options. A homemade database is more flexible in the long run, however, because you can always add another field.

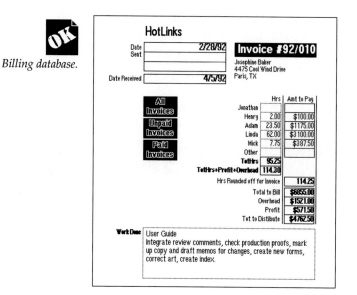

Billing database.

Estimating Spreadsheet.

	Deliverable	Pages	Milestone	Hours (Estimate)	Cost (Estimate)	Hours (Actual)	Cost (Actual)	Difference	
8	*User Guide*		Outline	300	$18000.00	316	$18960.00	-$960.00	
9			1D	150	$9000.00	138	$8280.00	$720.00	
10			2D	150	$9000.00	143	$8580.00	$420.00	
11			Final	80	$4800.00	80	$4800.00	$0.00	
12			Proofing	30	$1800.00	26	$1560.00	$240.00	
13			Index	40	$2400.00	37	$2220.00	$180.00	
14		150		750	$45000.00	740	$44400.00	$600.00	
16	*Quick Start*								
17			1D	80	$4800.00	76	$4560.00	$240.00	
18			2D	20	$1200.00	20	$1200.00	$0.00	
19			Final	20	$1200.00	19	$1140.00	$60.00	
20		20		120	$7200.00	115	$6900.00	$300.00	
22	**Total**	170		870	$52200.00	855	$51300.00	$900.00	

Questions and answers. These are definitely database material. On complex, highly technical projects, a question and answer database can help you make sure you and everyone on the team has the correct information. When you discover that a previous answer was wrong or has become outdated, you can go back and let that source know about the current answer and situation. You can track: When did the question arise? Whom did you ask? Who answered, and when? What was the answer? Which questions remain unresolved?

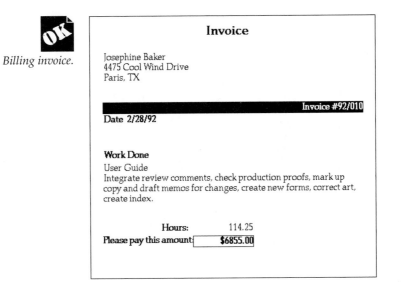

Billing invoice.

Invoice

Josephine Baker
4475 Cool Wind Drive
Paris, TX

Invoice #92/010

Date 2/28/92

Work Done
User Guide
Integrate review comments, check production proofs, mark up copy and draft memos for changes, create new forms, correct art, create index.

Hours: 114.25
Please pay this amount: **$6855.00**

Glossary database.

text ruler

Definition—Original from source

In word processing programs, a graphic representation of a ruler on which you set the format for the document, such as right and left margins, line spacing, and tabs.

Source of Definition
Amos Otis

Date Added
1/13/92

Date Changed
1/13/92

My Definition

The HotLinks text ruler appears at the top of message documents.

Change:
HK

Used in Project Glossary
HotLinks

OK

Bibliography database.

author	Cohan, L.A., & Newsome, S.L.	21 Feb 91
		Revised
year	1988	Subject Context
booktitle		Online Help
		Documentation
book Article		Design
		Windows
City/Publisher		
		Include:
		Bibliography Reprint
journal article	Navigational Aids and Learning Styles: Structural Optimal Training for Computer Users	Online Help No
publication	Sigchi Bulletin	
vol. & page	20, #2: 30-32	Master copy on file Yes
	Ability to navigate through an environment depends on two types of spatial knowledge: Route knowledge—the specific memory of actions that guides people from one place to another via a known path. Survey Knowledge—Memory of a more global structure with some understanding of the relationships between particular landmarks or local regions of the environment. Study tests what type of spatial knowledge subjects acquired when they studied either a global or partial representation of a heirarchical menu structure.	Reviewed Yes

Checklist

As you work to make your manuals more convivial, you:
   Collaborate with other writers and team members

☐ Cultivate a collaborative attitude

☐ Stimulate collaboration via computer

   Develop your own sense of design

☐ Learn to communicate with design professionals

☐ Plan your effects

☐ Make the most of your medium

☐ Help craft page designs that reflect your intentions

☐ Work with production specialists to ensure the design is carried out consistently

☐ Learn what makes an image attractive and meaningful

   Develop your document's structure

☐ Focus on the outline

☐ Make each draft complete

☐ Annotate drafts as you go

Polish your drafts before delivering them

☐ Check the formatting for consistency

☐ Check the spelling

☐ Check the punctuation

Take advantage of style guides and macros
Create your own database and spreadsheet tools

PART TWO   *Writing*

Openers—Tables of Contents and Introductions

I've stopped in mid-sentence. I'm starting off this long section: and I realize that exactly what I need at this point is a clear and concise summary statement of precisely what it is I'm going to say. And with the realization comes a trickier one: I cannot say clearly and concisely what it all amounts to.

—Peter Elbow

Few people begin their involvement with a manual by reading page 1. Some flip through the whole book, looking only at headings. Others skim the table of contents or turn to the index. Still others read the first paragraphs of a chapter, wondering whether to bother with the rest. A few settle down and read your introduction to learn how to use the manual. Tables of contents, introductions to your book, and introductions to chapters and sections offer you an opportunity to start your readers off on the right foot.

In this chapter we'll explore

- How to make your table of contents reveal what's in your book
- How to steer readers to the sections they need
- How to get people started
- How to introduce the product itself
- How to introduce a major topic or chapter

Make your table of contents outline the material

For many people the table of contents is their primary reference tool. No matter how short your manual, people count on the table of contents as an outline of the material, as an indication of what you consider the major and minor topics, and as a map leading them to the information they need. At a minimum, your main table of contents should include chapter titles and the first level of headings from each chapter, along with page numbers. Remember that your readers may look at most of the pages in the manual only once, but they will look at the table of contents dozens, perhaps hundreds, of times. Think of the table of contents as the first chapter in your book.

Give your audience an idea of what's in each chapter

All chapter titles should make sense to a beginner. These can be rather broad: "Introduction," "Tutorial," and "Reference" are traditional, somewhat old-fashioned, but safe and comprehensible. "Setting Up," "Working with Files on the PC," and "Printing" are more specific, but their meaning remains accessible.

Whenever possible, first-level headings also should target beginners. "Connecting the Cables" or "Displaying the Contents of a PC Hard Disk" are meaningful to people with little experience.

As you descend to the lower-level headings and begin focusing on the more specific workings of your subject, you may find some jargon unavoidable. "Connecting Directly to a BOTTOMS Flash-Card through the Slow Charger" won't mean much to anyone who isn't familiar with the details of the subject or the context, but it does name the relevant task for someone who is.

Take a diagnostic approach and put troublesome issues in headings so customers can spot a description of their problem quickly.

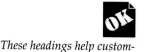

These headings help customers find answers to their questions.

> **Freeing Up Memory**
>
> **Coping with Smears, Smudges, Lines, and Fuzzy Spots**
>
> **If Your Document Won't Print**

Make sure these headings represent problems the way customers think about problems.

> **Paper Delivery Mechanism Release Implementation**

> **Clearing a Paper Jam**

Use verbs, not nouns

Verbs suggest the reader can do something with the hardware or software. And when you employ verbs commonly used within the task domains of your readers, you help them connect their current skills with the new ones you're writing about.

This bunch of nouns looks like a list of topics to study.

The Delete Function

Implementation of the Copy Function

Understanding the Move Function

The Search Function

Use verb phrases to liven things up.

Deleting Words and Phrases

Copying Text

Moving Text

Searching Through Text

In general, try to construct headings that are parallel in form at any one level. Once you've started using gerund phrases, keep it up. You might recast a series of headings from "Unpacking, Setting Up, Planning, Data Security," to "Unpacking, Setting Up, Planning, Safeguarding Your Data." But don't be straight-jacketed into inventing convoluted phrases just to be consistent. At times a single word such as "Printing" says exactly what you mean.

Avoid headings consisting solely of key words. Who wants to find out what ACK, STAT, REN, and PIP mean? If you think some people will look up commands in the table of contents, then include them—but only as an afterthought. First use English and then append the acronym.

Use noun phrases for concepts or command references, as in "The Nuclear Option," or "The Kill Command."

This table of contents for a BASIC manual doubles as a quick reference card, but only if you do this for every command and function.

Should you ask questions?

Questions make interesting headings, as long as you don't ask too many. They don't all have to end with a question mark, either. When you have an introductory section that explains the ideas behind the topic you're about to detail, questions can emphasize the point.

Why Device Drivers?

How to Decide Which Driver to Use

Why It's Called a Handshake

Keep titles short enough to scan

Short titles and headings let readers understand what you mean at one glance, not three or four.

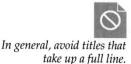

In general, avoid titles that take up a full line.

> **Using Logical and Physical Devices**
>
> > **Printing with the LST Command**
> >
> > **Simple Uses**
> >
> > **Advanced Uses**

Keep the layout simple and uncluttered

Differentiate major and minor topics clearly. Indicate the scope and importance of a topic by varying type sizes and styles: big and bold for chapter titles, small and plain for less important headings. When you want to suggest intimacy and informality, italics may be appropriate—but only if you are sure the slant and curlicues don't interfere with legibility.

Always use upper- and lowercase letters; uppercase letters alone are hard to read. If you need the extra emphasis that uppercase letters convey, use large and small caps. Use indentation to indicate less important topics.

Don't preface every line with a string of numbers such as 2.13.166A. You're not writing a legal brief or military drill (unless you're writing for the government). Often the numbering system is a carryover from an early phase of outlining and organizing. Numbers distract from the meaning of the words in the titles.

Use chapter tables of contents only when you must

Chapter tables of contents set up an extra stop along the way in a reader's search for a particular piece of information, so avoid them when you can. People begin to wonder, "Which table of contents has more information? Which one should I use?"

The main question to ask yourself is, What topics do people want to look up? When chapters are very complicated with many levels of headings needed to help organize and clarify fine-grained detail, a single table of contents at the front of the book may not suffice. The book's main table of contents may have so many levels that it's confusing, or it may become so long that readers can't construct an overview of the book. If so, begin each chapter with a chapter table of contents providing the extra detail that readers can use to zip to the section they want.

Here's what the main table of contents said about some functions of an editor.

Here's how the chapter table of contents covered the same ground.

Show your audience how to use the documentation

People want to make sure they have turned to the part of the documentation that will inform them about the task, concept, or command they have in mind right now. They need signposts pointing them in the right direction.

Tell each group of readers how to proceed

Use your audience profile to make sure you provide routing information for each major group of readers.

- Beginning computer users
- Old hands
- People who haven't used this type of application
- People who know the type of application but not this particular one

Make the access routes to information clear. Create a table up front to catch readers as they enter the book and send them to the right location.

After each "If," give readers the "then"—where to turn for the information. Include the component title (if you have a documentation suite with more than one element) and chapter, section, and page numbers, so they can turn there immediately,.

To do this	Turn to this section
If you've just set up your computer	Read your owner's guide for general information about programs and disks
If you're new to computers	Read Chapter 2, "Introducing Treasure Trove Utilities, "a hands-on tutorial for first-time users
If you're experienced	Read Chapter 1, "What's New in this Version"
If you want to look up a topic	Scan the table of contents or flip to the index.
If you think you're in trouble	Turn to Chapter 10, "Troubleshooting"

When your manual has an unusual layout or you want to clarify an intensive use of graphics, an illustrated tour—pictures of pages from each section of the manual with callouts—can get across the major features effectively.

Tell your audience what they need to get started

Include a packing list in your first booklet if manufacturing does not automatically provide it with the product. That way the nervous can assure themselves they have all the pieces before beginning.

Identify what's included in the product package and what equipment people must provide. Many people worry about not having the right equipment.

Bulleted lists are simple, economical, and effective.

> Before you start using Relate-a-File, make sure you have the following:
>
> - A PC with 20 megabytes of RAM and a hard disk of at least 200 megabytes, running Windows or OS/2
> - The Relate-a-File Installation Disk
> - The Relate-a-File Program Disk
> - The Relate-a-File Sample Files Disk
> - A printer (optional)

Since many people are impatient, you might tell them what they should do first—make backup disks, for instance. Then go on to tell them what else to do to get started, even if you go over that in a tutorial.

In the early pages of your manual, tell people what you expect them to know before beginning to use the product or manual (for instance, common accounting procedures or COBOL), and reference any other necessary books. You'll warn the unprepared before they get stuck and save them from a frustrating experience that might prejudice them against the product or manual.

Introduce the product

Often it makes most sense to write intros last, when you know the product best. By the end of the project, marketing has figured out the main benefits of using the product, you've discovered the most adroit way of describing new features, and the team has dropped several functions you might have struggled to explain, if you started writing your introduction when you started your first draft.

Tell people what the program can do for them

You'd be amazed how many writers forget to do this. Maybe they figure that because readers bought the program they must know what it's good for. Not necessarily. Remember that the boss may have bought the program and turned it over to someone else who has no idea what it's for.

Here's an example of a high-speed, condensed, general introduction.

> This electronic version of the dictionary will provide you with more information faster than you could manage with the printed copy. You can still look up how to spell a word, how to divide it into syllables, what it means, and what its origins are. And, when there's some debate about the best way to use the word, we give you our recommendations. But because this version of the dictionary is electronic, you can ask much tougher questions of the dictionary than before; for instance, you could say, "Find me all the musical terms that derive from the Italian." (You'd find more than 150 words that come from Italy.) Or you could say, "Tell me which words include quotes from Shakespeare as example texts." Basically, we've taken the book and turned it into a database. In the next few pages, you'll learn how much more power that puts at your fingertips.

Another question to answer quickly: How does it work? Provide just a thumbnail sketch of the way the program works— a few paragraphs or a few pages.

In the introduction to a manual on a spreadsheet, the writer starts with the metaphor of accounting paper to give a broad context.

> **Where Do You Work?**
>
> WhizziCalc unrolls a piece of accounting paper 82 columns wide and 354 rows long, giving you a total of 29,028 cells into which you can enter numbers or text.
>
> You look through a window on your screen at a part of this gigantic electronic worksheet. With a few simple keystrokes or clicks of the mouse, you can move left, right, up, or down. So you can set up an income statement in one area, an expenses statement in another, and flip back and forth. Or, if you wish, you can open one window to look at income and another window, right next to it, to study expenses.

If the program can't handle some things that readers might expect, say so here, so they don't waste time looking through the documentation. Tell readers about customizing the program for different purposes and arrangements of software and hardware. Indicate where the manual explains how to make the changes.

Introduce major topics

Start off chapters and large sections of your manual with a brief overview. An overview helps casual readers, who can glance at it and recognize whether this is the chapter they're after. When the chapter does deal with the topic readers are after, an overview answers most of their initial questions about the topic in a general way. Start with principles, then follow up with necessary detail. Make sure that you keep the introductory material brief—don't frustrate your reader with false starts.

Provide overviews to establish context

When you introduce a chapter, you may include topics such as

- What readers have learned so far, and what they will learn in this section—how this chapter grows out of the ones before it and leads to the next ones
- What the chapter does and does not discuss
- How different users can best approach the chapter. For instance, which sections an experienced user can skip
- Where to turn for information about related subjects

Remember that some people will pick up your manual and start right here—even though it's the overview to the fourth chapter. So be especially careful of jargon. If you must use it, make clear what it means and indicate where else you discuss the topic. If a chapter has several subsections, include an overview for each subsection that needs one. You'll feel like you're repeating yourself. Fine. Few people will read through all the sections in order as if they were literature.

Creating a Report

By now you know how to enter data, edit it, sort through it, and find the facts you need. You're ready to put some of that information into a report.

The first step in creating a report is picking one of the preset report formats; the next step is telling Relate-a-File which fields to include, and which records. You then specify font information for each of the fields. You can also create a header or footer, and a variety of summary parts to summarize the contents of subgroups or all the records. You can then print the report.

You can use a report format only once, or you can save it and use it again.

This chapter shows you how to

- Choose a report format
- Specify fields and records to use
- Specify fonts for the report
- Create headers and footers
- Create summary parts
- Print the report
- Save the format of your report

Don't strain to write meaningless introductions to subjects that don't need them just because most other subjects do have introductions. Your readers won't miss the unneeded introduction that customarily would have fallen between the level one and level two heads. If you do include unnecessary introductions, readers may be encouraged to skip all the introductions as a waste of their time.

Don't duplicate material you present elsewhere

Tell people what they must do and why, but don't tell them how in an introduction or overview. Save the hows for the steps of your procedure or tutorial. Telling them something about how in both places can create ambiguities later about where they can find needed information.

Don't treat an overview as the place to discuss exceptions, obscure qualifications, warnings, or frightening jargon. Keep in mind that you're offering readers a chance to look over the broad landscape before they go down into the twisting streets full of detail. It's a beginning, not an afterthought.

Checklist

A useful table of contents

☐ Gives your audience a clear idea of what is in each chapter

☐ Uses verb phrases, not noun phrases

☐ Keeps titles short

☐ Keeps the layout simple and uncluttered

☐ Appears in one place only—at the beginning of the book

At the beginning of your documentation, you should

☐ Show your audience how to get the most out of the documentation

☐ Tell people what they need to get started

☐ Introduce the product

At the beginning of discussions of major topics

☐ Provide an overview to establish context

☐ Predict what you will discuss, without repeating it all

Getting Users Started

**You become a good writer just as you
become a good joiner: by planing down.**

—Anatole France

9

Starting out is a critical time for users of any computer product, because their first impressions can color all their subsequent experiences. Imagine the situation: The purchaser has just torn off the shrink-wrapping and opened the box. Half a dozen manuals, as many disks, perhaps a few cables, stickers, and hardware parts lie amid the styrofoam peanuts and antistatic plastic bags. What now?

The customer looks for something meeting his or her expectations and needs. Each group in your audience—the timid beginners, the cautious intermediates, the confident experts—should find something they can recognize as a meaningful first step in learning the product. In most cases your audience analysis will have prompted you to include some of the following materials:

- A **Welcome** or **Read Me First** booklet or section presents paths through the information about the product for each segment of the audience, telling them where to start and where to go next.

- An **installation guide** explains how to get a product ready to start and use.

- Beginning and intermediate users may need a **Getting Started** chapter or booklet to ease the shock of a new product's complexity. Instead of diving into deep water and swimming, they may need to dip a toe in first and enter one step at a time.

- If you have a lot of experienced or especially brave users, provide a **Quick Start** guide, telling them how to get going fast.

- For people fearful of computer work, a **disk-based guided tour** can rehearse them without any chance of getting into trouble using the real software. A tour shows them how the program works and gives them a chance to practice in a safe environment.

- If you have some amazing new features and tricks to show people, create a **video** so they can see, in motion, how to do some of the important tasks the product makes possible.

You may not write all of these yourself; in fact, for video or computer-based tours, you often rely on people in other groups, such as audio-visual or training. But you do need to plan the customer's first experience—don't leave it to chance or guesswork.

Welcome your readers

Your readers need a clear path through the plethora of materials that come with your product. People may not know where to begin if you offer a tour on a disk, a chat with your company president on video, a guide to installation, a quick start, and several manuals. You want to keep them from picking absolutely the wrong place to start: for example, the manual on programming tips for advanced developers will only confuse the beginner.

Be bold and blunt. Issue a welcome section or booklet that captures each audience and sends them on the right path.

This welcome greets newcomers and tells them what to do first, based on their interest and experience.

Welcome

Thanks for buying All-at-Once, the complete statistical and charting package for the busy executive.

If you're new to statistical software, please use the Introduction disk. Put it in your floppy disk drive, and when the disk icon appears, double click it to see what All-at-Once can do for you. Then turn to the tutorial book called Getting Started All-at-Once.

If you're familiar with other statistical software and just want to get started, please turn to the Installation Guide for setup instructions, and then use the Quick Start. Later, as you work, you will want to look up procedures in the User Guide.

If you've used earlier versions of All-at-Once, please insert the disk marked UpGrade in your floppy disk drive, double-click its icon, and then double-click the icon for the Installer. Your software will be upgraded. Then turn to the booklet titled What's New for news about the great new features we've added. You can get right to work; please turn to the User Guide for information about new procedures.

Such guidance helps the newcomer get moving quickly. Your readers will feel grateful that you have actually imagined their situation and thought how to help them recover from packaging overload.

Soothe harried installers

One thing is certain in this uncertain world: Before you can use a computer, you must put its various parts together, and to use a computer program, you have to install it. Consider how much is involved: Very often, to install software, you must configure it; set parameters and preferences; create directories or folders; type in registration numbers, phone numbers, part numbers, port codes, and code numbers; choose from lists of printers; decide about saving, replacing, renaming, rewriting, or overwriting the CONFIG.SYS file; understand the scheme of copy protection and whether backup versions are expected, allowed, or encouraged; and—oh yes—consider whether the operating system is the proper version anyway.

You may have heard engineers joke about having potential users take a test, and only those who pass would be allowed to install their program. Such humor serves as a way of coping with a truly problematic situation:

- Software installation is the number one technical support problem.
- Some computer software companies change the installation procedures without changing the installation instructions!
- Installation *instructions* often must be written at the last minute, because managers put off installation *decisions* until they know how big the program actually is, how many disks are used, what kind of copy protection or compaction scheme is most appropriate, and so on. They say, "There isn't enough time to test the instructions with real users."

People connecting equipment and installing computer programs are anxious; they may quickly get into trouble. The more you keep this in mind, the more understanding you can bring to the task of helping them along. The best way to write these instructions is to try to install the product yourself, write up the instructions, and then have a novice user try the installation based on what you have written.

Aim the installation guide at all users

Installing software on a computer's hard disk or hooking up a piece of hardware can have implications for all the other programs the computer runs, particularly the operating system. But only rarely is a product aimed at users who understand all or even most of such implications. Generally, every kind of computer user will be installing your product. (Don't believe the myth that every customer's company has an in-house expert who just lives to install a user's new software or hardware. This myth usually crops up precisely at the moment when management is arguing that you don't need to tell people how to install anything, because the process is "so obvious.")

Reasonable companies make installation as automated as possible. In an ideal world, users can run one program that takes over the chore of transferring files to a hard disk, presents lists of the necessary choices, provides complete instructions, changes the relevant system files, prompts for additional disks, and perhaps even uncompresses compressed files. The ideal installation instruction is, "Start the installation program, and follow the directions on the screen."

However, as the writer of installation instructions, you often need to provide the context for your readers:

- the equipment and system software for which the software has been designed
- how the user can customize installation for a particular computer
- what information the user must provide during the installation process
- a list of any special codes or telephone numbers the user must look up

Given some form of automated installation, you can offer two kinds of installation instructions: detailed for novice users and general for experienced users. You can create a Quick Start guide for those who are confident about their own ability to install software and want to do so with a minimum of guidance.

Make it complete

Your job is to provide everything your reader needs to start using the product. You needn't teach the theory of operations, but you must include every step.

If the installation process has a potential glitch, highlight it and provide the information necessary to get around it. Remember, installing the software is the solution to a problem your reader might express as, "How can I get the application to start?" Also, consider that the installation instructions (the information and procedures) will form a troubleshooting guide if the installation should fail. If actually printing the information in the front of the manual seems to ruin your structure or interrupt its flow, be sure to print the instructions in a separate book, section, or appendix, and clearly point it out to the user.

Final copy for much introductory material can't be written until the end of the project when the last pesky details of the interface have been settled and the interface is frozen, the actual process of installation gets finalized, and marketing finally positions the product in the marketplace. Therefore you will probably have to rush the writing for any installation guide, and probably a Quick Start guide as well.

Anticipate problems so they never arise

Help your readers avoid problems by recognizing them as you try out the installation process yourself and then providing a solution. Ask yourself what a reader needs to consider before and during installation, and then be sure your instructions respond to those concerns, or that the installation routine anticipates them.

Tell people what information to gather before starting to install the program:

- What code numbers are required?
- Where will the program be stored?
- What computer configuration is required? What is the optimal setup?
- How much disk space is needed?

Help users anticipate the results of installation to prevent them from damaging the current settings. For instance, suppose the installation routine for a program creates a directory on disk and places the program in it. If a directory with the same name currently exists on the disk, it would be overwritten unless you warn the user to rename the directory before installing. If you work with the team designing the installation routine, you may be able to suggest that the installation routine pause to give users the opportunity to rename the directory.

Discuss related problems that may stem from other hardware or software. This may take a little extra research, but it makes a big difference to the ordinary customer, who cannot easily distinguish your product's failure from an operating system bug. The customer doesn't know how to diagnose the situation and may mistakenly pin the blame on your product.

For example, when a customer shifts from a dot matrix printer to a laser printer, he or she needs new font files to print with the laser printer. Because the font files come from another manufacturer, however, the laser printer manual ignores any problems customers might encounter with fuzzy printing or crashes when using their old font files. Customers don't know which manufacturer to blame, so they call the laser printer's customer support line. In revising the laser printer manual, the writers might include the suggestion, "Make sure you have the right font files for a laser printer," as part of the setup process.

Keep it simple

Installation instructions follow the same principles as other procedures. Provide clear directions, separate the steps users must perform from the explanations of why and the descriptions of results, and test the sequence of instructions again and again.

To Connect the VeriColor Hardware

With the VeriColor computer attached to the color copier, you are ready to connect the remaining VeriColor hardware.

1. **Place the monitor and keyboard on the top of the VeriColor computer.**

   Make sure you position the monitor so none of the VeriColor computer's ventilation areas are blocked. Don't put papers, manuals, or other items on VeriColor or the monitor.

2. **Plug the monitor's video cable into VeriColor's monitor socket.**
3. **Plug the monitor's power cord into VeriColor's monitor power outlet.**
4. **Plug the keyboard cable into VeriColor's keyboard socket.**
5. **Attach the BNC "T" connector to the thin cable Ethernet socket at the rear of the VeriColor computer.**

   Make sure a 50-Ohm cable terminator is attached to each arm of the "T." The VeriColor computer will not start up without them.

Continued

Continued

Make sure that the VeriColor computer's power switch is set to Off.

6. Plug one end of the VeriColor power cord into VeriColor and the other end into a grounded electrical outlet.

Warning: Plug VeriColor's power cord only into a three-hole, grounded AC outlet to ensure that VeriColor is electrically grounded. The grounding plug is an important safety feature.

Don't give gratuitous choices! Find the single best way to perform an action, and tell people to do it that way. For example, the installation routine may offer users the options of typing a number to choose a command from a menu, moving a highlight and pressing Return, clicking the item with a mouse, or touching the screen. Unless such options are an integral part of the standard interface offered by the computer for which the program is designed, skip the opportunity to wow users with trivial options.

Avoid the siren song of marketing, too. Detours into blurbs about neat features defeat the purpose of an installation guide. Tell marketing they have to wait until the customer has the software or hardware working before they can advertise special features. Your introduction should include a brief overview of what the product does, though, because these instructions may be the first and last booklet the user reads.

Start beginners smoothly

People who need a structured introduction to a product deserve a Getting Started section. For products with a unique interface or concept, this section would be necessary for virtually all users. But for any product, certain users may benefit from a paragraph of welcome that addresses their special situation:

- Their boss knows the product and gives it to them.
- They've just been hired and need to learn this program for their jobs.
- They've just been promoted, and people at the new level use this program.

- The entire department is learning this program as a new way of doing business.
- They used a different program for this application but have recently switched.
- They used the previous version.
- They're not comfortable exploring on their own.
- They're evaluating the software for possible adoption company-wide.

What is Getting Started?

A Getting Started section or booklet is a structured introduction to using the product. It can take many forms. As a tutorial, it might take a user by the hand and introduce the product's major features. As a set of procedures, it could point people in useful directions and suggest ways to proceed further. Some combination of explanatory material to introduce new concepts and tutorials to guide a user through an unfamiliar interface can change an attentive neophyte into a beginning student, informed and enthusiastic.

In almost any program, *80% of the work is done with 20% of the tools or features*. This 20% is the subject of the introductory material. If you can't demonstrate all the tools, demonstrate the central ones and point at the rest. Ideally, the material you label as Getting Started should do exactly that—get a user from standing still to moving.

Aim the content precisely

Tasks you set up for users to do during a Getting Started tutorial ought to be central to their understanding of the product and realistic for the work they will do with it. Your audience profile better be up to date, because the introductory material must be pitched exactly right, geared to the kind of product and the person who will be using it.

For example, suppose you are introducing a relational database product to people who don't know what a database is. You decide to walk them through a sample database with two data files. You explain fields, records, data entry, importing data, searching, sorting, and reporting. You create a sequence of lessons on these basic tasks, and leave lessons on more advanced tasks such as data validation or passwords to a separate book or section.

On the other hand, you must take a very different approach if you are introducing the same relational database product to people who know quite a bit about databases and have purchased this one to become advanced database designers. You decide to provide a fairly sophisticated but small database with four related data files designed to be used as part of a multi-user network. You write a short introduction to the example showing how to explore it, and then walk users through a tutorial about creating the file structure. In this case you explain enough about the theory of database design to illustrate how standard terms apply to this program.

Equally important is setting the example in an appropriate context. For a database program aimed at academics and collectors, the example database could be a museum collection tracking system, but for a business audience, an invoice database is a better choice. When you face a large, amorphous audience, you'll need to brainstorm with marketing to find a context that will appeal to many people without offending any.

Provide a completed example

One of the most useful ways to introduce the features of an application is to guide the learner through completing an example you've started but not yet finished (you've entered all the text so they don't have to type a lot)—an example that is practical, interesting, and handsome. When users are done, their completed example can stand on its own as an illustration of the capabilities of the program and as a model to examine and emulate. As an introduction to programming languages or other complex tools, a few good examples often are all that an advanced user needs.

Give advanced users a Quick Start

Aim a Quick Start at people who are better off without much talk, who prefer being pointed in the right direction and like to explore on their own. Knowledgeable, experienced, and confident, they are sometimes called power users. They don't want to be slowed down by explanations; they just want the steps, and they don't mind a little condensation.

- They may know an earlier version of the same program, so primarily they want to know about new features and how they fit in with the old ones.
- They may be familiar with the task domain and are experienced with similar products, so primarily they are interested in how this program handles familiar tasks.
- They are in a hurry to benefit from the product.
- They read only the minimum necessary to get going and use the manual primarily to look up unfamiliar procedures and reference materials.

A Quick Start provides these power users with a road map.

What is a Quick Start?

A Quick Start booklet (rarely a manual section) typically provides a bare-bones installation guide, a general overview, and a quick set of basic procedures. You're saying something like, "The gas tank is full, here's a map, watch out for those tigers over there, and good luck!"

The secret to a good Quick Start is condensation and centrality. The guide provides the absolute minimum information necessary to start, and then focuses on the most important aspects of the program.

Start the booklet by qualifying the reader: Explain, as politely as possible, that this guide is for power users only.

> If you're familiar with word processing software in general, and PreViouS software in particular, you can use this Quick Start to install KnewWrite, and get right to work.
>
> If you want more detailed explanations and support, please use the Installation Guide and the KnewWrite tour disk.

A good Quick Start wins you the appreciation of a tough and experienced audience. They deserve their own path through start-up.

Quick Install

A stripped-down version of the installation instructions depends on users following (and understanding) the on-screen instructions. The written guide may do no more than list the information to be gathered before installing and provide page references to the complete instructions in case a problem arises. (The full installation instructions may require a separate booklet or chapter.) As a rule of thumb, if the Quick Install instructions are more than a page long, they are perceived as a Slow Install.

A Quick Install is most successful, obviously, with a well-designed installation program that performs most housekeeping and setup tasks automatically.

Follow the Rule of Three

In general, try to follow the Rule of Three, which is, give the user only three things to remember to get going:

1. Here are the menus for these functions.
2. Here are the commands you will use most frequently.
3. Try this first, then make your own choices.

More than three ideas are too many to keep in mind. If absolutely necessary, you can expand the number to four, but recognize that you are placing a larger burden on rapidly firing neurons than you should.

Use broad strokes

As you work on the Quick Start, keep in mind that your audience is confident and competent, so you can concentrate on the large picture. Tell them how to set up what needs to be set up, how to operate the program, and how to finish with a printout or some other desired result. Remember—these people are interested in productivity.

If the interface employs a critical sequence of actions, or if the program requires a particular concept to be grasped, place the subject in its own section. Take the time to explain—briefly—what a user needs to know. You can assume these people know the meaning of most technical terms, but you may need to explain the new twist your engineers have put on those old concepts.

Brainstorming a Quick Start

Here is a case study of how a Quick Start booklet evolves to answer a real need. Imagine a software product designed to make some business activities a lot more flexible, interesting, productive, and convivial. Unfortunately, the product has a complicated installation procedure and requires some knowledge of modems, and the customer must set up a series of files and create customized printed forms to take advantage of its capabilities.

You may start out thinking your first directive should be, "Set aside a minimum of four hours," but this is clearly anathema for business people on the go. What can you put in a user's hands that will be of use? A pointer to the appropriate pages in the manual? A diagram of the program structure? A flow diagram of possible approaches to the task of starting out? A decision tree?

As you ponder these possibilities, you put yourself in this user's place and picture him or her sitting in front of a computer with the open package. The person has been looking forward to using this product and has an appointment (a presentation, a meeting, a business trip) in 45 minutes. Is there anything to do now?

The Quick Start booklet in this case must be aimed at an experienced user who can install software with a minimum of help, whose modem already works the way it is supposed to, and who knows where to find the files stored on the hard disk. This user's only problem is time. So the Quick Start is set up in stages. Each stage offers productive use of the software and builds on the previous stage, so the user gets increasing use out of the product over time.

At each stage in this example Quick Start, the user sees how to do something productive, building on what went before.

Here the writer has fallen down on the job, leaving it to users to determine what some basic tasks might be.

1. **Install the program.**
2. **Leave the computer running.**
3. **Access the computer from the field via modem to perform the most basic tasks.**

Now the writer has added some bare-bones steps so users will know what to do, to use the basics of the program.

2. **Set up a couple of records for colleagues, and enter their addresses and fax numbers.**

3. **Leave the computer running, and go out into the field.**

4. **Access the computer from the field to look up the file Test Run, and send the file to the addresses on the records.**

Finally, the writer expands on step 2 to make the exercise more challenging. Rewriting step 2 means that users must do more in the office, so they can do more later in the field.

2. **Set up a couple of address records and a couple of directories to hold particular files.**

3. **Leave the computer running.**

4. **Access the computer from the field to perform basic tasks, send results to addresses, and retrieve files from the designated directories.**

Guide readers on a tour

A guided tour is an introduction to the look and feel of a program, like viewing a city through the windows of a bus with an informed guide describing and explaining the features of the landscape. You glance at all the high spots so you can decide what to spend time visiting in depth later. The tour is built around the features that distinguish the program and the benefits that flow from making use of them.

A guided tour can illustrate and explain a program's interface using a series of pictures: screen shots with callouts, diagrams of the program structure, short descriptions of key benefits, and perhaps summaries of some key activities. Devoting half a dozen pages to a guided tour is a very effective use of manual space.

For instance, to introduce a word processing program, you might show the basic window in which people work; the ruler they use to set tabs, alignment, margins, and line spacing; a number of key dialog boxes (dealing with the formatting of the page, finding and replacing, checking spelling, and using the thesaurus); and finally, in miniature, the printouts of a memo, a business letter, a resumé, and a newsletter. Callouts would emphasize how the authors have taken advantage of many great features. This type of introduction reminds people why they bought the package, shows them what the software can do, and previews what they will soon be able to do. This foreknowledge shapes their conceptual model of the product, and motivates them to learn.

Remember that many people simply get handed a piece of software and don't really know what it can do. In this circumstance a seven- or eight-page tour can set out the main features and benefits for them so they begin with a sense of opportunity rather than a feeling of being burdened down.

Consider other introductory materials

Video and interactive tours on disk provide an accessible and attractive introduction to a product. They can suggest a productive attitude to take toward the product, educating users about the features and interface, indicating unusual benefits, and showing how the program approaches the work task. At a basic level, such materials can show people what the program looks like. Include a tour in the documentation suite when you want to

- Present the program's main features and intangible qualities, such as ease of use, by showing them in action.
- Powerfully illustrate the benefits of the program by presenting finished examples.
- Communicate the feel of the program, typical sequences of actions, and whatever users see onscreen.
- Overcome the reading problems of a particular audience.

Have users start with a video

An imaginative videotape can sometimes solve a particular problem. For instance, one database company knew their typical users often jumped into programming without first doing any planning. They emphasized the benefits of planning and how to go about it by producing a video tape demonstrating how to create a database plan, from beginning a system analysis through the final specification. Another company, introducing a drawing program with a never-before-seen technique, videotaped the boss using and talking about it. After viewing the tape, many people came to the conclusion, "Well, if he can do it, I can do it." That's where your tutorial can begin.

Coordinate your work with a disk-based tour

Computer-disk tours let users choose which material to cover, rather than making them sit through the whole event, as with video. ("I can play this for ten minutes, quit, and then come back and jump into the second unit.") Users look at a mock-up of the real software, so they can learn about the interface while whizzing through a presentation of the program's major features and functions. They have no risk of getting into the type of trouble they might get into if they were using the actual software. Such tours do not train people to use the product, but they do give a strong sense of its value, suggest what people might want to do with it, and help them build a conceptual model of its structure and interface.

Some interactive tour disks are meant to serve as presales tools. They focus on features and benefits, but do so primarily to subtly one-up the competition. There's a big difference between a tour done for people to look at before they buy and one for people after they buy. The after-purchase tour starts training people in ways to understand and use the product, even while introducing the same features advertised in the presale tour.

Materials such as video disks and disk-based guided tours must be developed at the same time as the documentation, often by the training department, the audio-visual crew, or the marketing department. If you can possibly do so, stay in close contact with that development team during the project—their presentation and yours should use the same language. At a minimum there should be no discrepancy in approach. Ideally, the two projects will support one another.

Make the introductory parts of a manual build on the other materials. Pick a specific spot in your introduction and recommend people go off to view the video or play the disk-based tour. In turn, to keep people from playing the video or disk and skipping the manual until they get into trouble, urge those teams to add a little message referring users to other relevant parts of the documentation (such as your manual).

Checklist

Welcome your readers

☐ A Welcome section or booklet gets them on the right path fast.

When getting users started, your installation guide should

☐ Address both expert and beginning audiences

☐ Leave nothing out

☐ Anticipate most problems and avoid them

☐ Make the process simple

If you prepare a Getting Started booklet, it should

☐ Illustrate central aspects of the product

☐ Engage people with realistic tasks

☐ Tell people exactly what to do first, second, and third when beginning to use the product

If you prepare a Quick Start, it should

☐ Aim at advanced users

☐ Use broad strokes

☐ Tell users where to go next

☐ Tell beginners what to use instead

As a tour guide, you should:

☐ Point out the highlights

☐ Familiarize newcomers with the lay of the land

☐ Record your message in the most appropriate medium for your subject and your audience

Tutorials

*Our tutors never stop bawling into our
ears, as though they were pouring water
into a funnel; and our task is only to repeat
what has been told us. I should like the
tutor to correct this practice, and right
from the start, according to the capacity of
the mind he has in hand, to begin putting it
through its paces, making it taste things,
choose them, and discern them by itself;
sometime clearing the way for him,
sometimes letting him clear his own way.*

—Michel de Montaigne

With a tutorial you teach people how to perform a handful of basic tasks using your product. The users have decided—or been ordered—to learn how to use the software for their job, so they set aside their usual work to do the tutorial. Along the way, they learn, almost incidentally

- What benefits the product offers
- What some of the key terms mean (the product's own terms for actions and objects)
- How to move around in the interface
- How the product is organized (you help users gradually build a conceptual model of the way it works)

The essential purpose of a tutorial is to teach the basics. In many cases you expect that people—with the support of your great manual and online help—will pick up additional skills as they use the product for their work. For a product crammed with features, though, you may decide to provide a series of tutorial lessons, beginning with simple, easy-to-comprehend functions and then moving on to increasingly complex tasks. Readers return to the tutorial when they're ready to learn more or go through only those sections that teach the tasks they want to learn.

Whether you're writing a tutorial that introduces a product or teaches how to use advanced features, identify the key tasks you will teach and set firm limits on how much you will cover. Few people want to endure a 100-hour visit to every feature in the product. Use the preface or part of the introduction to set readers' expectations and tell them where to find information not covered in the tutorial.

Should you create a tutorial?

When you're deciding whether or not to write a tutorial, you may have a number of questions or face them from the development team or from marketing:

- Why have a tutorial in addition to procedures?
- How about creating a tutorial *instead* of procedures?
- The training group already has training materials—why write another type of training document?
- Is the best choice a paper tutorial instead of an onscreen one? Would it be better to create computer-based training (CBT)?

Weigh the advantages and limitations of tutorials, and consider what makes them different from other types of documentation and training materials.

Tutorials meet different needs than procedures

Many people confuse tutorials with procedures because both offer step-by-step instructions and focus on user tasks. But tutorials and procedures address different needs, and sometimes different audiences (Figure 10-1).

Figure 10.1
Tutorials and procedures compared.

Tutorials	Procedures
People take up a tutorial when they wish to learn something new and they approach it in a receptive frame of mind.	People look up a procedure when they need to find out how to complete a task. They approach impatiently, oriented toward productive work; learning is secondary.
People allocate time for a tutorial in advance. They intentionally set aside a block of time in which to learn—15 minutes, half an hour, maybe an hour.	People's need to learn a procedure is unforeseen, unplanned, and they usually want to allocate as little time as possible for it.
The steps in a tutorial follow a scenario and explicitly tell people what to do in the context of the scenario.	Procedures give general steps that people can easily apply to their own situation. That's why tutorials rarely work well as a substitute for procedures: the specific details often differ too greatly from the user's own work.

The following example shows how instructions for the same task are presented as a tutorial and in a procedure.

If at all possible, you should provide both a tutorial and a set of procedures for your product. (You'll find complete information about writing procedures in Chapter 12.)

In a tutorial, the steps are specific.

Now that you have set up your standard letter, called Market Letter #1, you are ready to bring in names and addresses from your database. You do this by inserting the names of those fields, within brackets, to tell Writorama that you intend it to print a new letter for every record in the database, using the entries in those fields.

1. **With Market Letter #1 open, click two lines below the date, at the beginning of the letter.**
2. **Choose Open Merge Data File from the File menu.**
3. **Select Market Addresses from the list of documents, and click Open.**

    The Merge Field dialog box appears, displaying the fields in your database called Market Addresses.

4. **Click the First Name field, then click Insert Field Name.**
5. **Press the space bar once, then insert the Last Name field.**
6. **Press Return, and insert the Company Name field.**
7. **Press Return, and insert the Street field.**
8. **Press Return, and insert the City field, press the space bar, insert the State field, press the space bar, and insert the Zip field.**
9. **Click OK to close the Merge Field dialog box.**

    You have now set up Market Letter #1 so that the first name, last name, company name, street address, city, state, and ZIP code for each correspondent in your Market Addresses file will pour into these slots in your standard letter.

In a procedure, the text is generic.

To Insert Fields in Your Standard Letter

1. **With your standard letter open, click where you want to insert data from the database.**
2. **Choose Open Merge Data File from the File menu.**

    The file-handling dialog box appears.

3. **Select the database document that contains your names and addresses and click Open.**

    The Merge Field dialog box appears (Illustration).

4. **Click the name of the field that contains the information you want to bring into your letter, and then click Insert Field Name.**

    You may continue inserting as many field names as you want in this location.

5. **When done, click OK.**

A paper tutorial is convenient for learners

Even if a company provides classroom training, a self-paced tutorial on paper will be appreciated by many people. Here's why:

- They can do the tutorial whenever they want, fitting a lesson in before lunch, doing another during an afternoon lull.
- They don't have to leave their desks to go to a training facility.
- They can proceed at their own pace, unhurried by an instructor, freed of the need to wait for a slow class to catch up.
- When in doubt, the learner can turn back a few pages and compare sections without losing track of the current lesson (as sometimes happens with an on-screen tutorial, called computer-based training or CBT).

Of course, a live instructor can tailor explanations, amusement, and sympathy to suit an individual's needs.

Providing a paper tutorial can reduce support costs. If the company doesn't already have classroom training, a good tutorial can help avoid the cost of hiring a trainer, setting up a training room, and preparing and delivering stand-up training. With a good tutorial, you're also reducing the number of calls to the hotline.

Paper tutorials are familiar

For some products you may have to choose between creating a paper tutorial or computer-based training. Both have advantages and disadvantages.

Sometimes paper works better than the screen for instructions and explanations:

- Paper is reassuring. People are used to learning from a book and believe they learn more from paper than from a screen—any screen.
- Paper is stable; it does not go away when a customer reads the next instruction. A person can flip back and forth easily. In computer-based training the previous instruction disappears; with effort the user may be able to get back to it, but not as easily as in a book. With paper users never feel "I ought to memorize this because I may never see it again."

- Paper can be reviewed without the computer. Some people like to read through steps before they do them, or review them afterward, away from the computer.
- Paper tutorials take less time to write, don't demand programming support, require less extensive testing, and so cost somewhat less to create.

CBT has advantages, too. For instance, readers don't have to look back and forth between a book and the screen. During CBT you seem to be doing the task itself, not just reading about it and imitating it. And CBT can keep users out of trouble by giving them a subset of the product to work with, instead of the real software. CBT costs more to produce because it is a kind of software, but once created, it costs much less to duplicate and distribute. (A disk costs less to reproduce and weighs less in the box.) If you must choose between a paper tutorial and CBT, read this chapter and the next one on computer-based training before deciding.

Producing excellent tutorials

Your customers read your instructions in the tutorial booklet, and then follow them using a keyboard, mouse, electronic pen, screen, and the product you are teaching. They must move their attention from one medium to another several times a minute. They need your help to keep them focused and to learn one step at a time.

To avoid media migraine and create an excellent tutorial, follow these steps:

1. Identify the tasks customers need to learn. (When they see the point, they see how all these tools work together).
2. Create a story line to relate what they learn to their regular work by analogy.
3. Organize tasks so customers can build on what they know, as they go.
4. Introduce the whole tutorial and each lesson.
5. Write the steps and explanations so anyone can see where each step begins and impatient or experienced users can just do the steps. Make the explanatory paragraphs stand out from the instructions, so even the most anxious customers can find them.

6. Keep people out of trouble. Try to anticipate every doubt and question they may have, and do something to answer or reassure them.

7. Offer time for free play. Encourage users to explore when they are ready to do so.

8. Summarize and point out what users have accomplished so they recognize how much they have learned.

The rest of this chapter shows you how to carry out these basic strategies.

Identify the key tasks to teach

Figure out what tasks are basic to the work your readers want to do with the product. Begin by reviewing the audience profile you created as part of your document plan. With a word processor, for instance, customers might say the minimum they expect to be able to do when they start is write a memo and a two-page letter. Those are large-scale tasks.

Make a list, and break the large-scale tasks into their component medium-scale or small-scale tasks. Writing a memo involves (at the minimum) typing, correcting mistakes, tabbing, and starting a new paragraph. Writing a two-page letter might require, in addition, adding a header and footer; centering; creating hanging indents and bulleted lists; automatically entering page numbers and dates; and changing font, style, and size. And you still haven't taught copying and pasting.

This tutorial teaches key tasks in writing a memo by focusing on editing a partially completed document.

Lesson One: Editing a Memo

    Opening the Memo

    Moving the Cursor

    Selecting the Offending Word

    Deleting the Word

    Typing a Substitute

    Looking Up a Better Word in the Thesaurus

Continued

Continued

This tutorial teaches key tasks in writing a memo by focusing on editing a partially completed document.

Placing the Better Word in the Memo

Adding a Few Blank Lines

Tabbing Over

Saving and Printing

The audience for your tutorial may include absolute beginners (people who have no experience with the task domain, the computer, this type of software, or your product), sort-of beginners (they may have used the competitor's product for a few months), intermediate users, and—at least for a browse—expert users. In a tutorial your first responsibility is to beginners; if you have only 50 pages, focus on first things. Then if you have time and space enough, you can create a few additional lessons for newcomers from another product or old hands who used a previous version; such lessons ensure that you are providing some training for a wide range of customers.

Beginners want to feel comfortable with the product. They want to get going quickly, but they are willing to go slowly if you can guarantee they won't run into trouble, get confused, or hit a brick wall. By creating a top-notch tutorial, you're doing more than teaching tasks; you're instilling confidence. You show beginners that the program actually works the way the dealer or their boss said it should.

Use these rules of thumb: Exclude advanced features, don't duplicate features (if you try to teach two ways to do the same thing, people usually do not learn either one), and exclude functions that do not apply to the basic tasks. Plan to cover no more than a third of the wonderful features contained in the product.

Create a story line

Although you want to present tasks in a distinct, logical order, you don't want to march people through one task after another, giving instructions like a drill sergeant quickstepping a squad of recruits through the swamps.

Put what your readers will learn into a meaningful context by inventing a scenario with which they can identify or empathize: "You're going to write a letter to an insurance company," or "You're going to set up a budget to see if you can afford a new car." Sue Espinosa, who has supervised the development of dozens of tutorials, stresses "things to do, not functions to memorize. If a single story line can carry through the entire tutorial, so much the better." A good story line suggests goals to people before they type their first keystroke, clearing up the why before the how.

Your story line helps people relate each new step with real-life tasks facing them at work. Adult learners, particularly, tend to test everything they read to see if it has some immediate use; if it does not, it rarely gets beyond short-term memory. Your unfolding story helps show that what they are learning will be useful later, when they face a situation analogous to the one you're describing.

Not that this story should be elaborate. Too many twists and turns become distracting, even annoying. The point of the story line is its analogy, not its plot and characters. The story should stress a series of needs—what users need to do now—and the actual steps should answer those needs.

Throughout, says Espinosa, you should "cultivate a sense of coherent architecture and forward momentum. The end should be visible from the beginning. One activity should follow another naturally and logically. Keep to the point." In this way the imaginary story shows readers how each step forms part of a meaningful task. Without such a frame of reference, readers are more likely to lose track of the relationship between steps in a task or forget them entirely. The story helps people remember.

Here's how you might present your plan for a scenario to the project team:

The Scenario for Our Tutorial

After many meetings the project team has agreed on a scenario for our tutorial. We imagine that users work for the Fast Return Tennis Racquet Company. This is a small firm—about 15 people all told—just like those in which the majority of our customers work. (The focus study shows 72% of our users work in firms with less than 20 people.)

The user has to do a little of everything—listing contacts in a database, balancing a budget of about $1 million, writing up reports, and working on the logo for the next racquet model. (Again, this reflects the Focus study, which shows that our customers tend to do some work in each of our applications during the average week.)

Continued

Here's how you might present your plan for a scenario to the project team:

Continued

The tone of the place is upbeat, exciting, athletic, smart. That's the image our customers would like to have of themselves. This imaginary situation appeals to their self image and lets us exercise the basics of every application so a beginner can get up and running with just five lessons.

Here's the story: Fast Return is about to release a new model. The customer has to enter the results of two calls to excited dealers in the database; write them letters confirming the sales at prerelease discounts; tweak the final drawings of the new racquet; and update the release budget to take into account the new location at a penthouse racquet club in midtown.

We know that our story line reflects our own picture of our customers, so we want to make sure everyone in marketing and sales concurs. Deadline for comments is next Tuesday's staff meeting. Thanks for your help.

Organize tasks so they build, one on another

Plan the sequence of tasks as you might lead a gradual climb up a mountain. Start with tasks that echo actions learners already feel familiar with, tasks that don't require understanding a lot of new ideas at once. People learn best by comparing new ideas with what they already know. For instance, in a tutorial for a word processor, you might start by showing them how easy it is to delete and insert a word in an existing document, and postpone the complexities of setting up the margins and styles for a new document.

Work backward as you order and reorder tasks, so that customers learn simple skills before they progress to the tasks that put those skills together. Keep asking: What comes before this? What must they be able to do first? When you've answered these questions, you should be able to say why each task has its unique place in the sequence of tasks. If several tasks can be done in any order, consider which way an expert might do them. When you're sure that the order is something more than a personal whim, follow it.

If you can follow a perfectly realistic sequence of events in using the product, do so. But don't lead beginners into complex considerations before they are ready or bore them with housekeeping chores. Many writers start a tutorial by showing a user how to create a brand new document; but that task is often time-consuming, involves finagling with the system software, and gives readers the feeling that years must pass before they get to do anything meaningful. You're better off using an existing document (include the file on a disk that comes with the tutorial), letting users open it, modify it, and print it. Then you can propose they start a new document. Toward the end of the tutorial, they will have a better idea of where they are headed and why they have to do all these apparently arbitrary actions along the way. Do not feel compelled to follow real usage in every aspect.

Show only one way of doing a task

Do not show people two ways of doing the same thing unless you know they're both very important. If you find you must give two alternative methods, do so with a long pause in-between, so that people have a chance to absorb the first method, try it out, and assimilate it before approaching the second method as a clear alternative. As Sue Espinosa says, "Don't present six ways of doing the same thing. The new user remembers part of one, part of another, and then flubs up with the product. Save alternatives for asides or the reference manual. From a family of functions, teach just one function."

Cut or postpone supplementary, optional, or fascinating tasks. Resist the temptation to cover every function. "Your motive may be golden," says Espinosa. "But the result will be leaden—a 250-page opus that is exhaustive and—for the user—exhausting. People don't usually have the time or the energy to sit through more than an hour of material. They want to use the software fast."

Divide your material into modules

A module is a small-scale task that takes about five to seven steps. Each module should focus on teaching customers one task, not two or three. Don't force people to move too fast. Combining three or four different tasks in one module can make them lose track of what they are doing; they forget their aim, and the different actions blur together, soon to be forgotten. As a fairly experienced user, you may feel you are moving too methodically, taking too long with each simple task; but don't let your own impatience lead you to skimp on the time and attention your readers really need.

You may want to group several modules in a section devoted to a single large or medium-scale task. Depending on the size and scope of the task, the section might stand as an entire chapter, or you might group several sections together into a chapter. A reasonable tutorial could contain half a dozen chapters, each with two or three sections or medium-scale tasks.

Somewhere in your tutorial take a moment to introduce people to online help and paper documentation so they know where they can turn for assistance later, without calling the hotline. Make this an event. Present them with a challenge—a task that few will know how to do. Then turn their attention to the documentation, show them the table of contents, and have them use the index to locate the correct procedure, then have them carry out the steps. They'll learn to use the documentation and come to trust it.

Introduce the tutorial and each section

You can start readers on the right track by offering them introductory overviews. At the beginning, introduce the whole tutorial:

- List the equipment, disks, and supplies readers need.
- If the tutorial is organized so people can dip into different sections without having to work through all of them consecutively, make it clear who should go where. Start with a description of the person or purpose, then say which lesson to turn to. If each lesson should be done in sequence, say so.
- Define the level of competence users can expect to achieve—from flexible beginner to battle-hardened veteran.
- Name specific work tasks they will be able to do after completing the tutorial.
- Predict how much time they will have to put into each section.
- Describe the story line very briefly. (Don't go into details.)

Introduce each chapter with a précis of the story line, the challenge the reader faces, and the skills she or he will learn in this chapter to meet that challenge. Essentially you are making a contract with the reader, saying: If you put in the time, you'll be able to do x, y, and z on this program."

At the beginning of each module, introduce the particular task the users are about to do:

- Refer back to what the users have just done and point forward to their overall goal. In other words, fit this task into the sequence.

- Tell people what they're about to learn to do—not what they will feel, appreciate, understand, or imagine. (Take one or two sentences, no more.)

- Paint just enough of the scenario to have them look forward to what they are going to do.

- If necessary, show how they can tell that it's time to do this particular task.

Clearly stating these objectives focuses readers' minds on what's important about the task and provides them with a way to recognize that they have in fact accomplished their goal.

Here's an introduction to a module.

Finding and Changing Tabs

You have tightened up your letter by using the Find/Change command to locate repeated words and replace them with better words. But, as we noticed before, the letter still has the list of prizes indented much too far. Evidently, when the boss was drafting this letter, she pressed Tab four times to start each line describing a prize. You're going to use the Find/Change command to locate each sequence of four Tabs and change it to one. This editing will make the list look more businesslike.

Write the steps and explanations

Put yourself in your readers' shoes to understand what will be claiming their attention from moment to moment. Consider what they may be thinking, doing, or wondering about at each second. You're giving instructions to people who would be asking lots of questions if you were there in person to answer them. You don't have to anticipate and answer every possible question, but do put in all the information anyone would need to keep moving through the tutorial successfully.

Better yet, test each draft on people who are similar to those in your audience. As you watch them try to carry out the tasks, make notes directly on your manuscript and don't interfere except to save them from a crash. You'll find places where you've left out a key instruction or led them to choose the wrong command. Only usability testing can guarantee that you really have all the steps—and explanations—people need.

Tell people what action to take

Put one meaningful action in each step, and number each step. Like a step in a procedure, this instruction should be separated from any additional explanations, so a brave reader can just do the steps. The less adventurous can at least distinguish between the text indicating what to do and the text to read.

You may find it helpful to storyboard a particular module, chapter, or the whole tutorial. Use paper preprinted with a series of TV screens, if you like, and sketch each action someone will take, one step per frame. You can show your team exactly what people will see and do throughout the tutorial, and test out the storyboard before you get into the detailed writing. You'll often find you have left out a few steps—a fatal error in a tutorial. Make sure, by testing and retesting, that you haven't left out anything a reader might consider a meaningful action. For instance, we once watched 24 people get stuck at the same screen because we thought it was obvious that they should press Return after an instruction. For them, pressing Return was a step they expected to be asked to perform.

Make sure that you show rather than tell. For example, if you want to get across the difference between relative and absolute copying in a spreadsheet, first have people do a relative copy, allow them to digest that information, and later present them with a situation in which they make an absolute copy. Do not indulge in any lectures about the difference until they do the absolute copy.

Explain, explain, explain

Experts and programmers sometimes sneer at all the "hand-holding" that goes on during a tutorial, but many people need it. The impatient ones can always skip the explanations and just do the steps.

Explain

- What you meant in the instruction, if you think any doubt might arise in your readers' minds.
- Any new terms.
- What they learned before that may apply here, if you feel they may not recognize the direct application.
- What happens now (show the screen if it changes dramatically, and say what the change means).
- What they should do next.

Anticipate their every move, including goofs. What might happen if a user presses Escape at this point, instead of choosing Quit? How can users recover? Wherever possible, offer polite advice about how to get back on track.

Be alert to anything that might puzzle users. It's helpful to keep notes on your own first experiences with the product. What confused you? If it confused you, it's likely to bother other users, too. You owe your readers instructions that steer them away from trouble and an explanation that tells them how to get out of the mud if they do fall in.

Point out anything that may violate users' expectations. For instance, people who come to your program from another may be surprised when a certain feature does not operate as it did in the previous program. Point out the way it operates and acknowledge that this may not be quite what they expected.

Separate what to do from what it means

Some people like to skim through a tutorial, entering all the commands and seeing what happens. They get the general idea and don't want to get bogged down in descriptions. To make it easy for them to take the fast lane, you should adopt a book design that clearly separates the instructions from the explanations. The simplest way is to put the numbered steps in boldfaced text.

Inserting a New Record

Now that you have revised Julie Aaron's record, you are ready to add the information the boss handed you about the potential client, Casper Gutman, to your database. You need a new record to hold that information.

1. **Press Escape to leave editing mode.**

   You've been editing Julie Aaron's record. Now you will add a record, and you need to be in the File mode.

2. **In the Command bar type F for File mode and press Return.**

   At the bottom of the screen, the menu changes and you see that (R)ecord is an option.

3. **Type R and press Return to work with records.**

   The menu changes again, offering you the (N)ew option.

4. **Type N and press Return to create a new record.**

   The new record appears. You can now enter the information about Casper Gutman, the art collector.

If you have the time and the budget, you might put instructions in a left-hand column and explanations in a right-hand column. Impatient readers can read down the left column. Other people want to understand exactly what you mean; they want to confirm they are doing the right thing every second. These people can read both columns very carefully.

Inserting a New Record

Now that you have revised Julie Aaron's record, you are ready to add the information the boss handed you about the potential client, Casper Gutman, to your database. You need a new record to hold that information.

1. **Press Escape to leave editing mode.** — You've been editing Julie Aaron's record. Now you will add a record, and you need to be in the File mode.

2. **In the Command bar type F for File mode and press Return.** — At the bottom of the screen, the menu changes and you see that (R)ecord is an option.

3. **Type R and press Return to work with records.** — The menu changes again, offering you the (N)ew option.

4. **Type N and press Return to create a new record.** — The new record appears. You can now enter the information about Casper Gutman, the art collector.

Include lots of illustrations

Many people want to make sure they are in sync with you. Include illustrations to show what their work should look like after every major step.

Particularly at the beginning of the tutorial, pause after every action your readers take to show them what the result should look like. This reassures people that they are still following you and that nothing has gone wrong.

Screen shots confirm a reader's progress in learning a tutorial. Diagrams orient readers, showing them where the lever or the power switch is, for example. Use conceptual illustrations to get across ideas.

When introducing the idea of mail merge in your tutorial, you might show the standard letter emerging from the word processing software, and the address, emerging from the database software, merging together onto the final customized letter.

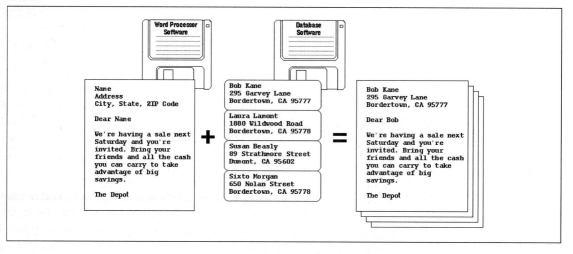

Define your terms as you go

Teach key vocabulary as you go, not only at the beginning. Too many terms up front terrify some users.

Introduce each bit of jargon as a new idea, and define it. People don't mind some inside lingo if they feel they are learning something more than a nasty acronym; they like to know what it really means. What they hate is jargon that snubs and bewilders without explanation.

If you have a lot to say about a term but your explanation is aimed only at beginners, you might put the information in a note or sidebar so experienced users can skip it. If it's a definition they're likely to forget and will need again, be sure to include it in the glossary.

Include alternate steps for varied situations

Anticipate a variety of conditions your readers may find themselves in. What if people have only one disk drive? What if they use a hard disk? If you're teaching how to use a program that works with several different types of computers, and the differences show up in almost every step, then assign each computer its own section in the tutorial and just repeat the instructional material. Make sure you take a page at the beginning of the tutorial to tell people which section to use.

If the differences only occur occasionally, however, you might come up with a stylized representation or icon to indicate each type, and break away from the regular flow of text with a boldface phrase such as, "If you are using Motif, ..." Then put the icon in the margin, and write the specific instructions for Motif users.

Users may run the Gardener's Designer on a Macintosh or custom PC, so they need an installation procedure for each situation.

Installing the Gardener's Designer

You install the Gardener's Designer by copying the software to your hard disk and making a few other minor adjustments. The process differs, depending on what kind of operating system you are using.

If you are using a Macintosh

1. **Insert Disk 1, the Installer, in your floppy disk drive.**
2. **Double-click the icon of the Installer.**

    That starts the installation process. As needed, the Installer asks you to insert Disks 2, 3, and 4.

3. **Insert disks when requested by the Installer.**

    When installation is complete, you see a message confirming successful installation. You're now ready to use the Gardener's Designer software.

4. **Click OK.**

    You're ready to use the Gardener's Designer.

Continued

Continued

If you are using our special Gardener's Greenhouse computer

1.   **Create a directory called Gardens, and copy all the files from the Garden Utilities disk into that directory.**

     These files represent all potential gardens. You'll use these designs as templates.

2.   **Create a directory called Plants, and copy all the files from the Plants disk into that directory.**

     These files contain detailed information about most of the vegetables, flowers, bushes, trees, and ground covers that you might want to plant in your garden.

3.   **Copy all the files from the Program Disk into your root directory.**

     These files include the program itself, GARDEN.EXE, and various supporting files, such as the local maps you ordered with the product.

     Once you've loaded these files, you are ready to start using the Gardener's Design software.

Keep people out of trouble

In a tutorial, above all, you need to keep people from getting into difficulty. Wherever testing shows people becoming puzzled or stuck, rewrite the instructions and add explanations to clear up the problems.

Show how to escape

Very early in your tutorial, show users how to escape from tangles and how to go back to the surface—the main menu, the opening screen, or the operating system itself. You're letting people use the real software, and you can't imagine how many wrong turns they can take, even with your careful instructions. So show them how to exit within the first few pages.

Offer remediation

Tell them how to recover from errors, and if you think they might trip again, tell them again. You can do this subtly, politely, but insistently—and whenever users get into trouble, they'll appreciate your insistence. You might, for example, have a running footer that tells what page to go to for advice, or a banner that says "Typing error? Turn to page 39 to find out how to correct a mistake." This doesn't condemn readers, but it doesn't leave them pounding the keyboard in frustration, either. You're just getting them back into the tutorial as quickly as possible.

> **1   Type your first name in the field.**
>
> If you make a mistake, press the Delete key to back up and erase what you have typed, and then type over.
>
> **Note**: Any time you make a typo, you can erase it by using the Delete key, and then retype.

Allay anxiety to prevent freeze-ups and frustration

If a frightening message such as "Non-standard parameters: Exception OK?" is likely to pop out at them, tell people not to worry. If the next few steps are going to be complicated, admit that they are—even for you. If you're stuck with some awful term like *fatal error*, show that you know it sounds terrible: "This message indicates that the software encountered some internal problem so overwhelming that it was unable to continue; in effect, it died. Start the software again, and use the Recover command to reload your document."

Show sympathy. Whenever you see the program getting nasty, recognize that people will feel scared. Crack a joke. It's OK. After all, this is just a tutorial.

If your company worries about letting any humor creep into their manuals, confine your jokes to the sample files and illustrations. As long as your introductions and instructions are free of even the slightest attempt at levity, you can usually get away with parodies, puns, and absurdities in the examples.

Ensure that each user gets to start with the original tutorial file

When you're teaching software, it's a good idea to provide sample files for people to use as they step through the tutorial. That way they don't have to spend a lot of time typing just to learn a few commands.

Often several people will use your tutorial. You want each user to find the sample file in pristine condition when he or she begins. Have users save their revised files as a step or module in the tutorial, telling them explicitly to change the filename. Or have them make a copy of the original file before they begin.

Give people a break

It can be hard work learning all these new concepts, strange terms, and contorted procedures using the computer. Don't wear people out.

Make it easy for people to stop with a feeling of accomplishment. Introductory modules ought to be doable in about five to seven minutes, tops. One lesson—several modules in a row—should be completed in half an hour, maximum.

Design the tutorial so readers can save the file after completing each major task, so they needn't lose their work just because they have to quit to attend a meeting. Show them how to do this and encourage them to stop whenever they have to.

Encourage real breaks, too, where users can get up, walk around, and look out the window and shake their wrists. You are teaching good practice, and you should endorse the precautions people need to take against sore backs, eyestrain, and carpal tunnel syndrome—the occupational hazards of computer users.

Offer free play

Once you're sure people understand the basics, encourage them to explore on their own. Creative and reflective people in your audience will enjoy applying what they have learned to a new situation. And the effort they expend in carrying out the new idea will help reinforce their learning.

Present them with a challenge. Show them what they should be aiming at—a document, an image, a model of what their spreadsheet should look like. Then set them off on their own to reach that goal.

Offer some hints in a separate box. That way they can ignore them if they're feeling confident, but if they get in trouble they can get some help. Some writers even put the detailed steps (the answers) on a separate page.

You can't make such exploration entirely safe. Experimenters may trash their sample files, crash the system, or damage something on the network. So warn people not to play around until they are ready, and caution them about the problems they could get into if they wander far from your exercise.

Now that you have completed your investigation of the DOS users bulletin board on our online service, you may want a tougher challenge.

To test your online skills:

1. **Locate the Baseball Card Collectors Corner.**
2. **Find the Online Price Book. (Hint: It's a resource).**
3. **Find out how much a 1989 Jose Canseco card from Blear is worth. (Hint: He played outfield for the Oakland Athletics.)**

For an even tougher challenge, try to find this in less than five minutes.

(For the complete path to Jose, turn the page.)

End with a summary

Make it clear when people have finished a task. Congratulate them, or at least point out when they have finished. Recognition of their success helps people solidify what they have learned. Knowing that they are done, they can wrap up the task in their mind and remember it as a whole.

When you reach the end of a chapter, bring about more closure than a sentence of conclusion. Review what you've taught so people can recognize that they've learned it. Provide a table that summarizes the tasks you've taught in the modules. Make the steps brief, so people can go back over the steps while they're still fresh in their minds reinforcing what they learned.

In this lesson, you learned how to format a disk, back up a disk, and move a file using the Utilities.

Task	Technique
Format a disk	Press F for File, and then D for Disk; insert the disk, and press F for Format.
Back up a disk	Press F for File, and then D for Disk; insert the disk, and press B for Backup.
Move a file from Disk A to Disk B	Put Disk A in Drive A, put Disk B in Drive B, press F for File, and then M for Move, type the pathname for the file to move, then Return, and the pathname for the filename of the new location, and press Return.

At the end of sections and chapters, point the way to the readers' next large-scale task. At the end of the tutorial, tell them what degree of competency you think they have achieved, and encourage them to go off and use the real software, turning to the documentation for any further support.

Checklist

An effective tutorial should

- ☐ Focus on teaching the basic tasks a customer needs to get started using the product in ordinary work
- ☐ Create a story line that shows users how the skills they're learning apply to their own jobs
- ☐ Build on what people have already learned
- ☐ Present one way of doing a task, not several at once
- ☐ Divide the material into a series of short modules, so users have a series of quick successes
- ☐ Introduce each module

- ☐ Separate steps from explanations
- ☐ Explain at length, for beginners
- ☐ Include illustrations to confirm their progress
- ☐ Define terms as they come up
- ☐ Keep people out of trouble
- ☐ Show how to escape
- ☐ Allay anxiety
- ☐ Ensure that future users get to start with the original tutorial file intact
- ☐ Offer free play at the end
- ☐ Conclude with a summary

Computer-Based Training

I fear explanations explanatory of things explained.

—Abraham Lincoln

When people tear the wrappings from a new machine or a fresh piece of software, they usually want to play with it immediately, poking, prodding, learning, investigating—but not studying. Eventually they will settle down and work with the product, but at first they just want to push a button and get a reaction.

A paper tutorial offers a problematic means of exploring because the paper gets in the way. You have to locate the right book, prop it up, skim past some introduction, locate the tutorial, and then start the software itself. The process can be clumsy.

Putting a tutorial on a disk gets people going faster; they can pop it into the computer and in a few seconds start exploring. Learning about a computer on a computer seems right to many people; in fact, some feel cheated when they turn to printed materials for further information.

Computer-based training (CBT) fits into the overall suite of documentation in just about the same place as a paper tutorial—somewhere very early in a customer's experience. Similarly, the success of CBT depends upon your organizing the material into a series of meaningful tasks, chunking them, and building people's skills gradually as you lead them from the simplest to the most complex. You define your behavioral objectives in the same way: "By the end of lesson 3, learners should be able to do x, y, and z."

Good computer-based training gives people the feeling that they are interacting directly with the real software—there's no book lying between their keyboard and the screen. But in reality most CBT lessons run on some other software; they imitate the software you are teaching but rarely let learners risk getting into trouble with the product itself. That way learners will have a good first impression, no matter what.

Although learners are safer, they are also cocooned. Some of them report shock when they graduate to the actual software: It's so much more puzzling, surprising, and inconsistent than the CBT was.

With CBT you face new challenges:

- You are writing for the screen, so you must say more with less.
- You are creating an application, so you may also have to invent or modify a user interface for your CBT.
- You may need to learn an authoring program or language in order to produce your effects. Many of the first authoring systems were developed by teachers who wanted to create

minilectures followed by quizzes, all on the computer. These systems limit you to rote drill and practice. More sophisticated authoring programs let you capture screen shots, dialog boxes, even the moment-to-moment action of the real software, and reproduce it when needed.

- You may have to devote 100 hours to a 20-minute training disk.

- If you have not come to technical writing from teaching, you may need to team up with an instructional designer to ensure that you reveal ideas at an appropriate pace, without overwhelming your viewer.

- You can catch most mistakes a user might make, so you need to anticipate them and create helpful messages showing what the learner should do to correct the mistake and go on.

- You may have to develop a way to confirm that users have learned what you expect they will to justify the expense of creating the computer-based training.

Begin on target and in focus

Your CBT should open with a screen that announces your subject. Like the cover of a book, this opening screen advertises what is to come.

Here the welcome screen does double duty by also advertising the objectives of the training.

Welcome to

Learning IndexWorks

In 20 minutes, using this disk, you'll learn how to

- Start IndexWorks
- Open your document
- Perform an index
- Save the index to a separate file
- Quit IndexWorks

Please press Return to go on.

Teach navigation first

Make sure people know how to move around in your CBT. If you can't count on them knowing that they should press the Right Arrow to move to the next screen, make it your first priority to teach them how.

Introduce them to navigation gradually. Don't cram a list of every action they can take into one screen. Instead, during the first lesson, take the time to focus on one function at a time so people can master each technique before moving on to the next one. With careful planning you can show how to use even an over-buttoned interface (Next, Previous, Return to Main Menu, Retrace Your Steps, Pause, Quit, Volume, Run Example, or WhatNot) in five or ten minutes.

If possible, limit the number of interface elements you have learners use at the very beginning. For instance, you might start with only a Next button and ask users to press that for more information about the lessons. When they press Next they see the main menu, the Next button, and an additional Back button. You tell them, "Click a menu item to go to that lesson, or click Back to go back a screen." Add any remaining elements as you need them during the course of the first lesson, so their purposes are clear and you do not overwhelm the newcomer with a jet airplane's control panel.

Make a menu outlining what people will learn to do

Menus in a CBT perform the same role as a table of contents does in a book, previewing the material and presenting the structure. However, your menus won't give someone as clear an idea of the total length of your CBT as a table of contents would, because you don't have any page numbers on the screen. If you can, suggest how much time the training will take and then invite people to choose a module. In constructing your menu

- Define your objectives in terms of actions, and use those as the headings for your modules.
- If you want people to go through your modules in order, number them. If you have really designed them so people can start any module without knowing what's in the earlier ones, say so in your instructions and do not number the modules.
- When someone has finished a module, flag it in the main menu so they can see their progress each time they return.

- If possible, when someone clicks a module title, clarify what's in that section by showing the subtopics within or giving a brief description.

- Make sure your instructions tell people how to choose the menu item they want. (Too many times we've seen beginners staring patiently at the menu, waiting for something miraculous to happen.)

- If a module has several subunits within it, create a submenu for the module and make sure it works the same way as your main menu.

Your main menu should outline what people will be able to do in each lesson.

Learning FreeDraw Plus

We recommend you do these lessons in order, but you can skip any you think you're familiar with and begin anywhere.

Double-click the lesson you want to turn to, or press the Right Arrow to begin Lesson 1.

1   Starting to draw
2   Using preset forms
3   Placing forms precisely
4   Editing what you draw
5   Combining drawings
6   Putting drawings into other documents
7   Leaving this tutorial

If your lesson has more than one or two sections, you may need a submenu at the beginning of the lesson.

Lesson 4: Editing what you draw

In this lesson you'll find out how to revise the objects you have created.

Double-click the module you want to go to, or press the Right Arrow to begin the first module.

- Reshaping a polygon
- Resizing an object
- Moving an object
- Changing the preset fill color and pattern for an object
- Selecting several objects at once
- Aligning several objects together
- To return to the Main Menu
- To leave the tutorial

Involve the learner

Early computer-based training was numbingly repetitious. They tended to follow the pattern of behavioral conditioning à la B.F. Skinner. You got a paragraph explaining what you should know, followed by a multiple choice, true/false, or fill-in-the-blanks question in which the answer would be blindingly obvious. You proceeded from one stupefying frame to another and if you had patience enough to make it through to the end, you indeed learned new vocabulary terms and sometimes some new skills. A major danger, though, was falling asleep and having your head crash into the keyboard. So make sure that you teach actions, not just ideas, and that people must do, not just think, different things from one frame to another.

Note that we're not saying you should indulge in spurious originality, coming up with a dozen different ways of saying, "Press the such-and-such key." No, the point is that you must make sure that your users get to vary what they do, physically, from moment to moment.

Make every segment short

Keep a module between five and fifteen minutes. Don't try to teach more than two or three key skills in one module. Pare the explanations down.

For one important action you might take a few screens to show each part of it; later you could use one screen for a repeat of the same action. But never cram more than one significant action into a single frame. When people hear about two important things at once, they tend to forget both.

Encourage interaction

Alternate between any necessary lectures and exercises. Let users do something, read, then do again. As the experienced instructional designer, Jon Butah, says, "Keep a rhythm between the user reading something and the user doing something, so you don't have long stretches where the reader is pressing Return and reading text, pressing Return, Return, Return. That's deadly."

If you really have to talk at length, put that material on paper for people to read before they come to the computer-based training. You might create a Getting Started notebook with conceptual overviews, a section sending the users to the CBT, and exercises for them to perform when they return.

Encourage guessing

Once you've shown how to do one function, see if you can lead users to guess correctly about how to do the next one. If they get it, their confidence grows and their understanding of the program is confirmed. If they don't catch on, your response can steer them onto the right path.

Elizabeth Weal built a number of modules around a series of mock quizzes in which she encouraged people to take a stab at the answer even though they had not been instructed yet. In showing that databases resemble the way people store information in an office, she asked, "Each individual piece of information in a record is called a: a) tidbit, b) entry, c) smidgen." The wrong answers are just funny enough to warn most people off. If users happen to pick a wrong answer, they get the response, "Not quite. Try again." That goes on until everyone's got it right.

In computer-based training designed to teach students the way diplomats carved up Europe after World War I, a map shows central Europe, and the program poses a series of questions. If students guess wrong, they get corrected and can try again until they get it right. The point is not to punish (or grade) them for wrong answers, but to nudge them along so they learn the right ones. The drawback: if there's nothing but guess-and-point, you may just be teasing their minds without gradually building up a skill. Also, you should set a limit on the number of wrong guesses people can take before you step in and give them the right answer.

Some employers like to use CBT as a kind of qualifying exam for promotion, so they want to get a set of grades for each user. You should put any quizzes that count at the end of the section, after you've reviewed the module, to give users the best shot at passing. (Really, their grades are your grades; if you've done a good job, they'll all get 100.)

Lesson Review

If you want to go back over the main skills you learned in this lesson, press the Back arrow.

If you're ready to test yourself, click the Forward arrow.

Lesson Review

Click the box next to the best answer to the question.

Question One:

When you want to set up a series of form letters, you write the letter, and then open a document containing the names and addresses of your correspondents. To open that data document, you use the command:

    a) Mail

    b) Mail Merge

    c) Form Letter

    d) Print Merge

Offer remedies

If the learner does make a mistake, you haven't written the instructions clearly or explained things simply enough. You have a responsibility to do something more than beep at learners when they goof.

Your code should catch any mistakes and disarm their effects so that your CBT doesn't go haywire. As Elizabeth Weal says, you ought to "Make provisions for every conceivable error that users can make. Give people constructive suggestions when their responses indicate they're not understanding what's being explained."

If they guess wrong, encourage another try. If they make the same mistake two or three times, give them the answer or the opportunity to have the action done for them so they can move on.

Be as specific as you can in commenting on their responses. But if you and your programmer can't interpret what a user types, admit it and say something like, "That wasn't what we were looking for. Could you please try again? We want to know what you call an application that uses your computer to edit documents." Then if they still wander off track, you could give a suggestion. "Hint: It begins with a w."

Keep your remediation free of blame; avoid terms like *error, mistake, foul-up*. Don't even imply criticism of the users for their responses. After all, they were trying to follow your directions. And you are not a teacher grading them on what they picked up in an earlier lecture.

Write real responses

Vary your responses and make them specific to the tasks. When every error gets the same response, people soon learn how limited your CBT is and how little attention it really pays to what they have done. If possible, escalate your responses, so that if someone makes the same mistake twice, you say something more helpful the second time.

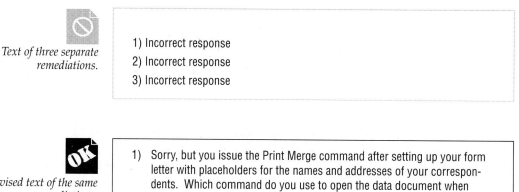

Text of three separate remediations.

1) Incorrect response

2) Incorrect response

3) Incorrect response

Revised text of the same remediations.

1)   Sorry, but you issue the Print Merge command after setting up your form letter with placeholders for the names and addresses of your correspondents. Which command do you use to open the data document when inserting those placeholders?

2)   No. Print Merge actually prints the letters. But before you can print, you have to set them up, inserting placeholders for the names and addresses to come from the data document. What command do you use to open the data document?

3)   Sorry. You use the Mail Merge command to open the data document when preparing the standard letter. You use the Print Merge command later, when you want to print the form letters, drawing the names and addresses from the data document.

Too many CBT courses overreach themselves in trying to be conversational; they reveal that the programmer has no idea what the learner has just typed or done. For instance, in a CBT course designed to train students to think through their material before writing a report, the program asks them to choose a topic and then answer a number of questions about it, based on the categories of classical rhetoric. So far so good. But then the CBT enthuses, "That sounds really interesting. Please say more about that." We begin to hear the fake good cheer of an official greeter. The student may fill in two answers, but type gibberish in the last, just to move on. Imagine what the student must think when the CBT responds, "Number 3 is excellent."

Do the boring stuff for people

If you want people to see what a filled-in spreadsheet looks like, have them type a few entries, then say, "OK, we'll do the rest for you." You are teaching spreadsheets, not typing.

Encourage free play

Some authoring systems let you launch the application itself, so users can venture into that more extensive, tangled, and (possibly) treacherous world to try out what they have learned in your safe environment. Or you can construct a miniworld and present a small challenge for users to solve. As Jon Butah says, "The ideal would be to present the material under very close control, and then to put them into a much freer situation and give them a general goal to go for, and say, 'You've learned to move around and delete letters and paragraphs. Now here are a couple of letters. Move the first paragraph to the end.' And we leave it totally open to them to try it."

Free play costs money—essentially your programmers have to develop a working reproduction of at least one module of the actual software. That way your users will only be able to act within the limits you set. One alternative—having them bring up the real software and experiment—will work only after you have trained them on opening the software, launching a document, and other basics.

Work within the constraints of the screen

The screen is the environment in which you teach. But in many cases users have half a dozen windows open, and your CBT is just the one on top. You need to distinguish your CBT from the real software (so people don't expect to issue commands and have them obeyed), and you need to devote different areas of the window to navigation tools, text, and the imitation software.

Keep the CBT world distinct from that of the software

Create a distinct area for the control panel. You may have navigation buttons (Next, Back, Fast Forward), control buttons (Volume, Pause), location indicators (Lesson One, Opening a Document—Screen 5). Clump together the elements of each group, and then put all these groups in one area to keep them distinct from the software, which appears to be running in the background. After a few screens your users will recognize that this is the place to go for information about what they can do and where they are.

Navigation buttons should appear in the same place on every screen. If the graphic alone does not make clear what to do, add a text label, such as "Contents."

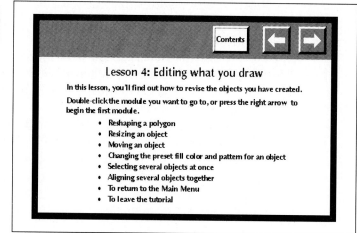

You need another distinct area for your words, if they appear on the screen. (You might, of course, have a narrator talking over the computer's speakers, so the words would be invisible). You might box your onscreen text in front of the imitation software. You need to set off your words so they do not blend in with the background and get lost. If you have to work with a small screen, you may have to bounce this text box around to reveal key parts of the software underneath—not a great practice, but one you may have to follow in tight circumstances.

Your comment needs to be set off from the background document. If possible, your text should appear in the same format and location on each screen.

| | | Contents | ← | → |

	EXPENSES			
2	**EXPENSES**			
3				
4	ITEM	Month	Year	
5				Now that you've entered all
6	Auto	50.00	600.00	your income and expenses,
7	Auto Insurance	110.00	1,320.00	you're ready to prepare the
8	Cable	30.00	360.00	chart you need, showing what
9	YMCA	86.00	1,032.00	percentage of expenses went
10	Water Company	25.00	300.00	to each account.
11	Food	400.00	4,800.00	0.00
12	Life Insurance	160.00	1,920.00	0.00
13	Medical Insurance	250.00	3,000.00	0.00
14	Miscellaneous	200.00	2,400.00	0.00
15	Mortgage	1,405.00	16,860.00	0.00
16	Mortgage Disability Insur.	41.25	495.00	0.00
17	Newspaper	9.00	108.00	0.00
18	PGE	100.00	1,200.00	0.00

Inside your text area you will often start with an explanation of what has just happened, and then offer an instruction for the next step learners should take. For the impatient or nervous, do as you would in a paper procedure—separate the instructions from the explanations. On screen that often means dropping down a line or two and putting the instruction all by itself in a line at the bottom of the text area. If you follow this convention consistently, people know where to look for the action to take.

Imitate the real software

Let people feel as if they are using the software as they would in real life. Show them the real screens and dialog boxes, and when something beeps or flashes in the original, make it beep in your CBT. You are faking the events so you can catch people when they trip. But you can make your imitation look just like the original.

Write for the screen

People don't like to read much on the screen; they have difficulty making out the words because the characters don't yet have the resolution of a book. As you write your CBT, you'll find that every time you see your words on the screen, you can edit, trim, and toss away a sentence here, a phrase there. Whole paragraphs boil down to a sentence or two. Get your language out of the way.

Because the CBT program responds to people, the series of interactions seems like a conversation. Jon Butah says, "It's a dramatic dialog between you and the program, so there's a natural tendency for people to anthropomorphize the program or the computer. They're going back and forth with it." Think of what you write as a form of dialog. You don't want to get cute ("Hi there, I'm your computer!") but you want to be less formal, briefer, and more conversational than you would be on paper. In this low-key drama, you have even less chance to discourse on interesting sidelights, similar functions, and advanced features. No detours, please.

Your original text is often too long when read onscreen.

| Contents | ← | → |

First Quarter

Anderson	$50,700
Anderson	$63,250
Anderson	$27,900
Anderson	$43,600
Subtotal	$185,450
Chavez	$52,900
Chavez	33,150
Chavez	37,400

Your screen changes, showing the results of sorting by Quarter, and then by Sales Representative. You see all the records for the First Quarter and, within that group, all of Anderson's records. You can now preview and print your report, with subtotals for Quarterly sales and, within each quarter, for each sales representative, as you had originally planned. Choose Preview from the Edit menu.

Your tone conveys an attitude toward the material—and that attitude should be neutral, confident, at ease. You aren't selling anything. You are leading people through the product's interface so they become aware of the way the product is organized.

Revise to make sentences shorter, but not so short as to be incomprehensible. Count on people being able to see the file behind your text; whatever they can see, you do not have to describe.

First Quarter		
Anderson		$50,700
Anderson		$63,250
Anderson		$27,900
Anderson		$43,600
	Subtotal	$185,450
Chavez		$52,900
Chavez		33,150
Chavez		37,400

Contents ← →

The database groups records by quarter and by sales representative, so you can collect subtotals by those fields in your report.

Choose Preview from the Edit menu.

Gradually you help them build a conceptual model of the product itself. Just as your words seem to be embedded within the product on the screen, your words speak for the product. But you need to maintain your own identity as a commentator on the software rather than the voice of the product. You're the learner's assistant, friend, mentor—not the voice of doom.

Format for the screen

Format your text so it can be read easily. Some designers make their text 24 points; at that size, they can display only a sentence or two at a time—too little text for most training. The bigger the height of your "x" (the x-height of a font at a certain size), the quieter your tone can be. With many fonts 14 points is about right. Try not to shrink any smaller than 12 points; you want people to absorb what you say without squinting. If they can't read it, they'll ignore it.

Don't use a variety of typographical styles, either. If you use italics, bold, underlining, and color, all in the same paragraph, you make the screen jump around. The point of such devices gets lost in a welter of flashes.

Provide summaries

People learn just as much on screen as they do on paper, but perhaps because the information is so evanescent on screen and so similar to TV, people don't recognize how much they have learned unless you point it out to them. Summaries help people remember what they have learned. In fact, if your users say "It was fun, but I don't know how much I learned" after the first tryout, add a quiz after the summary.

In a quiz people have to act. As Elizabeth Weal says, "Some people like to test themselves. Others don't. That's why quizzes should be optional." But for the people who want to test themselves, a quiz can prove they've really learned the material. And some companies insist you set up real exams at the end, to prove that their employees have really been paying attention. Many authoring programs are built to capture the users' responses and, based on the percentage you set for mastery, pass them or flunk them.

Tell people where to go next

At the end of a module, and at the end of the disk, tell people what they should do next. Don't leave them wondering whether to start the program, open the manual, or go to lunch. As Jon Butah says, "We have to make our directions very explicit on the disk. We say, 'You're finished now with the disk. Go to the tutorial.' It's very important to set people's expectations: 'What do I do next?' You may be sending them to the program, with advice to use the manual for assistance; to a tutorial; or to a conceptual overview in the beginning of the manual. But whatever you think they should do next, say it loud and clear."

Checklist

Begin on target and in focus

☐ Announce your subject in the opening screen and advertise what is to come

☐ Introduce navigation first and gradually

☐ Make a menu to serve as a table of contents

Involve the learner

☐ Teach actions, not just ideas, so that people do, not just think

☐ Keep each module between five and fifteen minutes in length

☐ Encourage interaction by alternating between lecture and exercises

☐ Encourage guessing

☐ For incorrect responses, offer remedies that encourage another try and that lead to the correct response

☐ Keep your remediation free of blame

☐ Write responses that are appropriate to the learner's actions

☐ Do the boring tasks for people so they can focus on essentials

☐ If you can, encourage some free play

Work within the constraints of the screen

☐ Keep the CBT interface distinct from that of the software interface

☐ Let people seem to use the software as they would in real life

☐ Write interactions as if they were conversations between you and the learner

☐ Format for the screen

☐ Provide optional self-assessment quizzes at the end

☐ Tell people where to go next

Procedures

Everything should be made as simple as possible, but not simpler.

—Albert Einstein

12

Procedures are the heart of a good manual. Conceptual explanations may get basic ideas across, and reference sections may define commands, but procedures encapsulate the skills of experienced users in a way that lets novice and intermediate users acquire those skills quickly—whenever they need them.

A procedure is a step-by-step plan for carrying out a small-scale task—a part of customers' usual work or a part of their set-up work in preparing the product to do what they want. A task is something customers mention when you ask, "What do you do here?"

Procedures must give customers all the information they need to carry out the task and, ideally, nothing that's irrelevant. To make your procedures effective, break the information into four major components:

- **Name**—identifies the task and tells people what the instructions enable them to do, what the goal is.

- **Introduction**—when needed, explains unfamiliar ideas, and when to use the procedure. An introduction may precede the numbered steps or introduce a group of procedures gathered under a mid-scale task heading.

- **Numbered steps**—spell out a sequence of discrete actions people take to accomplish the goal of the procedure.

- **Explanations**—when necessary, follow a numbered step to explain the instructions, identify likely errors (and show how to recover from them), confirm the result, or provide a context for the next step. Screenshots showing the customers' progress provide additional explanatory material.

In this chapter we'll explore each of these parts of a procedure.

Give each procedure a meaningful name

Most of the time people use procedures when they are in the middle of their own work and want to look up how to do something. They know what tasks they've done so far, so if you organize the tasks in the manual in a sequence that matches the way they work—and name the procedures carefully—your readers can find the instructions they need easily and quickly.

Start with tasks

In preparing your profile of your audience, you collected and organized a list of tasks at different scales.

Scale	Example	Amount of space
Large-scale task	Entering data in a database	Chapter or part
Mid-scale task	Formatting text	Section
Small-scale task	Changing the font of selected text	Procedure

Factors such as rapidly evolving software, unexpected changes in marketing strategy, or emergencies may have prevented you from maintaining the list. In that case now's the time to make sure you've included all the tasks your customers may look up.

People also resort to procedure sections when they are in trouble—they've been formatting some text and something's gone wrong. An aptly named procedure that's part of a section on formatting can lead them to the correct instructions for carrying out the particular formatting task.

Make names meaningful to readers

The name should reflect the customers' thinking, not the product's terms or some engineer's ideas. Meaningful names are those names your audience recognizes easily. Stress the goals that users have, not features, commands, or neat options of the product.

If possible, choose one grammatical form for all procedure headings—an infinitive phrase, for instance, or a gerund—and use that form only for procedures so customers begin to recognize that the phrase "To begin a manufacturing schedule" indicates that the section contains step-by-step instructions.

This table of contents uses different grammatical forms for similar procedures, forcing readers to question whether the differences are significant or not.

Drawing

The Selection and Deselection Process

Parallel form makes skimming easy—a plus for the impatient reader. The second part of each heading signals the different objects being dealt with.

Drawing

Selecting and Deselecting

Make it easy for people to distinguish between similar procedures, too. Repeat whatever they have in common, and then stress the differences.

The last two headings empha-size the difference between procedures in their first few words, but parallel form in their endings to show what the procedures have in common.

Recharging

To Decide If You Should Recharge

To Recharge

To Set Up a Routine for Recharging

To Change Your Routine for Recharging

Introduce the task

You need to introduce a procedure or provide an overview for a large or mid-scale task when

- Users are unfamiliar with the concepts.
- Users need to know the appropriate context or prerequisites.
- Users may not know which procedure to pick when there are several similar procedures
- Users need to know about the logic behind the order of the procedures within a section. Explain why the procedures are grouped together or arranged in this particular sequence and what they have in common.

Introduce large or mid-scale tasks with an overview for beginners

A large task is one that involves several mid-scale tasks, each of which includes a half dozen or more individual small-scale tasks. Chapters or parts devoted to major tasks should start with an overview for beginners, who need to understand the reason for the mid-scale tasks, the sequence of mid-scale and small-scale tasks, and the exact spot where their particular job fits in or where they should start.

Your overview should follow the organization of the chapter. If you have three Level one heads in the rest of the chapter, those should figure prominently in your overview.

A lousy overview: An expert probably knows all this, but the people who will most certainly turn here for information are beginners. First they get a warning, and then the text focuses on details that are already covered and apply only if they've gotten into trouble. The writer adds a little extra note at the end so beginners realize that they do not have to reinstall .qinit every time they launch.

Starting the Quotient System

Caution: Quotient will not launch if you have not placed a customized version of the .qinit file in your home directory. See the beginning of this chapter for details.

Invoking the Quotient System from a menu brings you to the graphic display known as the Command Interpreter Window, but if you want, you can run a SKILL routine and bring up a nongraphic and noninteractive window; or, if you start at the command line, you can bring up the Command Interpreter Window. You'll find instructions for all three methods in the following sections.

By the way: You should already have invoked the X Window System, if it does not appear automatically, and run the QT Window Manager, if it does not appear automatically. You will find instructions for these tasks earlier in this chapter.

Before You Start

You should already have customized the .qinit file and placed it in your home directory. Quotient uses this file during startup. You only need to place this file in the home directory once, and Quotient will use it from then on.

Here the writer spells out the normal routine before alerting the reader to any potential problems or prerequisites. The writer also stresses the major choice facing the user, then lists the procedures available in the chapter.

Starting Quotient

Normally you log on, enter the UNIX environment, invoke the X Window System, if it does not appear automatically, and run the QT Window Manager, if it does not appear automatically.

At this point you're ready to launch Quotient. You can enter Quotient by bringing up the Command Interpreter Window, a graphic and interactive environment; or you can enter Quotient with a nongraphic, noninteractive window in which you can write and run SKILL routines.

By the way: Make sure you have a customized version of the .qinit file in your home directory so the Quotient software can use it during startup. If you do not have the .qinit file in place, please go back to Chapter 1 for instructions.

In this chapter, you'll learn how to

- Log on to your system
- Enter UNIX
- Invoke the X Window System, if necessary
- Run the QT Window Manager, if necessary
- Choose to launch Quotient with the Command Interpreter Window
- Choose to launch Quotient with the SKILL window

Limit the introductions to procedures

Decide in advance what topics you want to cover in your introductions to individual procedures, and stick to that decision. Don't use an introduction as a dumping ground for material you can't seem to fit in elsewhere.

Be sure you don't narrate the entire procedure or offer any step-by-step instructions in your introductions—people try to follow these denuded instructions and often run into trouble.

Customers like to jump right into the actual steps. If possible, clear introductions out of their way. Don't write introductions just because other manuals always seem to have them. Introductions to procedures and groups of procedures are often written to maintain a rigid notion of consistency—if any procedure has an introduction, every procedure must have one.

For small-scale tasks, you can usually cut the introductions...

Scrolling Up or Down One Line

You will often want to scroll up or down one line at a time. Using the scroll bar makes it very easy. Be sure you use the correct arrow on the scroll bar so that you scroll in the direction you desire.

- **Click left on one of the arrows at the top or bottom of the scroll bar.**

     The text moves up or down one line.

Scrolling Up or Down Continuously

You can also scroll up or down continuously when you need to move more than one line at a time. Be sure not to scroll too far or else you will have to scroll back to find the correct location.

1. **Press left on one of the arrows at the top or bottom of the scroll bar.**

     The text moves up or down continuously.

2. **Release the mouse button when you reach the part of the file you want to see.**

Scrolling Up or Down One Line

• **Click left on one of the arrows at the top or bottom of the scroll bar.**

   The text moves up or down one line.

Scrolling Up or Down Continuously

1. **Press left on one of the arrows at the top or bottom of the scroll bar.**

   The text moves up or down continuously.

2. **Release the mouse button when you reach the part of the file you want to see.**

Stick to the present

To avoid ambiguities about the exact sequence of events, march forward chronologically, from prerequisites to the current context. Don't get into the future with phrases such as "You'll learn how to...." Stick to the present tense when stating what they need to know or do before carrying out the procedure.

The future tense raises the question, when?

You'll need to name the output pins.

Compaction will be an iterative process.

Before comparing, you'll need to...

Keep the introduction in the eternal present.

Name the output pins.

Compaction is an iterative process.

Before comparing, you must...

Put instructions in distinct steps

If procedures are the heart of a good manual, instructions in the numbered steps are the heart of the procedure. Each step specifies an action readers take on the way toward accomplishing their goal.

When you make the steps clear and easy to follow, you make them memorable. Jumbled, jam-packed, irrelevant, or confusing steps lead readers to make mistakes, slow down, and increase their sense of helplessness.

If a step needs hand-holding advice, decide where you're going to put it—in an introduction or in an explanation. Don't dilute instructions with explanations.

Number the steps

Most often you'll write sequences of steps. Number each step so that readers can keep their place easily. Even when they can't tell you what step they're on, people rely on numbering. Adding numbers to a set of steps almost guarantees fewer mistakes (skipping a step or doing the same step twice).

Numbering as you write also helps you spot a sequence that is becoming too long.

Here the writer has jammed too many actions into a single sentence to make the procedure look simple. Result: confusion.

- **Locate the Instance menu, select the Init command, then issue it, complete the form, and initialize the instance.**

    In the form, enter the purpose of your device in the Function field. (You may already have defined the purpose of the device when you created an instance of it; if so, that purpose appears in the field.)

    Define the physical type by selecting an item from the scrolling list that appears when you click in the Type field.

Now the writer has separated out the significant actions, devoting one step to each and proceeding in chronological order.

1. **Issue the Init command.**

    You may issue the command from the Device menu, or from your Design Flow.

    The Initialization form now appears.

    [Art]

2. **Enter the purpose of your device in the Function field.**

    You may already have defined the purpose of the device when you created an instance of it; if so, that purpose appears in the field.

Continued

Now the writer has separated out the significant actions, devoting one step to each and proceeding in chronological order.

Continued

> **3. Select the physical type from the scrolling list in the Type field.**
>
> **4. Click OK.**
>
> The software now initializes the instance.

In a one-step procedure, use a bullet for the instruction to indicate that what follows is an action step. Numbering the first step of a one-step procedure makes some people think that step number two will follow.

Use bullets when a procedure consists of several alternate single steps, each equally important. (If one of the options begins to spawn substeps, you're looking at a separate procedure.)

Limit the number of steps in a procedure

Most people can remember only five to nine items at a time, so don't overburden them. When you set a limit on the number of steps in a procedure, you help people to grasp and remember the entire sequence. Too many steps make people feel the process is endless and arbitrary; they may have a hard time spotting meaning in the sequence.

Avoid a series of trivial steps that trap the reader's attention in what seems like busywork.

Instead of...

> **To Display or Hide Gridlines**
>
> 1. **On the Layout menu, click Rulers.**
>
>   The Edit Rulers form appears.
>
> 2. **In the Edit Rulers dialog box, highlight the display Gridlines line.**
>
> 3. **Indicate whether you want to display the gridlines.**
>
>   • **Type y for yes.**
>
>   • **Type n for no.**
>
> 4. **Press Return.**

...write significant steps only.

To Display or Hide Gridlines

1. **On the Layout menu, click Rulers.**

   The Edit Rulers dialog box appears.

2. **Highlight the display Gridlines line.**

3. **Type y to display, or n to hide, and then press Return.**

At first glance the revision might seem insignificant because we've removed only one step. But the new step is a meaningful unit now. Getting rid of a step or two in 50 or 100 procedures results in a leaner, smarter manual.

If the number of steps in a procedure goes into double digits, break the procedure into several procedures. First make sure that you've consolidated several partial steps into a single complete action, wherever possible. Carve the sequence into phases and consider each a small-scale task.

These instructions go on too long.

Verifying Rules

1. **Choose Set Up from the VR menu.**

   This command allows you to set up the environment for a Verification.

2. **On the Set Up Form, confirm or change the default options for Run Directory.**

3. **Type in the File name, Block name, and View Name.**

4. **Choose Run VR from the VR menu.**

5. **To specify every kind of error you want selected, choose Select Error Types from the VR menu.**

6. **To define the type of error you want considered active, choose Display Options from the VR menu, and set the Active VR Error Type.**

7. **To specify which types of errors you want highlighted, choose Display Options from the VR menu, and set the Error Options.**

8. **To zoom the window to show the current error, choose Show Current Error from the VR menu.**

9. **To have an error explained, choose Message from the VR menu.**

The long procedure can be carved up into a series of shorter ones.

Setting Up the Environment for a Verification

1. **Choose Set Up from the VR menu.**

   The Set Up Form appears.

2. **On the Set Up Form, confirm or change the default options for Run Directory.**

3. **Type in the File name, Block name, and View name.**

Running the Verification

- **Choose Run VR from the VR menu.**

Examining the Results

- **To specify every kind of error you want selected, choose Select Error Types from the VR menu.**
- **To define the type of error you want considered active, choose Display Options from the VR menu, and set the Active VR Error Type.**
- **To specify which types of errors you want highlighted, choose Display Options from the VR menu, and set the Error Options.**
- **To zoom the window to show the current error, choose Show Current Error from the VR menu.**
- **To have an error explained, choose Message from the VR menu.**
- **For a report on the errors found, choose Error Status from the VR menu.**

If several procedures begin with the same three steps, consider removing those three steps from each procedure and making them into a separate procedure of their own.

Begin instructions with imperatives

Begin most instructions with words that tell people what action to take. Do not use passives ("The Hue operation is now implemented"). People wonder, does the operation just occur, or should I do something to make it happen? Do not issue permission, either ("You may delete or clear the text, if you wish"). Here people wonder whether they should, or must, or if this choice is purely optional, if they may skip it altogether. Use the imperative ("Choose Hue from the Color menu" "Choose Delete or Clear from the Edit menu").

Here are just two of several procedures that repeat the same instructions for selecting an object.

Moving Objects

1. **Click left on the Objects menu.**

    The Objects menu appears.

2. **Click left on Select.**

    The Select submenu appears.

3. **Click left on Add to select one object.**

    This command adds the object to the selected set.

4. **Click left on the object you want to move to select it.**

    The object is highlighted.

5. **Click left on the Edit menu in an icon editor window.**

    The Edit menu drops down.

6. **Select Move.**

    You are asked to enter the origin point.

7. **Click right on an origin point.**

    The origin point is usually some point on the selected object.

8. **Move the cursor to the new location.**

9. **Click right to place the object at the new location.**

Copying an Object

1. **Click left on the Objects menu.**

    The Objects menu appears.

2. **Click left on Select.**

    The Select submenu appears.

3. **Click left on Add to select one object.**

    This command adds the object to the selected set.

4. **Click left on the Edit menu in an icon editor window.**

    The Edit menu drops down.

5. **Click left on the object you want to copy to select it.**

    The object is highlighted.

6. **Select Copy.**

    You are asked to enter the origin point.

7. **Click right on an origin point.**

    The origin point is usually some point on the selected object.

8. **Move the cursor to the new location.**

9. **Click right to place a copy of the object at the new location.**

Here, we've extracted the instructions for selecting an object and placed them at the beginning of the other procedures. If a sequence of steps is namable, it's useful on its own.

Selecting an Object

1. **Click left on the Objects menu.**

     The Objects menu appears.

2. **Click left on Select.**

     The Select submenu appears.

3. **Click left on Add to select one object.**

     This command adds the object to the selected set.

4. **Click left on the object you want to select.**

     The object is highlighted.

Use the name in place of the steps you've removed, as here in the first step.

Moving an Object

1. **Select an object.**

     The object is highlighted.

2. **Click left on the Edit menu in an icon editor window.**

     The Edit menu drops down.

3. **Select Move.**

     You are asked to enter the origin point.

4. **Click right on an origin point.**

     The origin point is usually some point on the selected object.

5. **Move the cursor to the new location.**

6. **Click right to place the object at the new location.**

Copying an Object

1. **Select an object.**

     The object is highlighted.

2. **Click left on the Edit menu in an icon editor window.**

     The Edit menu drops down.

3. **Select Copy.**

     You are asked to enter the origin point.

4. **Click right on an origin point.**

     The origin point is usually some point on the selected object.

5. **Move the cursor to the new location.**

6. **Click right to place a copy of the object at the new location.**

Here the steps begin with a noun or a confusing introductory phrase. The second step isn't an action at all.

1. **The triangle under the Imitate step should be clicked, not the step itself, to bring up the Initialize Imitation Environment Form showing the current library path (the default) and the library path defined in the imitation environment file (im.env).**

2. **You may want to modify one of these library search paths.**

   To add or delete a library in the current library path, choose Set Search Path from the Design menu, and edit the path, then return to this window.

   To add or delete a library in the imitation environment search path, use the vi editor to edit the im.env file, and then return to this window.

3. **It is possible to specify the library path defined in your imitation environment (im. env) file, if you want, by clicking the button next to the question about it.**

   Clicking Apply approves the selection but leaves the form displayed; clicking OK approves the selection, but closes the form.

The first and fourth steps begin with verbs. We've revised the introductory phrases so they set the scene or briefly explain the purpose for the action. And the fourth step is unearthed from where it was hidden in the old step three.

1. **Left click the triangle under the Imitate step.**

   Do not click the step itself.

   The Initialize Imitation Environment Form appears, showing the current library path, which leads to the default library, and the library path defined in the imitation environment file (im.env).

2. **If you want to modify one of the library search paths, do so now.**

   - To add or delete a library in the current library path, choose Set Search Path from the Design menu, and edit the path, and then return to this window.

   - To add or delete a library in the imitation environment search path, use the vi editor to edit the im.env file, then return to this window.

3. **If you want to use the library path defined in your imitation environment (im.env) file, left click that button.**

4. **Click Apply to approve the selection and leave the form displayed, or click OK to approve the selection and close the form.**

   The Imitation flowchart appears.

> When done, press the middle mouse button.
>
> On the x menu, choose y.
>
> To complete the drawing, click the middle mouse button.

For similar steps, use similar language

When you want people to do the same thing twice, use the same phrase twice. When you invent variations on the same idea, you raise doubts in people's minds: Is this the same action? Is there some significant difference?

Here the steps are actually similar, but the language makes them look very different.

1. **Use the left mouse button to click on Tools in the command menu banner at the top of the design window.**

2. **Select Analysis from the Tools menu.**

3. **Choose Imitation from the Analysis menu.**

    The Imitation Run Directory Form appears.

4. **Type the name of the imitation run directory, and click OK.**

    The Initialize Imitation Environment Form appears.

5. **Left click the triangle under the Imitation step.**

…using similar language for similar steps confirms readers' assumptions that their actions are the same.

1. **Left click Tools at the top of the design window.**

2. **Left click Analysis on the Tools menu.**

3. **Left click Imitation on the Analysis menu.**

4. **Type the name of the imitation run directory, and click OK.**

5. **Left click the triangle under the Imitation step.**

Handle branching with if clauses

You're going along fine through the first three steps. Then in step 4, your audience diverges. The ones using the old printer have to do one thing, and the ones using the new printer do something else. They're both initializing the printer, but they do it differently.

Make the common action a step. Then put the alternatives in bulleted items. Begin each one with an if clause, spelling out the conditions under which someone should carry out this alternative.

4. Execute the Init file for the Model 100, or choose Initialize from the Options menu.

The Init file is located in the Print.Com directory. **By the way:** The Initialize command applies only to the Model 150.

4. Initialize your printer.
- If you have a Model 100, execute the Init file, located in your Print-.Com directory.
- If you have the newer Model 150, choose Initialize from the Options menu.

Remember procedures aren't tutorials

In writing procedures, you are responding to your readers' needs for quick instructions when they get stuck in the middle of their own work—instructions focused on a particular task, not buried within a series of lessons, each of which builds on the one before. In this situation they just want to get on with their work. On the other hand, people pick up a tutorial when they choose to learn; they may have deliberately set aside a half hour or so to explore the product.

Since procedures and tutorials both offer step-by-step instructions, some desperate customers facing a manual without any real procedures turn to the tutorial for help. They may find some useful instructions, but often, at the key juncture, the tutorial veers off in another direction. A tutorial focuses on a specific example, helpful for training, but not so easy to adapt to the customer's particular job. A tutorial is usually very specific, while a procedure must be generic.

Organize the explanations that follow numbered steps

Always separate explanations from the instructions contained in numbered or bulleted steps. That way novice users can recognize the actions they must perform, and experienced people can skip the explanations entirely. Include only what is necessary for someone doing the step, but be sure to include all that's necessary.

Counter-intuitive parts of the product may force you to make extra explanations. Be aware of the potential for your readers encountering a frustrating experience, but be careful that you don't fall into expressing your own frustrations by actually complaining about the product's odd habits. Guide readers through the maze as carefully as you can.

In any explanatory paragraph, put the main point first. Leave sticky details for later in the paragraph.

Keep to a standard organization in your follow-up paragraphs

Follow the sequence of decisions or actions a user must take:

1. Put any warnings right after an instruction that could lead users into danger.

2. Explain any ideas that crop up in the instructions.

3. Display or discuss the results of carrying out the step. Discuss the results when customers are faced with something new, unusual, unexpected, or subtle and hard to notice. Include "how it works" **only** if user must infer what is going on inside the machine. Avoid lots of cross-references so customers needn't look elsewhere. Go-tos are bad practice in writing as well as programming.

   Use screen shots to show the results, even if you need to repeat some pictures. Sometimes you need art to show the result of one action and then the location of the next step's action. Rely on callouts to point out several parts of the same illustration, but don't get ahead of the instructions.

4. Whenever the sequence is not obvious, suggest why customers should take the next step. The explanation should help motivate customers to continue.

When in doubt, proceed chronologically.

These explanatory paragraphs start off by telling you what you can do after you quit, and then go back and tell you how to quit.
The caution ought to go into the introduction before anyone starts to quit, or right after the instruction telling how to quit.
The Quit Form may not appear if users just saved their block. The writer assumes it always appears and then apologizes, saying, "Oh, if you made no changes, then you can exit immediately," implying but not stating that the Quit Form will not appear.

1. On the Design menu, choose Quit.

You may restart Quotient software at any time, following the directions at the beginning of this chapter.

Caution: Quitting will take you out of the Quotient software, not just out of the Design.

On the Quit Form, make sure both answers are set to yes, and then click outside the form.

If you modified the block since the last time you saved it, the Quotient software displays a quit form with the name of your block, asking if you want to save your block and if you really want to quit.

[*Art:* the quit form]

The Design menu can be reached via the Flat or Depth Edit menu. Just choose *Design.*

If you made no changes since the last time you saved your block, you exit the Quotient software immediately.

The Entry Window closes, and returns you to UNIX, and the window manager.

Now that you have stopped using the Entry Window, you may want to run some of your PROLOG routines at this time, using a nongraphics window. If so, type opus-nograph in an xterm window.

In the Quit Form, the phrase "Save/your_path/inverter/depth/current" describes the elements that will be saved if you choose Yes.

In revising, the writer uses branching. If you made no changes, this happens. If you did make changes, that happens.
The writer also puts all results or actions users can take after quitting after describing how to quit.

1. On the Design menu, choose Quit.

Caution: Quitting will take you out of the Quotient software, not just out of the Design.

If you made no changes since the last time you saved your block, you exit the Quotient software immediately. The Entry Window closes and returns you to UNIX and the window manager.

If you modified the block since the last time you saved it, the Quotient software displays a Quit Form with the name of your block, asking if you want to save your block and if you really want to quit.

[*Art:* the quit form]

Callout: Elements that will be saved if you choose Yes.

Continued

In revising, the writer uses branching. If you made no changes, this happens. If you did make changes, that happens.
The writer also puts all results or actions users can take after quitting after describing how to quit.

Continued

On the Quit Form, make sure both answers are set to yes, and then click outside the form.

Now that you have stopped using the Entry Window, you may want to run some of your PROLOG routines at this time, using a non-graphics window. If so, type opus-nograph in an XTerm window.

You may restart Quotient software at any time, following the directions at the beginning of this chapter.

Anticipate what someone might do wrong when following instructions

Tell people how to spot a problem and how to recover from it. In a procedure introducing the use of the menus in a command-line system, testing showed that customers followed the onscreen prompt to "Select an option and press Enter" before reading the next step, which told them what option to select. As a result, customers ended up in the wrong part of the program and wondered how to get out. The writers rewrote the manual cautioning people to wait when the prompt appears, and read the instructions on the right option to choose. They also added a screenshot, showing what customers should see, and this remediation:

If you do not see this screen, you may inadvertently have pressed Enter and proceeded to a screen you do not want. To go back one screen, press Escape. Escape always takes you back a screen.

In another company some customers ruined their SIMMs by opening the container before reading the instructions thoroughly. The writers emphasized the danger, and the solution, by pulling the caution out of the mass of text and making it instantly visible.

Caution:

Do not remove the SIMMs from the special antistatic plastic bag until you are ready to use them. You might inadvertently ruin them by discharging small amounts of static electricity into the chips. To make sure you are not carrying any static electricity, touch a grounded metal object such as your desk before you open the bag.

At the end, tell customers what to do next, if you know

If people should generally perform some other action after a procedure or series of procedures, say so.

In large systems with many interlocking applications, you should probably also indicate what people **can** now do, because they are deep in the thicket and may not recognize the trails leading out.

7. **Type all holiday dates, indicating whether each is a full-day holiday (F) or a weekend holiday (W), and then click Print.**

Your new manufacturing schedule is now saved and printed.

You may want to check the Just-in-Time schedule of deliveries and shipments to make sure that you are taking these new holidays into account. If you have scheduled shifts to work on holidays, you will probably want to look at the Compensation by Shift database to make sure you have planned overtime and time-and-a-half payments for these new holidays.

Checklist

A successful set of procedures has

- ☐ Names that are meaningful to the users
- ☐ An overview of the large-scale and mid-scale tasks
- ☐ An introduction to the actual procedures, when absolutely necessary
- ☐ Instructions in distinct, numbered steps
- ☐ Instructions that start with an imperative verb, when possible

- ☐ Similar language for similar steps
- ☐ Branching with if clauses
- ☐ Explanations kept separate from instructions
- ☐ Explanatory paragraphs that follow a recognizable order, similar to the sequence of the user's decisions or actions
- ☐ Information about what to do next, if necessary

Reference Materials

Every compulsion is put upon writers to become safe, polite, obedient, and sterile.

—Sinclair Lewis

Traditionally engineers wrote hurried notes about what their product could do, and slightly edited versions of those notes formed the contents of a four-inch-thick three-ring binder—the ultimate reference manual. You had to read the whole book to find out how to do one thing; and you had to figure out for yourself how all the commands applied to your job. Your employer assumed that if you knew what every command would do, you could figure out how best to put the product to use.

That may have been true when the only readers were fellow engineers. But to nonengineers who began using computers, the traditional reference manual came to seem an annoying tease—plenty of information, but very little an ordinary person could use. So writers added step-by-step procedures to allow people to look up a method for doing a task using the product. In essence, the procedures answered the vital question: How do I … ?

But procedural sections don't answer questions such as

- What is this …?
- How does this element of the product work?
- What are its limits?
- What information does it need to work right?

People still need to turn to a reference section for answers when they wonder what actually goes on during some process, how to use a particular tool, what impact a particular button will have, or how one command differs from another.

Beginners usually prefer procedures to reference material, because they don't know what features may accomplish the task they have started. But intermediate and expert users can already do a lot with the product. They consult reference sections more often because they understand a lot about the way the product works, and want to know how to use an unfamiliar parameter or anticipate the results of an obscure command. No one reads a reference chapter from beginning to end—at least, not voluntarily.

What to put in the reference sections

Four major kinds of information go in reference sections.

- **Controls**—ways to control a product. On hardware these include switches or levers. In software, commands on menus, icons on palettes, or buttons in windows.

- **Language and formulas**—programming language elements, commands in command-line programs, and formula elements that have to be combined to perform functions.

- **Troubleshooting**—guidelines and diagnostic procedures for problems of any sort.

- **Technical specifications and details**—the facts that may come into play under certain conditions or may never be necessary to an ordinary user; but someone, somewhere, may need one key fact.

In the rest of this chapter, we'll explore these areas.

Put information about controlling a product in a command reference

Knobs, buttons, levers, and switches control equipment. Commands control a software product—starting processes, performing functions, bringing up dialog boxes for further information, and so on.

The reference section explains what every physical button, every command, and every option on every menu does. You need to say something about each item—at least to define it. Essentially you must cover every choice a user can make.

Follow the organization of the hardware

To describe all the parts of a piece of hardware, start with a visual overview showing where the major functional areas are located. Don't do what VCR manufacturers like to do—show one picture with a hundred tiny callouts and lines pointing at some fuzzy things down in the shadows. Begin with the bigger picture: the print area, the control panel, the power box.

Follow up with exploded diagrams of the parts of each functional area. Walk people through the pieces explaining things in the order people need to use them. If there isn't a set order, follow the geographical pattern—top to bottom, left to right. If you can cram all the facts into the callouts, fine.

If some programming has been built into a piece of equipment, it may have a push-button panel with numbers 0 to 9 and a little LCD display capable of showing up to 20 characters. This innocent display might be hiding a few hundred different options and combinations of options. Don't jam all that description into the middle of your overview. Instead, devote a separate chapter to them in which you can follow the structure of the software, because you are really dealing with the software itself.

Organize the commands the way the software does

Don't just list every command from A to Z; that's what an index is for. Organize your reference section to give readers a model of the way the product is organized. Doing so makes clear what the major parts of the product are. Later, when people become familiar with some of those parts, they can use their knowledge to locate the facts they need—for instance, by looking up a menu they recognize to get to an unfamiliar command.

Even if your product is an old-fashioned mainframe application with no menus, the commands fall into functional areas. If you consult with the team, they will tell you which commands belong to which module—and in many cases those modules reflect some major functionality such as accounts receivable or checking in an inventory.

These fields in a form are listed in the order they appear, left to right, in a mainframe inventory application. The sequence makes little sense.

Palette size

Vendor name

Loading factor

Vendor address

Units per box

Vendor contact phone

Boxes per palette

Size of this unit

Palette weight

Product name for this unit

Recommended shipping method

Unit package type

Brand name

Unit price

Batch price

Box price

Palette price

Here are the same fields, organized by the functional areas in which they appear. This is easier to follow.

Shipping
- Palette size
- Loading factor
- Units per box
- Boxes per palette
- Box weight
- Palette weight
- Recommended shipping method

Product identity
- Brand name
- Vendor name
- Vendor address
- Vendor contact phone
- Size of this unit
- Product name for this unit
- Unit package type

Pricing
- Unit price
- Batch price
- Box price
- Palette price

Commands presented on menus are already grouped for the user. So if you can, adopt those groupings and sequences. For instance, if the main menus appear in a menu bar from left to right across the top or bottom of the screen, follow that order. That way readers won't have to keep a finger in one section while flipping through the manual to find out what the submenu offers.

If one of the commands on the main menu opens up to a submenu, deal with all those commands under the main menu's command. (This may take 10 pages or more.)

If you are working in an environment in which several similar products have been stitched together, resulting in overlapping menus, menus that do similar but not quite the same things, or choices that erase one set of menus and offer another, you need to follow the hierarchical order very carefully. Listing all commands alphabetically would make it hard to tell on which menu a command appears; people might confuse two similarly worded commands that appear on menus at opposite ends of the universe.

If a command brings up a form or dialog box, march through every option in that dialog box as part of the command's description. But if half a dozen commands bring up the same dialog box, describe the dialog box once, under the first command, and just refer folks back to that description. You needn't be as mechanical as the software.

Be sure to explain how different paths to a function affect the way it works. A function performing a multilayered task in one situation may have fewer options in a different situation. If a command or function operates oddly in an exceptional circumstance, tell your reader.

Some products offer additional opportunities to organize topics in useful ways. For example, one area of a standard screen may display current information about the system; another may be used for data entry and editing; a third area may offer specific commands for performing related tasks; and a fourth area may provide commands for saving, copying, and screen handling. In presenting information about these functions, you can follow this spatial organization.

Your product may also carve up functions into various modes. If you're in data entry mode, you can't print a report; and if you are in layout mode, you can create a layout for a report, but you can't see one with some data in it. Those modes may offer you a large-scale organizing device: Perhaps you need a chapter on data entry commands, another on reporting commands, and a third on layout commands.

Describe each control

For each button, gizmo, or command, people like to find a complete description including:

A definition. (What is it?) The definition should come early so readers can be sure they've reached the right place. Stress the main function; put it first and leave secondary functions for following paragraphs.

Context. Where is the control, and when should people use it? Say where the knob is or what menu the command appears on. Say when someone should use the command and when they shouldn't. If a command works in sync with another, point that out. For example, in a product controlling an image scanner, one particular setting (Resolution, perhaps) may have important consequences for another setting (say Halftone Pattern). Point out how they work together.

Requirements. Include any other information needed to make sure the command is carried out properly: prerequisites, preferences, settings, or whatever. If a dialog box appears, show it and explain how to fill it out.

A little explanation of the process. (How does it work?) In some cases, you may have to explain exactly how the command works behind the scenes. What processing does it trigger? What levers flop down, and what dials spin? Where is the current flowing?

The results. How can people be sure the command has been carried out?

An example. Illustrate a typical use. Use an example to illustrate the function, context, and process. The example you provide should be large enough to provide an understandable context, but small enough so the reader can spot the command itself, highlighted, perhaps with boldface type.

Warnings about dangers and exceptions. Yes, include cautions. When you point out potential problems and exceptions, you're not just being considerate. Such information is absolutely necessary to anyone trying to understand how the command works (or, very likely, hasn't worked as expected).

Possible shortcuts. If there's a shortcut, display that prominently at the beginning or end.

An entire command description.

GROUP (COMMAND-G)

The **Group** command consolidates a set of selected objects into one object. You can manipulate grouped objects as a single object rather than as several individual objects.

Purpose: You can use the Group command to consolidate a complex image composed of multiple objects into one object. For example, you might group several lines and a square into a single object that forms a chair. Group is also useful for keeping related objects together, such as a picture and a caption, or a room and the pieces of furniture it contains.

Prerequisites: Be sure to set the line widths, fill pattern, and pen pattern of individual objects before you group them, because you won't be able to work on them individually after grouping.

Continued

An entire command description.

Continued

> **Process:** Grouping puts the objects together into a group but does not wipe out their separate identities; hence, you can easily ungroup and recover the independent objects at any time.
>
> **Results:** After you group objects, a new boundary appears around the grouped object. Handles appear on the boundary of the group, rather than on the individual objects.
>
> **Exception:** You cannot group objects that reside on different layers.
>
> **Caution:** Once you collect objects in a group, you cannot change or edit the individual objects. You must choose Ungroup to make changes to individual objects within the group.

Once you work out a way to describe each command, be consistent. Readers who have figured out your approach can get information quickly, without having to struggle with the presentation.

Throughout, respect the details. You can't anticipate every question people may have about the product, but you can make sure you include every little fact that you have turned up—and dig for more. Keep in mind that people turn to the reference section when they have one or more of those annoying, obscure questions about the product—questions many manual writers dismiss as trivial. But small questions demand precise answers.

Since people are looking up a fact, not a theory, reduce the material to its essentials so they can find the fact on the surface of the page, not buried in prose.

- **Use a bulleted list** instead of several sentences to present a series of facts.
- **Use a table** instead of several paragraphs to present a group of related facts.
- **Use charts and diagrams** to condense a whole chapter into a few pages of essential information.

Separate reference material from procedures

If your book includes procedures for every task a user may want to do, resist the temptation to sandwich a few more procedures into the reference sections. Yes, in older reference manuals writers often included bloodless procedures (named, for instance, Implementation Procedure for Command Z), telling readers where to go to find the command, how to issue it, and what might happen next. But users want complete procedures that show them how to use commands to get a task done.

If you're revising an ancient reference volume containing these anemic procedures, cut them out. If any of them actually refer to work that customers want to do, expand the procedure and move it to your procedures section.

Procedures serve a different purpose and require a different format; mixing them with reference materials merely slows down access to each type of information. In looking up a procedure for printing, users should not have to flip through pages of tables; but the exact parameters for a particular printer code should appear in a table in the reference section, with no distracting numbered steps before or after.

Put information about creating programs in a language reference

Any product offering users the chance to create their own programming code (with formal statements, functions, scripts, macros, operating procedures, or formulas for calculating) should provide information in a reference format.

You may be documenting a programming language such as BASIC, Pascal, C, or one of the special languages that supplement high-powered software such as databases, spreadsheets, and telecommunications packages. Statements or arguments couched in these supplemental languages offer a tremendous range of possible combinations, depending on what a user wants to do.

Organize the elements in a recognizable pattern

The way you organize your presentation of this material depends on your understanding of how it will be used.

Alphabetical order. You expect readers will know the command and want specific information. This is the order of dictionaries and fits everyone's notion of a reasonable way to look up language. Be sure you have considered the reader's exact needs. Alphabetical order jumbles elements together without respect for their purpose and requires that the seeker know the name of the element, just as a dictionary requires that the seeker know how to spell a word. Before you decide on using alphabetical order, consider grouping the commands into functional groups.

Functional group. You expect readers will have a task in mind and seek the means of doing it. Dividing the universe of language elements into functional groups gives readers access to coherent sets of such elements. For example, in creating a spreadsheet formula to calculate the future value of an annuity, a reasonable user will find the right function more quickly among the eight entries under "Financial Functions" than in an alphabetical listing of all the functions offered to calculate any kind of result. Within the group you can organize the elements alphabetically.

Grouping language elements can make learning the language easier. For example, a database procedural language may offer the following groups:

- Records
- Printing
- Indexing
- Searching
- Importing and exporting
- Managing the interface
- Using sets
- Calculating

Users who want to know how to operate the program with its language can turn to an appropriate group to see all the related commands. Users understand the program's capabilities and assumptions better this way than when the commands are scattered around the alphabet.

Provide a unique format for each language element

Make sure that the book design makes it easy for a reader to skip some topics and find others. Use a special format for the command name and for syntax, but use the same level heading for other topics, such as parameters, warnings, and results. That way readers quickly become familiar with the format and can spot the information they want merely by glancing at the page.

Just be sure not to go overboard—don't try to account for subtle differences by providing a formatting nuance for every element. A book design needs to be legible when you first turn to the page without requiring readers to perform a detailed semantic analysis of the difference between six levels of headings.

This draft has only two formats—one for the command name and the other for everything else. As a result the various elements of the command description get buried in the running text.

> ### DELETE SUBORDINATE RECORD
>
> Parameter: subfile name   Type: subfile   Description: the attached or subordinate file from which you want to delete the record
>
> You can undo this command at any time, using the command Recover Subordinate Record, until you save the parent record.
>
> You must have the record open; this command only works on the current record. The result is that the record is deleted. If you do not have a subordinate record open, nothing happens.
>
> The aforementioned deletion of the subordinate record does not become permanent until you save the parent record again. (If you delete the parent record, you automatically get rid of all its subordinate records). An example: If you wanted to delete the current record from the subordinate file Customers, you would type Delete Subordinate Record (Customers).

Here the format makes each element stand out, so a reader can quickly zip to the facts.

> ### DELETE SUBORDINATE RECORD
>
> **Syntax:** Delete Subordinate Record (subordinate filename)
>
> **Example:** To delete the current record from the subordinate file Customers, you would type: Delete Subordinate Record (Customers)
>
> **Prerequisite:** You must have the record open; this command only works on the current record.
>
> **Result:** The current record is deleted temporarily. (If you do not have a subordinate record open, nothing happens.) You can undo this deletion at any time, using the command Recover Subordinate Record, until you save the parent record again.
>
> **Alternate:** If you delete the parent record, you automatically get rid of all its subordinate records.

Describe each element

For each element, you need to give details in the same order and format. Here is the minimum you should provide in a language reference.

Command or function name. Make the name visible, and make it the correct name. Don't call it "Save Record" if it is really "Savrec." If the program function is Int or Mod, use those names, and put the words *integer* and *modulus* in your definition.

Definition. Say what the command does. Make the definition functional. Explain how the element works, what it does, and the formula it uses if it calculates values. If there are similar commands, distinguish this one from the others. Refer the reader to all related commands and functions. This is particularly important in a strictly alphabetical presentation.

Syntax and parameters. Clearly identify the difference between required and optional values, what a user must key in exactly as shown and what can be variable. Also, indicate the exact technical specifications—the number of characters if limited, required character types, and so forth.

Prerequisites or context. Make clear what readers need to do before using the command. Say when it makes sense to use it.

Warnings. Provide cautions about potential problems, exceptions, and impact on other functions.

Example. The example should be long enough to show the command being used in context, but not so large as to disguise or obscure the command in question. The more technical your audience, the more they will appreciate your including lots of examples. "So often missing," the writer Meryl Natchez says, "examples make commands intelligible."

Here's an example in which the user uses a special language to increment a check number and sets the new balance in a check register database. As an example, it's useful to experienced developers, who may need to modify it only slightly to match their own circumstances.

Run Procedure: Balance

```
If (Before)
        If (Date=!00/00/00!)
            vNew:=1
            SEARCH BY INDEX([Constants]Record No=1)
            Record:=([Constants]Next Num)+1
            [Checks]Balance:=([Constants]Balance)
        Else
            vNew:=0
        End if
End if
If (During)
        [Checks]Run Total:=Balance+Deposit-Amount
End if
If (After)
        If (vNew=1)
            ([Constants]Next Num):=Record
            ([Constants]Balance):=Run Total
            SAVE RECORD([Constants])
        End if
End if
```

Put information about solving problems in a troubleshooting section

Unless future products are drastically different from those we know, you can assume that the product you are writing about will fail or surprise users with odd messages and unexpected behavior. A user needs a troubleshooting section specifically designed to help out when a problem arises. Such a section may be part of a small reference, a chapter on its own, or an extended appendix.

Recognize that you can't solve all the problems a user may face. Although many products can detect problems and announce them in an error or status message, many problems simply can't be anticipated. There may be an undetected bug in the software, or the hardware may fail due to a power outage. A disk error may prevent a program from even starting. You can't prepare messages for these truly unanticipated situations.

A troubleshooting section contains directions about what to do when something goes wrong, because either the software collapses, or the user tries to do something the designers never expected or warned users never to do. In the old days all such circumstances were lumped together under the heading, "User Errors."

Distinguish the problem from the cause and the solution

State the problem clearly, explain the probable cause, and write as detailed a solution as necessary. If one problem has several causes, list them and describe solutions for each.

Make a clear distinction between the problem and the solution in your page design. You want a reader to recognize the relevant problem statement quickly, without having to plow through irrelevant text.

In the following example the problem statement is bold, in its own column. The text in the right-hand column provides solutions in numbered paragraphs.

Problem	Solution
The PC does not respond	1. Make sure you are dialing the right number.
	2. Make sure the PC is on.
	3. Check that the PC has an AUTOEXEC.BAT file with the last line FONTURNON.

Create a diagnostic decision tree for complex problems

A diagnostic decision tree is a structured method for analyzing possible causes of a problem, guiding users toward the solution. Such a method is useful for problems requiring different courses of action depending on the cause. A first-aid manual is a good example of the format. It asks if an accident victim exhibits a particular symptom. Depending on whether the answer is yes or no, the reader is told what to do next.

The troubleshooting section for a supermarket checkout stand program talks the store manager through a series of questions, diagnosing what has gone wrong.

> Examine the following problems in the order listed. When you find one that describes your problem, please turn to the page indicated.
>
> 1. All checkout stands are inoperative (try each station)…Go to Page 3.
> 2. Two or more stations (but not all of them) are down…Go to Page 5.
> 3. Only one station is inoperative or malfunctioning…Go to Page 7.

On the page, the heading repeats the description of the problem, and then offers further branching.

> Page 3: All checkout stands inoperative.
>
> **Do you have a backup computer?**
>
> > If **YES**, please turn to page 40.
> >
> > If **NO**, look at your computer's power indicator (the small light on the front right).
>
> **Is the power indicator on?**
>
> > If **YES**, go to page 17.
> >
> > If **NO**, check the power switch (the red lever in the back).

A decision tree narrows down the diagnosis by asking a series of questions. At each step the user moves onward based on the answer to the question.

Explain the product's own troubleshooting tool, if it has one

Many products contain built-in troubleshooting or debugging tools. For example, a debugging tool can display all or part of a program that is executing, provides a printout of all the operations as they are executed, or provides commands that start and stop execution at specified locations in the program. The tool may offer additional programming techniques for discovering the source of a problem. Provide a thorough introduction and explanation of such tools, including a tutorial, an annotated example, complete procedures, or all three.

For users who must work effectively with a troubleshooting tool, you should strongly consider adding a tutorial introduction that takes them through the solution of a common problem. This lets you guide newcomers through the hands-on experience of using what amounts to a subapplication within the larger product. Even experienced users can learn how to use the debugger quickly if you provide carefully thought-out examples. Consider the kinds of problems likely to arise and how the debugging tool can best be used to address them.

Similar considerations apply to a diagnostic tool for a piece of hardware. It may provide checks for calibration, electrical circuits, or power supply. But such modules are usually tongue-tied; to understand what's being diagnosed, users need you.

Explain messages

You've seen those messages that are nothing more than cryptic signals such as "Abort, Retry, Fail," "Error #33," or "System Error $1\neq2$." What's a user to make of such "information"?

To avoid the damning ("Illegal parameter"), the condemning ("User Error in Violation of Defaults"), and the downright taciturn ("Error 1030"), you should volunteer to rewrite all messages from the product:

- Error messages, pointing out mistakes a user has made, and recommending a solution
- Status messages, alerting a user to circumstances in the system, such as the printer being out of paper
- Warnings, pointing out that a user has reached a decision point and should consider the implications before proceeding.

Remember, the context for error messages is anger and frustration. No one likes being told about mistakes, whether they were responsible or merely present when things went wrong. First say, in a neutral tone, what has gone wrong; then say what to do about it.

Invalid numeric entry.

People need to know they have made a mistake, but you can also offer a way out.

You have entered a number that is too large or too small. Please enter a value between -32,000 and +32,000.

Even if you do get to rewrite the various alerts, beeps, and cautions, list them all in your reference section and provide fuller descriptions, explaining what is going on and what a user can do.

Make the explanations accessible by listing messages in alphabetical or numerical order. Unless the product has iron-clad operating environments (modes) or an absolutely invariable sequence, a user won't be helped by any other organization. For example, grouping by type or source of message is useful only to people expert enough to recognize most of what is going on when the problem occurs.

Use a consistent structure:

- Print the message

- Explain the problem or situation

- Provide a step-by-step solution

If there is no solution, say so. But say what to do next ("Turn off the computer and restart it"). If a user has to read some other section before continuing, be sure to say where the information is available ("See the Table of Appropriate Values in Chapter 6").

When a single message covers several problems, indicate what they are and how to solve all of them. For example, when a word-processing program announces that it has an input/output error, you could suggest that people fiddle with their disk drive doors, check the cable connection between the monitor and the computer, or see if the printer has any paper in it. Or you can ask a series of questions that suggest the solution, as in this example:

LABEL NOT FOUND -----> XXXXX

A Go statement contained the label argument XXXXX but no such label exists in the program.

- Have you spelled the label correctly in the Go statement? If not, type the Go statement again.
- Did you substitute the letter I for the number 1? the letter O for the number 0? If so, retype.
- Are uppercase and lowercase letters used identically in the label and the label argument? If not, retype the Go statement so they match exactly.

Organize troubleshooting sections in the order problems occur

Users must know what function misfired to look up a problem by function. If there's a warning, alert, or caution, they will look that up. If not, you have to help them formulate a name for their difficulty and find that. Arranging problems in a chronological order or within the task domain helps.

Make troubleshooting sections easy to find

Place a table of common troubles and solutions (or common questions and answers) at the end of a chapter of procedures, or at the end of the book.

Make a troubleshooting section look different, with bleeds, tabs, special boxes.

Include a variety of terms for each problem in the index, for easier identification.

Put a customer support phone number in several places, but say what to do before calling

Having a checklist that customers fill out before calling helps them focus on what's descriptive of their problems, calms them down, and leads to a more useful response from customer support. That promotes all-around satisfaction. And it saves your company a lot of time they would otherwise spend answering silly questions.

Put everything else in an appendix section

Almost every product contains information so narrow in scope or purpose that it doesn't fit in a larger category. Or else several pieces of information are so unified that they ought to be presented together, even when they apply to widely separated parts of the product. Sometimes a large amount of information can be condensed into a useful table that can stand by itself. An infinite number of reasons exist for creating an appendix, but the general rule is, "if it doesn't fit easily into the main organization of the reference, put it into an appendix."

An appendix section is usually short and self-contained. It often consists of only a chart or a list. Typically you use an appendix to provide technical details that you know will be important only once in the lifetime of one person:

- Housekeeping information, such as a complete list of system files created by the program, file extension conventions, a list of compatible programs.

- Limits—maxima and minima. The largest record size, minimum memory required, calculation limits, and so forth.

- Exact measurements. The size of the product, its power draw, manufacture date.

- Hierarchy of operations. If one command causes a sequence of operations, provide a list.

- Graphic symbols used. File icons, screen icons, and symbols for the cursor or pointer.

- A list of all language elements, with syntax, in short form. No explanations, just the format for every command and function. An appendix makes it easy for an advanced user to find the necessary minimum information.

- Analyzed examples of important tasks. If a product has a set of standardized forms to fill out, provide examples with callouts. If a product produces a set of standardized reports, annotate enough sample reports to make learning to read them easy. If a product can import and export data in a couple of unusual formats, give examples of how to do so.

- Formulas used for calculating. For any financial, statistical, or mathematical application, many users need to know the exact formula used by built-in functions for calculating. Place them all together for study.

- Keyboard shortcuts for menu choices. If a product is designed to be operated by means of choices on menus, there are probably shortcuts. Put them all in one place so that a user can look up the important one quickly.
- Information on how to connect with and set-up compatible equipment or peripherals. Computer users are also printer users, scanner users, modem users, and software users. The designers and engineers can provide all the relevant specifications for hooking up a system.

When in doubt, make a table

Creating clear, pertinent, carefully thought-out tables may take more work than writing a chapter. Tables and charts are staples in reference sections, and they are not easily slapped together.

Nearly every table benefits from an introduction, even if you use only a sentence or two. An introduction gives people a context. Also, add an example or two, either in the table itself or in a paragraph after the table.

A table lets you show the relationship between two or more related subjects.

SOUND [tempo]

When you issue the SOUND statement, you must assign a tempo. Here are the various tempos, with the beats per minute assigned to each by the language. (Actual performance by a human will vary enormously, so your computer will sound like a fairly mechanical student.)

Tempo	Speed	Beats per Minute	Clock Ticks per Beat
Largo	Extremely slow	50	20
Larghetto	Very slow	60	17
Adagio	Slow	75	15
Andante	Medium	100	12
Moderato	Medium fast	110	10
Allegro	Fast	130	7
Vivace	Very fast	150	6
Presto	Extremely fast	200	5

You should help people grasp the table's conventions by putting similar information in the same location (file names always on the left, for example). Even if there are slight variations, users quickly become familiar with a standard table format.

If people have to read across ten columns, give them visual help. You can shade every five lines, or skip a line every ten lines. These types of clues give a reader access to the entire width of a table.

Don't forget your own ability to describe things. Descriptive phrases and notes can make a table meaningful. Use the introductory paragraph, headings, labels, and any footnotes to help a reader distinguish among all the information in the table.

Checklist

Put information about controlling a product in a command reference

☐ Say something about each item—every physical button, every software command.

☐ Organize information about all the parts of a piece of hardware in the order people typically use them.

☐ Chunk the information into the major functional groups.

☐ Organize information about software commands the way the software does.

☐ Keep procedures in a separate section or chapter.

Put information about creating programs in a language or formula reference

☐ Whenever possible, organize and present the information by functional group.

☐ Use a special format for each element of the language.

☐ Provide details for each element in the same order and format.

Put information about solving problems in a troubleshooting section

☐ State the problem clearly so users in trouble can diagnose their situations.

☐ Explain the probable causes of the problem, from most likely to least likely.

☐ Create a diagnostic decision tree for complex problems.

☐ Provide a solution for each combination of problem and cause.

☐ Explain the product's own troubleshooting tool, if it has one.

☐ Explain error and status messages, and warnings, calmly and clearly, and tell users what to do about them.

☐ Organize troubleshooting sections in the order in which people are likely to encounter the problems, not alphabetically or by function.

☐ Make troubleshooting easy to find.

☐ Put a customer support phone number in several places, but say what to do before calling.

Put odds and ends in an appendix section

☐ Keep appendix sections short and self-contained.

☐ Consolidate and present information in tables whenever possible.

Indexes and Glossaries

The beginning of wisdom is calling things by their right names.

—Chinese proverb

14

As the eleventh hour tolls, when production deadlines loom and everyone's attention is turning to the next project, indexes and glossaries are often begun. The results look slapped together. But these tools are more important to many people than pages of text. Indexes and glossaries deserve your best planning and attention—not afterthoughts.

According to a series of studies by the American Institute of Research, about a third of your readers use the index as the first step in finding the information they need. (Another third look first in the table of contents, and the rest leaf through the pages.) A good index helps people find what they need fast, on the first try. The result: your manual becomes a frequently consulted reference tool instead of the last resort.

A glossary helps new users and beginners by defining terms and concepts needed to use the product. Experienced users can compare their usage with your definitions.

Plan your indexing method

You have three main options:

- Do the index manually.
- Use software to automate the task.
- Have a professional indexer do it.

If you create the index yourself, in most companies you will need to fight for more than a day or two in which to do the work. Some companies give you an afternoon—as long as you have nothing else to do. This stinginess almost guarantees that the company wastes most of the money they pay you, because users won't find their way to your writing.

If you index manually, budget time for indexing

As the author of the manual, you're in a good position to create a useful and complete index. You know the concepts and the material and because you have adopted the point of view of your audience, you have the advantage of being able to consider entries in the index as your reader might. You know the terms by which you decided to call things, as well as other common terms that you decided not to use but that a reader may look for. All are invaluable additions to the index.

Build a first draft of terms to be indexed into your beta or final draft. Just list every term you think should be included. Don't worry about page numbers. Ask testers to look in the list for any term they want to find out about; if they don't find the term, they should let you know.

Plan to begin indexing when you have a copy of text with accurate page breaks, so you can identify the page on which a reference appears. That could be when you turn your final over to production or, if they usually adjust pagination, when you get their first proof.

The production staff may want to know how many pages your index will be. That depends on the level of complexity of the manual—the more complex the book, the more detailed the index. It also depends in part on the page layout—indexes are often compressed into two or three columns, with type that's a couple of points smaller than the type used in the body of the manual. For a fairly complex manual, you may need between 1/50 to 1/20 the length of the text. That means between 5 and 12 pages for a 250-page manual. To estimate your own manual, flag a dozen typical pages, then see how many references you think you should include from each. Overviews might average 3 or 4 references per page; complex discussions, 12 to 15 references per page. Multiply your average number of references by your page count for a ballpark figure of the total number of lines (at one line per reference).

Allow enough time for a thorough job; how much depends on the size of the manual. If you've never done an index before, plan about three days for a 100-page manual (25 hours); about six days for a 250-page manual (50 hours).

When it's time to begin, clear your mind of last-minute details about the manuscript, such as catching misplaced commas and typos and the three features that were changed yesterday.

Avoid automatic indexing if you can

Indexing seems like one of those jobs you should be able to automate—after all, you're referencing information that for the most part is already in your text. A variety of word processing and page layout programs can gather text that you've flagged and generate an index. Your company may prefer that you use this approach and may even insist upon it as a matter of policy. However, we've found that automated indexing doesn't yet approach the quality that can be achieved manually. The drawbacks of automatic indexes include

- Few synonyms appear.
- Unless you code extra phrases, you'll get an index that only includes words in the text. If people don't happen to look up the exact word, they miss the reference.
- The organization tends to be helter-skelter and flat, not hierarchical and meaningful.
- Software that searches for all occurrences of flagged entries and includes every one in the index produces an index with more references to trivia than to significant information.

The more sophisticated word processing and page layout programs have improved indexing tools that let you insert synonyms, inverted phrases, and cross-references right on the page, adding special formats so they don't appear in the body of the manual. When you're ready, you tell the software to generate the index. The program creates an alphabetically sorted list and assigns the current page number to each item.

Unfortunately the resulting index still needs a thorough review and edit for completeness, redundancy, additional synonyms, and consolidation before it's ready to print. It may also need formatting to make it hierarchical. You perform this review without the benefit of having worked with an evolving list, so the time needed for reviewing and editing can approach that required for manual indexing. Automated indexing may save time if your manual goes through several editions with pagination changes. In that case automatic renumbering of entries is a blessing.

Automated indexes are most useful when you want to index early drafts of a manual. Ordinarily early drafts don't include an index, but your client may request one so that the manual can be used at beta test sites for product testing.

Keep in mind that if you code index entries in your text and create interim indexes, you're adding a documentation task. Don't expect to simply flag index entries as you write. The results won't be thorough or consistent. Rather, plan a complete pass through your text to add the codes. Such a pass, if you're thorough, may take an hour for every 20 or so pages.

If you use a professional indexer...

Indexing has become a science unto itself, and whole seminars are devoted to the subject. There are professional indexers who do nothing else for their living. If your schedule leaves you no time for doing the index yourself and your budget allows for expert help, consider using a professional indexer.

Make the arrangements well ahead of time so the indexer can schedule the job. When you farm out the task of indexing, you remove the benefit of your expertise from the task. Professional indexers are skilled at indexing subjects they know little about, but few other people are. Agree about the way in which the indexer's work will be reviewed. If possible, you should be given a chance to talk to the indexer before the job and after the first draft. Agree on the level of detail and the number of levels, up front.

Decide what to include

Planning what to include—if you do it ahead of time—can save you a lot of thinking time when you actually get down to indexing.

Make references count

A really useful index refers readers to significant information. Thoughtful indexing involves sifting the text to decide whether a word's occurrence is meaningful or incidental. How finely you sift is a matter of individual judgment and, perhaps, agreement between you and the product team.

Indexing every occurrence of a word would make for a long, frustrating, and stupid index. Many references would be trivial and people would have to go back and forth between the index and the text many times to find a kernel of information that really helps them. At the other end of the scale, listing a topic only when it's the central focus of a section (as when you index only your headings) may neglect references to many nuggets scattered through a manual. Such an index ends up being little more than an alphabetized version of the table of contents.

How finely you distinguish between related items is also a matter of judgment. For example, should you lump references to *external disk drives* under *disk drives* or provide a separate listing? Your familiarity with the product and the manual is probably your best guide to which distinctions are significant and which are not.

Include the main subjects, topics, and concepts

The main topics in your manual will probably stand out in the headings and subheadings of your table of contents. Because many people will turn to the index instead of the table of contents, include all these topics in the index, too.

Some entries generate additional entries. Invert phrases; if your main entry is *disk drives*, include *drives, disk*. When you encounter an acronym, list the long form in the index as well. If the abbreviation is used frequently in the text, putting the initials after the long form in the index will help readers.

BBS
bulletin board service (BBS)

Include synonyms and aliases. Ask yourself again and again, "How else might the user think of this topic?"

attaching the monitor cable
cables, connecting
connecting cables
connecting the monitor
equipment, installing
hooking up the equipment
installing
        cables
        monitor
        other equipment

Continued

Continued

monitor, connecting
plugging in
      cables
      monitor
      other equipment
setting up
      cables
      monitor
      other equipment

Providing aliases increases people's chance of finding the information they're looking for.

Once you're sure you've included every synonym your manual uses, browse specialized dictionaries in the field and manuals from your competition. These will suggest a few more ways of describing the same thing. And don't forget to use a thesaurus—you may even have one online. The point is that a user may think first of one of these terms, not the term you used; to help that person, you need to open all the doors, even if you decide to post a "Please see ..." sign just inside some of them.

Include all tasks your audience recognizes

Let readers look up any kind of task, large or small. Include every reason for using a particular command or sequence of commands. Then a reader can look up information by task, without having to know what command to use. Include all names by which the audience may refer to tasks, even if those names aren't used in the product or documentation.

The product uses the command Mail Merge, but that term is not the first that occurs to average users.

Mail Merge
      command
      data document
      letter

OK

addresses, merging
customizing letters
data document for form letters
form letters
       preparing
       printing
letters
       form
       standard
Mail Merge
       command
       preparing
       printing
merging information during printing
printing
       form letters
print merge
standard letters
writing
       form letters
       standard letters

Include all commands, options, and arguments

For example, the Paragraph Format command in a word processing program opens a dialog box that includes settings for left and right indents, space above and below paragraphs, tabs, borders, and more. Although one command opens the dialog box, the index might have a dozen or more entries.

alignment of paragraphs
borders
boxes
formatting paragraphs
 borders
 boxes
 indents
 margins
 spacing before and after
 tabs
indenting
 first line
 paragraph
margins
 document
 paragraphs
paragraph formatting
 borders
 boxes
 indents
 margins
 spacing before and after
 tabs
right indent, setting
right tab
setting indents
setting tabs
space, above and below a paragraph
tabs, setting

Include cautions

Readers may remember seeing a tip or a caution but not the context in which it came up. For example, say the operator's guide for a computer system mentions noises a disk drive may make and what they mean, and cautions you to turn off your machine if you hear a particular noise and take it to a dealer immediately. If your drive starts sounding strange, you want to find that caution immediately. It should be listed under several topics:

disk drive, sounds it may make
grinding noise in disk drive
hard drive
      sounds from inside
sounds the disk drive may make
maintenance
      when drive sounds like a garbage disposal
troubleshooting
      disk drives

Include references to key graphics

Include references to graphics that present important information visually, as well as named charts and tables. In an introductory networking manual, for example, put at least one reference to a diagram that helps users conceptualize how a network works. You may want to use a special font or format for entries that point to tables, diagrams, or screenshots.

You don't have to mention the graphic explicitly in the index entries. The point is to reference the information that the graphic presents.

Compile your list and organize it

When you begin your index, go through every page of the manual. You may prefer to mark entries in a paper copy with a highlighter and then, in a second pass, compile your entries into a list. Some writers prefer to go through the manual once, creating the list as they go. Or you can create the list directly in the word processing file, marking entries as hidden text and assigning a style that puts them flush left. Just root the terms out as you go through; then take a second pass, and collect all terms that stick out on the left.

Watch for additional subjects that should be included. You can jot synonyms and related topics in the margins or add them to your list as they occur to you.

Use appropriate software

When you're listing items, you'll save yourself hours of aggravation if you use a good program. You want to be able to create a list of items, move back and forth quickly in your list, hide some entries from view, sort entries alphabetically, and list items on hierarchical levels.

An outlining program makes a good indexing tool, because topics can be collapsed and you can sort the main list or within a topic. If you don't have an outliner, you can use either a word processor or a spreadsheet.

Programs that let you split the document window or open two windows of the same document enable you to compare related topics that may be pages apart in your list. For example, you can see what you've listed under *formatting* while making entries under *paragraph settings*.

If your word processor doesn't include sorting capabilities, consider using a spreadsheet program that can export to a text file. Put entries in one column and page numbers in another.

As entries add up, your list eventually becomes unwieldy. You have trouble scrolling to check whether you've already included a term and trouble finding existing entries to add more page numbers to them. This is the time to alphabetize the list and, if you're using outlining software, collapse parts of the list you're not working with.

Make your index hierarchical

Creating a hierarchy with subentries makes it easier for you to group information together and easier for users to find it. Identify each topic, instead of having a single term followed by a row of 20 page numbers.

If possible, limit your index to two levels under each letter. Only for a very large book about a complex product should you consider having three levels.

Some terms can stand on their own in an index. Others suggest broader topics that clearly have subentries. Start each subentry on a line of its own, indented under the main entry. Lines that wrap to the next line should be indented to keep entries and subentries clearly distinguished. A subentry may also deserve a separate listing so a reader can find it alphabetically.

Beginning with the topic formatting in a word processing manual, you quickly develop many subentries.

formatting
       alignment
       borders
       boxes
       character formatting
       fonts
       indents
       line spacing
       margins for document
       margins for paragraph
       page formatting
       paragraph formatting
       size of text
       space before or after paragraphs
       spacing of lines
       style
       tabs

Pick a main entry for a topic

When more than one entry refers to the same subject, make the entry most readers would look for first the main entry and list any subentries under it. Refer people to this main entry from alternate entries for the subject. Don't leave the alternates out, since they might help someone find the subject. Just add "*see* monitors, video" or whatever the main entry is. This way you indicate the standard term without condemning readers for not knowing it.

> displays (*see* monitors, video)
> monitors, video,
>> black and white, 37
>> color, 52-5
>> interlacing, 38
>> resolution, 40
> screens (*see* monitors, video)
> video monitors (*see* monitors, video)

Use *see also* to refer people to related subjects that they might not think to look up. Be sure the cross-reference leads to additional information, not the same information indexed under different headings.

Used thoughtfully, *see* and *see also* can provide a diagnostic resource in your manual. You can point to troubleshooting tips and solutions to problems, and also to tips about avoiding problems. For example, a reference to *printer jams* might include subentries for *fixing* and *avoiding*; it might also include a cross-reference to *loading paper*.

Place both *see* and *see also* references immediately after the index heading, in parentheses, and italicize both words.

Subdivide topics

When you accumulate more than a handful of page numbers for an entry, start making subtopics. Use the information in your notes and go back through the manual to pick out the best divisions.

For instance, after going through 30-odd pages, you may have a dozen references to reports. Going back through the manual, you might find those could be divided up into separate entries for *report, report catalog, report format, report menu, report name,* and *report title.*

Sort your entries

Of course, an index is alphabetized. But there are two ways to do it: letter for letter or word for word. We prefer letter for letter. In that method you don't stop alphabetizing a phrase when you come to the end of the first word. Instead, you ignore the spaces, any accent marks, and any capitals and look at the next letter, up to the first punctuation mark. If you alphabetize word for word, you arrange entries by the first word, then the second, then the third, and so on. Whichever method you use, be consistent.

When you alphabetize remember to put entries beginning with symbols at the beginning of the index, before entries that begin with letters. List the term again under the first letter. For example, list the software command *%include* before the *A's* and also under *I*.

```
%help
%include
%login
%logoff
...
I
...
illegal entries
%Include
initializing
```

List numbers alphabetically, as though they were spelled out.

Ignore words such as *the, a,* and *of* when alphabetizing. Instead, alphabetize the first significant word. Omit insignificant words from the entry if you can do so without sounding like a telegram.

Edit the listings

Once you've compiled and sorted your index, review and edit it. Carefully assess your listings and decide what's useful. If you've done your first pass well, you'll find lots of redundancy. Don't cut meaningful alternative terms. Do cut a term when a similar one appears right above it. And compress minor variations into a single term. For instance, if you have an entry for *spelling* and one for *spelling checker*, you can probably get rid of one of them.

Review each item to make sure it would make sense when a reader comes to it cold. Is its meaning clear enough? An entry like *codes* may tell the user nothing, while *codes, access; codes, formatting;* and *codes, ZIP* indicate what the user can expect to find.

Comparing your index to that of a similar product can give you an idea of how complete you've been and what you've left out.

Use consistent style

Consistency in the index helps the user, just as it does in the text of your manual. Here are a few stylistic issues to consider.

Singular or plural? Generally, make entries singular, but when in doubt follow the common expression. For instance, under *disk*, you might have subentries such as these:

> disk
>
>> backup (because it's a single process)
>> blocks (because no one's likely to care about one particular block)
>> file types (because there are several)
>> volume (because it's a collective noun)

Case and Punctuation. We prefer to make the first letter of each main entry follow the case used in the body of the manual. Don't put a comma between an entry and the page numbers. Instead, leave two spaces before the first page number.

- If an entry is modified, use a comma in the middle, like this: *menus, quick file 23.*

- Don't put a period at the end of the entry. When you use subentries, just indent them.

- If you have to include a numeric entry, spell it out so you can fit it into the alphabetical list.

Page numbers. Use page numbers, not section numbers, or chapter numbers (unless, of course, the page numbers include chapter numbers).

- If the text has the major discussion of a topic on four consecutive pages, use an en dash.
- If your book is numbered by chapter (1-1, 1-2, 2-2, 2-25, and so forth), you may have to use a slash, like this: *assembly language 3-25/3-28.*
- If the text treats another subject and just mentions the entry incidentally on each of those pages, list them separately: *assembly language 25, 26, 27, 28.*

Revising an existing index

When you've updated a manual, revising the index may be harder than creating a brand-new one. Going back to the text to verify every entry is tedious; if many sections of the manual have been reorganized or rewritten, every page number may be incorrect and many entries made obsolete by new terminology. Even professional indexers grow pale at the thought of revising an index.

If you haven't changed much of the text and you know exactly which pages you revised, you can search through your original index looking for those page numbers. See which of the original entries still apply and which should be changed or deleted. Here's where automated indexing can save time by recompiling the index from the marked terms remaining in the revised file. Manual or automatic, you'll need to make another pass to add new terms that crop up in the revised text.

If you've made extensive revisions that have forced repagination of a number of sections and you are indexing by hand, it's easier to begin your index anew. Don't just look for the key words you used before; keep an eye out for words and phrases you never mentioned in the first draft.

Include a Glossary—a Minidictionary

When you mention a new term for the first time, you can help beginners by defining it in the text. If you need to provide more information than you can in the context of a paragraph, give a more elaborate explanation nearby—perhaps in the margin or in a note—so experienced users who already know the term don't trip over the definition.

Put the term in a glossary, too, for the person who dips into your book without encountering that first reference and wonders what the word means. A glossary defines words that may be unfamiliar to some readers—bits of jargon, acronyms, commands, and phrases. The more inexperienced your readers, the larger your glossary should be.

To determine all the words that a novice might find puzzling, consider your early experiences with the subject matter and remember what puzzled you. To learn more definitively what confuses novices, test your manual. Ask someone who doesn't know the product to read through the manual and underline all words or phrases that seem obscure.

Accumulate entries as you learn the product

You need accurate definitions to document the product in a consistent manner. List expressions and their definitions as you learn the product, and then edit your personal glossary to create one for users.

Your glossary should include

- Key terms that are unfamiliar to users
- All technical terms
- Acronyms and abbreviations in their short and spelled-out versions
- Words used atypically in the product. For example, in a product using the word *include* to mean "make a file available from within the program," *include* is an important term to put in the glossary
- Any idea that may present problems to users or puzzles you

In the final glossary don't include terms not used in the text of your manual.

Set off glossary terms the first time they appear in the text

The first time you use a glossary term in the text, give it a distinctive format, such as boldface or italics. Early in the book—perhaps in the preface, or in the section on "How to use this book"—describe your highlighting method so readers will recognize when they can find additional information or clarification of a word.

Your definition of the term in the main text may be quite general. The glossary entry should provide more detailed information.

To select an icon, move the mouse until the pointer is over the icon and click the mouse button.
To click the mouse button, just press and release it quickly.

Here is an instruction in a software manual.

click   Rapidly press and release a mouse button. Unless a step explicitly specifies the right button, "click" refers to the left button. Clicking the mouse button when your pointer is touching an object selects the object; to select additional objects, hold down Shift and click them. (This is known as Shift-clicking.)

The glossary entry for click provides additional information:

Define without repeating the term itself

When writing a glossary definition, the first phrase should just define the term. (You can assume the verb *is* or *are* between the term and your phrase.) That phrase may have to be a bit dry to be precise. But after that you can loosen up and get a little more conversational.

port   You need a way to connect your computer with other devices, such as a printer or external modem. A cable from one of those devices hooks into the appropriate port on the back of your computer.

An instruction in a software manual for a product might say:

port   A connector at the back of your computer. You can plug a cable from a printer or other device into one of the ports. As you scan from left to right looking at the rear panel from behind the computer, your computer has a serial port (for your modem), an RS-232 Centronix port (for your line printer), a SCSI port (for hard drives or other storage devices that use the Small Computer Standard Interface), the Mouse port, and the Keyboard port. You'll see the name of each port engraved above it on the rear panel.

Add information to make the definition clear: the context or an example

If someone needs help badly enough to look up a word, they want more than a tight-lipped minimum. So add an example, like this:

> **device name**   The name used in our operating system pathnames to refer to a particular device, without regard to what files are associated with the device. Device names begin with a period and a letter, followed by up to 13 alphanumeric characters. For example, the device name of the disk drive built into the PortaNote is .D1, regardless of what disk is in the drive.

By giving a little extra in most definitions, you can make your glossary a lot more helpful than a dictionary—and a lot more specific to your subject.

Feel free to add a sentence or two of advice, as in this entry:

> **floppy disk**   A 3-1/2 or 5-1/4 inch flexible disk enclosed in a plastic envelope or case, used to store programs and their files. For the computer to read the information stored on a floppy disk, it must be inserted into a disk drive attached to the computer. Remember not to touch the magnetic surface of a disk by opening the envelope, or sliding the metal cover back; handle the disk only by its envelope or case when you insert or remove it.

Be sure you define the term in the context of what you're documenting. Don't be too general. For example, *distribution list* has a general meaning in offices. In a product with a graphic interface and icons, its meaning may be much more specific:

> **distribution list**   An item on the desktop that represents a container in which you can group individual recipients. You can send or distribute documents to all members of a distribution list in one step.

If you're in doubt about whether to include information in a glossary definition, it's better to err on the long side—include more information rather than less.

Include cross-references to similar terms, books, or sections

If a word you're defining is often confused with another term, clarify that in the definition. For instance, if you're defining both *indents* and *margins* in a glossary for a word processing manual, you might mention one in the definition of the other.

> **margins** The distance between the text and the edges of the paper. You set and change margins to determine where on the page your text will print, and how wide each line of text will be. To change the width of individual paragraphs instead of all paragraphs, change the *indent* instead of the margins.

Checklist

Choose an appropriate indexing method, and make a plan for implementing it

- ☐ If you index manually, budget time for indexing in your schedule
- ☐ Avoid automatic indexing unless you need intermediate drafts with indexes.
- ☐ Use a professional indexer when your schedule doesn't let you do the index

Plan what to include

- ☐ Refer readers to significant information
- ☐ Include the main subjects, topics, and concepts
- ☐ Include all tasks your audience recognizes, large and small
- ☐ Include all commands, options, and arguments
- ☐ Include tips and cautions
- ☐ Include references to graphics that present important information

Compile your list of terms and organize it

- ☐ Create a two-level hierarchy, three-level for a very large or complex book
- ☐ Pick a main entry for a topic and make it the entry most readers would look for first
- ☐ Subdivide an entry when it accumulates more than a handful of references
- ☐ Sort your entries
- ☐ Edit the list

Use consistent style

- ☐ Make most entries singular
- ☐ Make the first letter of each main entry follow the case used in the body of the manual
- ☐ Use page numbers, not section or chapter numbers

A glossary is a minidictionary

- ☐ Accumulate a list of glossary entries as you learn the product
- ☐ Set off glossary terms the first time they appear in the text with a distinctive format
- ☐ Define a term without repeating the term itself
- ☐ Provide enough information to make the definition clear
- ☐ Include cross-references to similar terms, books, or sections

Job Aids and Quick Reference Cards

The more you say, the less people remember.

—*Fénelon*

Job aids are technology's crib sheets—they're designed so people can look up facts they almost know, half forgot, partially recall. People turn to a paper tutorial when they are ready to devote an hour to learning how to use the product; they go to the manual for information about an unfamiliar procedure or a command they have never used; and they turn to job aids known as quick reference cards when they need to jog their memories.

15

Design to fit the conditions of use

Job aids started as index cards scribbled with reminders; some factories printed them for workers, and when computers appeared, many workers made up their own reminder sheets and stuffed them in their shirt pockets. One thing all job aids have in common: They're short. Like a student's crib sheet, a job aid is handy, easy-to-use, and definitely not the full-length original work.

Many companies favor a single stiffened sheet, printed on both sides, often laminated for durability. When there's more to say, some companies create accordion-like fan-fold cards that can be tucked into a folder, briefcase, or purse; these unfold to a larger format. Others offer a set of cards, loose or bound.

Tailor the physical dimensions of the card to the environment and circumstances in which your readers will need to use it. A job aid for computer software meant for use primarily in one location should fit next to the keyboard or under it. Unfolded, it can be propped up next to the screen or stuck into a shelf for ready access. This type of job aid can be the same size as the manual it accompanies; often it must be to fit in the product package.

If the job aid is meant to travel with a user, it should be easy to take along. If the card accompanies a piece of portable hardware, such as a notebook computer, or an electronic device with a limited function, such as a calendar or scheduler, size the card to fit in the same carrying case as the equipment. If you know your audience always carries a binder of a particular size, make the card that size. In some cases, you might want to make a wallet- or purse-sized, card, like the dialing instruction cards supplied by long-distance phone services.

The promise implicit in a quick reference card is that a user has crucial information at hand and can look up something immediately.

Your layout needs to reflect that purpose, too. Even though you may be trying to cram a lot of facts into a small space, make sure you use enough white space to separate categories of information (the command and its definition, the name of a procedure and the steps). You can go down to about 9 points in some sans serif typefaces; but a job aid isn't a phone book, so use plenty of leading between the lines and between groups of facts. In general, 10 to 12 points leading for 9 point text is readable at arm's length, by the light of the screen.

What to include

What goes into the job aid depends on what you think people will want to have handy. Traditionally writers who documented software thought customers just wanted to know what actions different commands performed, so they produced cards listing each command alphabetically, with a one-sentence explanation of its function. Later, as menus begat menus and customers wondered where little-used commands could be found, writers came up with menu maps—reproductions of all the menus in the product. When graphic user interfaces arrived, some writers reproduced them with labels indicating what each item was and perhaps what it did. Most recently these folded sheets, which have earned the name quick reference cards, have begun to include a condensed version of every procedure in the manual. So job aids come in four categories:

- A list of all commands, with a short definition of each one for any customer who wants to know what it does
- A reproduction of every major menu and submenu to show people where particular commands appear (menu map)
- An annotated tour of all the major interface elements (windows, tools, palettes, dialog boxes, buttons, levers, panels) showing what each part does
- A condensation of all the major procedures in your manual

You may want to provide some combination of these four elements in a quick reference card, but you will quickly run into the principal constraint: How do you fit everything on a single card or sheet without resorting to 6-point type? You may need to emphasize one of the categories and skimp on the others.

Listing the commands

Defining all the commands in the product with brief functional definitions ("Saves a file to disk") answers a user's question, "What does this command do?"

You need to decide whether to list all the commands, from A to Z, in one giant list or, if the product uses menus, to group commands the way they appear on the menus. In general, if the product organizes commands, your job aid should follow that model.

Include keyboard shortcuts, special macro commands, or neat tricks, perhaps on a separate panel. The expert user wants to move fast but may not remember the three-finger trick that applies the previous style to the current paragraph or the exact sequence of arguments needed for a database query.

Here are the commands on a menu devoted to Windows, with definitions, and shortcuts.

Working with Windows		
Close Window	Shuts current window	Option-C
Copy Window	Makes a copy of the contents of the current window and places that copy on the clipboard	Command-Option-C
Iconize Window	Shrinks window into an icon	Command-S-W
Open Window	Expands window from icon	Command-E-W
Print Window	Prints contents of current window	Command-P-W
Stack Windows	Arranges all windows in a stack, with current window in front	Command-S-W
Switch Windows	Makes next window active; if you have more than two windows open, cycles through all windows	Command-W

Mapping the menus

Some software products take the user through 20 or 30 major menus, each with submenus opening onto other submenus. The interface of a hardware product such as a fax machine may number menus and commands like the records in a juke box and display only one command at a time on the control panel. To cut through these thickets, you may want to provide a map to the commands, showing all the menus and submenus. Your whole job aid, then, becomes a series of reproductions of the various menus. If you have a little extra room, you may also be able to add a short phrase as a label, defining what each command does.

Menu maps are aimed at fairly experienced users who face as many as a thousand commands and wonder where to find the one they used three months ago. Maps to complex products won't leave room for any procedures. Make sure they appear in the manual or online help. And you probably won't have room to explain the interface elements; if users can't scroll, they'll have to read the manual or take training.

Here we see reproductions of three levels of menus, with annotations where needed. This menu map assumes readers are experienced enough to know which ISO set they need.

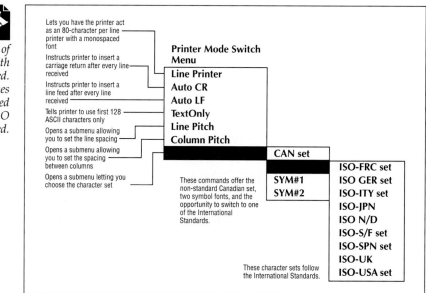

As much as possible, organize the maps to follow a person's experience with the product. Start with the main menu, if there is one, or the most obvious panel on a machine. From that point follow the organization of the product. If the first command on the main menu brings up a submenu, that submenu becomes your second illustration. Let your design indicate that this is a spin-off, a subset, a secondary menu.

If your product has dozens of keyboard shortcuts, employing every conceivable combination of function keys, you may want to show a diagram of the keyboard, with labels showing what to press to achieve what end. You may even want to make a template that fits over and around the keys, with reminders of what each key can do by itself and in combination with assisting keys such as Control, Shift, or Command.

Showing the interface

For newcomers to a graphical interface, particularly that of a product aimed at inexperienced users, you may want to focus on any complex or problematic elements in the interface. For instance, if your product has a complex ruler, a confusing tool palette, or an overloaded ribbon of icons, consider showing that, with callouts indicating what each part does.

This information manager's calendar uses notebook-like tabs for navigation among different views.

August						
S	M	T	W	T	F	S
			1 Planning ✦Review status of template	2	3 ✓BBS meeting.	4 ✦
5	6 ✓Meeting to review Links, Channel	7	8 ✦Call from Megan.	9 ✓Meet with JR, MP. ✓JP	10 ✓LNA July/Augu st stories due today	11
12	13 ✓Review template	14 ✦Call from Gina. Wants	15 ✓Dentist ✓Put notice on BBS	16	17 ✓Planning ✓LNA Newslette	18 ✦Work Meeting
19	20 ✓Called Dave, requested callback	21 ✓1d Ch12 MR to JP	22 ✓Bills ✓CW—Call from Dave	23 ✓SW 962 SFO>AB Q	24 ✓Meet with JP	25 ✦ABU ✓Work Meeting
26 ✦ABU SW ABQ>SF	27 ✓Call Gina	28 ✓OAK>SU SW Ramada Inn San	29 ✓Online Help Workshop Southern	30 ✓SD>OAK SW ✓Online Help	31 ✦Call from Casey	

Click a side tab to turn to see the view you want — **Year**

Click a day to see details — **Month**

Bullet indicates a To Do — **Week**

Checkmark indicates the task has been done — **Day**

Today

| To Do | Done | Appointments | Meetings | Calls |

└Click to see a list of tasks

Click to see a list of completed tasks

└Click to see scheduled appointments

└Click to see scheduled meetings

└Click to see calls made and received

As a rule of thumb, showing the interface can supplement one of the other approaches but not replace it.

Summarizing the procedures

Occasional users tend to forget the exact sequence of steps in procedures. Advanced users may seek a hint in order to try something they've never done before. They needn't crack a book if they have an aid to jog memory and intuition.

Group the tasks, as much as possible, in the same way you have in the manual or the online help. Use meaningful headings so people can find what they need by skimming. For the large headings use the large-scale tasks a customer might want to do; under those, for a complex product, add subheads for each mid-scale task.

Carve your page up into columns: Put the name of the small-scale task on the left so someone can find it quickly; on the right, put the steps, drastically condensed. When revising the steps, omit all but the essentials.

- If you think experienced users can locate any command on the menus, omit the phrase "on the such-and-such menu." If you want to make sure people recognize that something is a command, represent commands with a distinct font or style (small caps, white on black) or graphic (keycap, iconic menu).
- Omit all explanations of what happens, such as "A dialog box appears."
- Do not number the steps or put white space between them.
- Condense five or six steps into a single sentence.
- Reduce the amount of supporting detail, but leave in anything that's crucial or that could help people avoid errors.

In condensing your procedures, you may feel as tentative as if you were getting a new haircut or pruning a prize rose bush. You don't want to leave out a key detail; you are afraid to underemphasize something; you recall how much effort you put into a long paragraph explaining the circumstances in the book. Forget most of that. If people need the extra facts, they will open the manual.

Here's what the procedure looks like in the manual.

To Install a Font Card

Font Cards let you add special fonts you need for one job. In general, use only one font requiring a Font Card per document.

1. **Make sure the printer is OFF.**

   Use the On/Off switch on the back of the printer, on the right. If you do not switch off the printer, you can damage the Font Card, and you may short-circuit the printer.

2. **Remove any Font Card from the Font Slot.**

   Grasp the card with your thumb and index finger, and gradually increase pressure. It will come loose from its socket and then slide out swiftly. The red warning label, No Fonts, appears on the top panel display.

3. **Put the new Font Card into the Font Slot, label side up.**

   If you put the card in upside down, you may damage the pins that make the connection from the card. If a pin breaks off in the slot, you can make it impossible to insert another card until you have a certified repair technician replace the socket.

Here's the same procedure in the quick reference card.

To Install a Font Card

1. Make sure the printer is OFF.

2. Remove any font card from the Font Slot.

3. Put the new Font Card into the Font Slot, label side up.

Checklist

☐ Tailor the dimensions of the aid to the environment and circumstances in which it will be used

☐ Tailor the amount of information and level of detail to the needs of your audience

Online Help

Give me the ready hand rather than the ready tongue.

—Giuseppe Garibaldi

Online help supports people when they encounter a problem in the midst of their work. They're in no mood to study; they want to get on with their jobs. They need a reminder about a forgotten step or what a particular icon means, or they need to diagnose their situation and solve a problem.

Today's management wants more effective help facilities because good help saves money and sells products.

- Lets you toss out some sections and shrink paper manuals
- Reduces the amount of time and money spent on customer support
- Saves on production (it costs less to duplicate disks than print books)
- Saves on shipping (disks cost less to package and ship)
- Persuades customers to buy the product because of good reviews.
- Makes the product competitive.

When you provide effective help within a product, people experience the product as smart, even friendly. But if the help facility is difficult to use or lacks the information they need, people interpret that as a product failure and grudgingly turn back to the paper manuals or call the hotline.

Many people got burned by old-fashioned, so-called help. It was unresponsive, barely verbal, punitive, stingy, and sluggish—a series of telegrams from hell.

A sampling of "help" messages from earlier days.

Incorrect response, answer Y or N.
Cursor movement can be achieved by utilization of arrow keys.
Abort, Retry, Fail
Illegal parameter

Today's consumers want more effective help facilities built into products such as copiers and video recorders as well as appearing within the computer environment—not in paper manuals. The spread of networking means more new or intermittent users who lack manuals and need information online. More people are using software, doing a greater variety of tasks—and they expect more now.

16

In the remainder of this chapter, we sketch the entire process of creating an online help facility, a subject complex enough to warrant a book of its own. We introduce most of the issues you need to know about before starting your first project or when brushing up on the process.

What you do to create help

Here are the steps you should take to create a genuinely useful help facility.

1. Specify the help environment (define the audience, product, and the world in which help has to live—the display, the screens available, the system software, the networks, the application itself).

2. Design the help user interface—the ways people enter help, move around in it, and exit, plus the design of the help display.

3. Structure the content of help.

4. Prototype and test a sample.

5. Write and design the content.

Designing a help facility is an iterative process, with redesign occurring at every step. In designing the interface, for instance, you plan, propose a solution, test it out, evaluate the results, and go back to redesign. Testing takes place at every phase—or should. We describe these steps separately, but you'll find you cycle through them many times on the way to achieving a finished help facility.

Take a diagnostic approach

A manual usually describes a "healthy" system, but online help treats the system's "illness." In creating online help, think of yourself as helping the user to diagnose and treat a symptom—not just learn a subject. Remember that people come to you upset, confused, frustrated, and worried that they may not be able to finish their work on time. Taking a diagnostic approach can sensitize you to users' conditions when they seek help.

Incorporate help into the user's workflow

Make help an expected part of the usual course of work, not a last resort when trouble has darkened the screen. Something happens that interrupts the flow of users' thoughts; help should not extend that interruption. It should be fast enough so people remember what they were doing when they began looking for help. The less time it seems to take to get to the relevant help, the less it seems an intrusion, and the more likely it is that people will incorporate help into the context of their work.

Put help next to, not on top of, users' work. This lets people transfer information quickly from help to their real work—without memorizing it, writing it down on yellow stickies, or printing it. If you hide their work, they forget what they were trying to do.

- Use overlapping windows. The cognitive psychologist Don Norman says that when the help window overlaps people's work, they infer that help is secondary and can be put away when they're done. But don't use too many windows.

- If you can't use windows, use a set message area, rather than an area in which text flows and flows and flows.

If screen space is limited

- Present topics in a series of discrete screens.

- Let users toggle between the help display and their work display.

- Use a fixed message area (four to six lines deep) for messages, not the full display.

- Let users return to work where they left off.

Step 1: Specify the help environment

When creating help you need to make many of the same exploratory documents as you do when creating a manual. In fact, two documents may turn out to be just the same.

- The audience profile, including a list of the main tasks customers will be using the software for and task analyses

- The profile of the product itself

But there are two additional pieces of research you need to undertake for online help: a platform profile and an information profile.

Create a platform profile

To know what you can do in help, find out exactly what hardware and software the users have.

- What display will people be using? What size is it? Is it character-based or graphics-based? What is its resolution?
- How much memory can you expect to use within the computer and on disk to store the help materials?
- How fast does the operating system or network respond when someone calls for help? The help should appear quickly—but not so fast that people miss the change. Users compare onscreen performance with the ease and speed of flipping paper pages. If your system doesn't allow such speed, explain the delays and make them consistent; more people forgive a consistently slow system than an inconsistent one, where they begin by hoping for speed and then get disappointed over and over. Jef Raskin, the inventor behind the Macintosh, says

  > Most people don't use dictionaries and encyclopedias because it takes from half a minute to a few minutes to look something up. If a computer system is as slow or slower, it will be avoided as thoroughly as people avoid other reference systems.

- Is there enough screen real estate so that people will be able to see their work at the same time as help? They should be able to transfer information from the help facility to their work.

Describe the user interface you will be working with. The product sets up certain conventions you may not want to violate. If you are working with several user interfaces, describe the most limited user interface you must conform to. Does help have to fit into a corporate user interface?

Review and describe the constraints imposed by the help facility development tools. Your tools may include

- Writing and graphic tools (perhaps those used for manuals)
- Authoring tools (the software that lets you create help)
- Networking environments

- Runtime presentation tools (the software that lets you show help to the users)

Whenever possible choose authoring tools and runtime software that let you design a help facility that can be revised and reissued in a timely way. For example, revising may require that every hyperlink button must be relinked. (Hypertext environments, the basis for most help facilities, let you click a button and make a jump—through hyperspace—from one place to another in the help facility; these connections are known as *links*).

The constraints may remain unclear for a while and frequently change, and some will only surface late in the effort. A strong basic structure can make it possible for you to respond to late-surfacing problems with elegant solutions.

Create an information profile

Position the help facility in relation to all the documentation. Compare the content and delivery to that of

- Paper manuals
- Tutorial or training materials
- Marketing and positioning materials
- Customer support responses
- Documentation of companion or earlier versions

Make a strong case for providing as much information as the manuals. Make clear what you intend to include: procedures, reference material, advice about the application area, and troubleshooting. Make clear what you intend to leave out—exclude

- General overviews
- Hardware installation
- Hand-holding tutorials
- Marketing material, advertising

Stress the purpose of help. It's more than a reference. The team often comes to the help facility with memories of the old kind of help, so they may expect that—unless you disabuse them.

Define how much information will get passed back and forth between the application and help.

- Will there be a form in help where someone can type in and record the answer to a dialog box in the application?
- Will the application tell help what command the user just used?
- Will context-sensitive information be passed to help, or will it just lead to its own separate facility of quick help?

The goal of the information profile is to show the team exactly how help fits into the overall flow of information about your product.

Step 2: Design the help user interface

The user interface—the ways people can interact with your help facility—determines how successful they are at discovering help, moving around in it, locating the information they need, and retiring with that information to apply it to their work.

Craft a metaphor for help

Use metaphor to make it easy for customers to apply what they already know to using help. The metaphor helps people construct their own meaningful conceptual model of the software by representing one thing (unfamiliar) in the terms of another (familiar), such as

- A notebook with tabs
- An office
- A desktop or the objects commonly found on a desk
- A panel resembling audio controls or an airplane cockpit
- Tools and toolboxes
- Palettes

Users form their conceptual models from the system's actual interface, not from the conceptual model you have in your head. Surface appearances provide their most important cues:

- Physical knobs, dials, keyboards, displays

- Indications of intellectual organization: menus, tables of contents, the layout of each window
- Documentation, including instruction manuals, help facilities, text input and output, and error messages.

Interfaces are dramatic forms; like plays, interfaces act things out, while databases, manuals, and novels just describe things. Users are not a passive audience in this theater; they are participants—actors—who manipulate objects in the onscreen environment directly for some larger purpose (their work), forming a mental model of help from their experiences. These models are more memorable when the interface embodies a familiar metaphor.

If the system or application has been developed around a central metaphor, express it in the help facility. If the application has no particular metaphor, create one for help.

The metaphor should suggest actions, give meaning to the user's search. For example, a desktop metaphor suggests that users can do onscreen everything they've done at their desks.

The metaphor should enable components of the interface to be manipulated like real-world objects. The tabs in a help notebook, for example, suggest that they represent section dividers and can be somehow lifted up, or turned, to go to the section.

Users who see an onscreen notebook with tabs unconsciously associate it with real notebooks they've used and expect to find ways to turn the onscreen tabs.

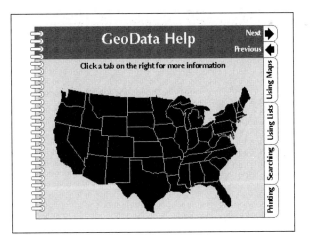

The metaphor should also suggest the breadth and depth of the help facility. For instance, a diminutive help notebook suggests it's a job aid, not the last word on the software.

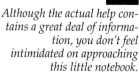

Although the actual help contains a great deal of information, you don't feel intimidated on approaching this little notebook.

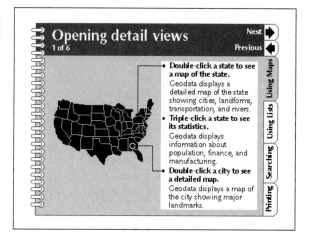

How people navigate in a help facility

The ability to navigate through any environment depends largely on two types of spatial knowledge.

Route knowledge—memories that guide people from one place to another via a path they have previously followed through an environment (Figure 16-1).

Figure 16.1

Some people prefer to get a general sense of the place and accept trial-and-error as a way to get from one major landmark to another.

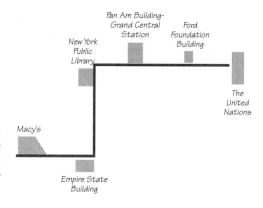

Survey knowledge—memories of the global environment with some understanding of the relationships between landmarks (Figure 16-2).

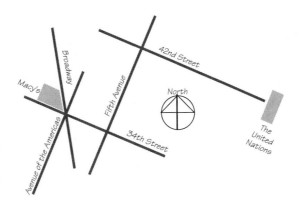

Figure 16.2
Other people like to know exactly how to get from one street to the next.

People often prefer one type of knowledge over another. They express their preferences in the kind of information they seek and in their strategies for getting it.

Encourage several strategies for acquiring information:

Reading every word—the least efficient technique, but one that some people still want to be able to do.

Skimming—an old favorite from book reading.

Browsing through linked or associated topics.

Looking a topic up in some kind of list. (Flat alphabetical lists such as an index or glossary are popular with beginners.)

Initiating a complex search for a specific topic. (People who once knew some facts prefer searching, because they already understand how the information is organized, but beginners hate searches.)

Answering questions about your current situation, branching to other questions, reaching a solution (diagnostic system).

Accessing help directly from the task context. (Such quick help provides information about the working of the software but rarely helps users accomplish their own tasks.)

Support various user information-acquisition strategies by arranging the information in several alternative structures:

Hierarchical lists, such as a table of contents, menus, a command reference, or an index, let users recognize an item on a list of alternatives rather than recall a command.

Flat lists, such as a glossary or dictionary, have no hierarchy and just one organization. If you know the term, you're in luck.

Visual or spatial hierarchies, such as images of folders and files, maps, graphic objects in the application interface, or buttons, let you access information that would not fit into a conventional table of contents.

Opening help: Rough out main routes to the relevant information

Establish the main routes by which you think users will want to travel as they enter the help facility and locate the information they need. Make these routes recognizable, memorable, and fast. (Figure 16-3)

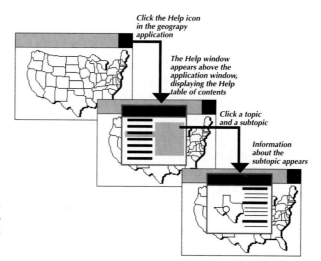

Figure 16.3
Diagram the routes in your help facility to work them out and aid team discussions.

Even when they can't recall exactly where it is or what the command might be, people can *recognize* a route. Recognition is more reliable than recall. To make access easy to recognize, keep a help button always visible, or make sure that a help command always appears in a standard location on a menu.

Keep the main route short—no more than four actions to get to the content.

Have users arrive at a meaningful location in the content

Announce the subject with a title so users know they've arrived. Don't plop them down somewhere in the middle of a page of information, forcing them to skim up and down to find the facts they seek. General rule: Never leave people in doubt about whether they've reached the fact they sought.

- If the section is organized as a sequence of displays or topics—start the reader off at the *first display in the sequence.*
- If the section is organized as a hierarchy—start the reader at the *top of the hierarchy,* either in an overview topic or at the table of contents for that section.
- If the software can detect the user's context—start the reader in the topic that corresponds (somehow) to the current conditions of the program, usually a *definition of the last command* or icon selected.

Keep users from getting lost

In your first prototypes you may find yourself getting lost—bad sign: If you can't find your way through your own structure, how can a user?

Avoid too many levels, too many steps to get to the relevant information. A shallow structure is easier to comprehend. Beyond five or six levels, most people cannot tell you what choices they made while descending to the lowest level, so they are more likely to become confused and disoriented.

In every screen of help, tell users where they are. For example, you can tell them they are viewing "1 of 3 pages."

Let users reverse their course, correct a mistake, or retrace a trail. Make it easy to go back to the top level, so people who have gotten lost or reached a dead end can quickly return to what many users call "home," which is often the main menu.

Getting around: Articulate paths within the help facility

Having entered the help facility, users want to find information by following various paths.

Let users move easily within the contents of one topic. For instance, you need to settle on a consistent way to provide extra details about a topic, such as pop-up boxes with definitions of key terms. If one topic does not fit in a single display, provide a direct route from one display to the next; for example, you could use Previous and Next buttons.

Let users navigate quickly and surely among several topics.

- Forward and back among topics at the same level
- To cross-references (along links)
- Back along a reading path
- To bookmarked topics (that is, topics the user has marked to return to)
- To the first-level of the help facility
- To the index

Plan a glossary as another way to move among topics.

- Provide some way for users to jump directly to the definition of a term—and then back again.
- You cannot link every glossary term with a particular display, because some terms appear in many different displays.

Plan the ways to reach the index, move through it, and go to a reference. Unlike a book index, an online index has only one "page number" per reference—that is, each entry leads to only one display. That means you will probably need to break the index up into at least two levels.

Plan the types of links. Hypertext is a general term for software that lets you set up links between parts of a document by building various paths through your material and encouraging people to jump from one topic to another without going through the table of contents or index. You needn't figure out every link in advance, but you should decide on categories—for instance, whenever you have a term you think people will want to look up, they can click it and go to the glossary item. Make all links two-way, so people can return without getting trapped in a dead end.

To visualize the paths between levels and categories of information, diagram the links.

This diagram shows how the help route parallels the application route in a context-sensitive help facility.

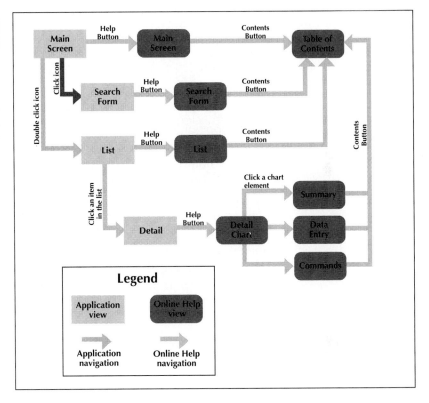

Use menus. Menus come in many forms, such as lists, pictures with selectable elements, and tool palettes. Because menus let people recognize what they want rather than recall a phrase they have to type, menus speed up every choice. But make sure you let people abandon a menu if they decide they don't like any of its options. Use pop-up menus to get at tiny details.

Polish your buttons. As you work out your interface, define and list all button types, what they are, and what they do. Test any iconic representation to make sure people understand it. Add a label where possible. And make some buttons visible at all times:

- Next
- Previous
- Index
- 1st-Level Menu
- Glossary
- Help on help

Leaving help: Exit gracefully

Help should lie open next to the actual work, so users can read and apply the information without having to put help away and reopen their document. But even when help coexists with the work, some people want to put it away.

Make it clear how to get out of the help facility. Users of an online system don't like feeling trapped inside the system, unable to exit. So make the command clear (Leave Help), or use the application's mechanism for closing windows or putting away documents.

Where practical, return users to what they were doing before opening help. If help disturbs the work, the distraction may make it hard for people to recall what they learned in help.

Design the help display

The screen is a less familiar medium than paper, and the way you design each screen must be different from the way you design a page.

- The online help facility display is often smaller than the paper page.
- The screen is often grainier, so text and graphics are rendered more coarsely than on paper. The lower resolution means you cannot use the same subtleties you can on paper.
- People read more slowly from the screen, and less accurately.

Because such differences exist, you should consider the following issues while designing your help screens:

Don't reproduce the pages of your manual for the screen. The effect is like looking at a book you can't quite touch. Depending on screen size, users may have to scroll through two or three displays to see "one" page; the empty parts of some pages fill the screen with nothing, making users think the system has crashed; and the shape doesn't quite fit. For all these reasons people find it's hard to get to relevant information, hard to move to the right location, and hard to switch from one topic to another. There are, after all, no physical pages to flip.

Specify a fixed size for the help display early: It's your basic unit. The size of the help display affects navigation methods and the way you chunk information. Many help facilities provide a scrolling display, so you never know how much information to expect on a particular topic, and even when you arrive at what is supposed to be the topic, you may have to scroll down, down, down, to find what you need. The resulting uncertainty and inconsistency makes some users feel actual motion sickness. So avoid scrolling whenever you can; work within a fixed space.

Don't allow resizing, either. Resizing and reshaping can ruin your carefully set-up relationship between art and text. Keep the size of your help display small enough to show the application itself behind or next to help, but large enough to show five or six steps of a procedure.

Make text legible

The more easily users can read your online help, they more often they will return, to use it regularly.

Use black text on a white background. Most people find black on white easier to read, easier to understand, and less open to mistakes than white on black.

Don't rely on any one typographic convention to communicate. Change at least two aspects of your text to distinguish between levels in headings, or purposes (such as captions, callouts, regular text). For instance, change the size and style from 12-point plain text to 14-point bold, for a heading.

Use fonts with clear, legible character shapes, such as Helvetica or Palatino. Look for a font with a tall "x" so that the bottom of each letter seems large; avoid fonts with very thin strokes. Don't make regular use of italics or all-uppercase words; they're very hard to read onscreen.

Increase line spacing and blank space beyond the conventions for paper manuals. Crowded lines blur the text, leading to eyestrain and confusion. Increasing line spacing definitely increases reading speed and cuts down the number of pauses the eye has to make on each line.

Keep lines short. Newspaper columns work well.

Left-justify text. Ragged-right text lets readers keep their place and read more easily than fully justified text.

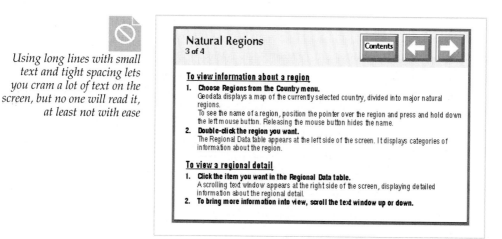

Using long lines with small text and tight spacing lets you cram a lot of text on the screen, but no one will read it, at least not with ease

Putting the text into narrow columns makes it easier to read.

Structure the help display to communicate consistently

Develop a layout that telegraphs the purpose of each element; make the whole screen seem obvious. That way people can quickly figure out how to "read" the screen. Then, if you stick to the same layout throughout, your consistency reassures people, and reenforces the skills they've learned.

Arrange items onscreen in a familiar, logical pattern.

- Position the most important items, such as key words, information you want the user to remember, navigation buttons, or commands, where they can't be missed.

- Organize lists of items in the groupings and sequences users expect.

Users learn to look in the same position in every help screen to find buttons that take them back to the main table of contents, back a screen, or forward a screen.

Users also become accustomed to seeing text appear in a constant location. The left side remains available for illustration—and in software with a graphic user interface, you must have art on almost every display.

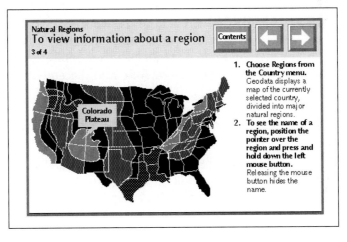

Divide the display into functional areas. Devote a particular part of the display to navigation, information about your position in the structure, running text, and art. Following a consistent structure like this will halve the number of errors people make. Within each area, group related items. For similar items

- Cluster them together and surround them with blank space.

- Draw a box around them.

- Apply similar visual characteristics, such as color.

Standardize the items in your displays. Put a title on every display, in the same place, so no matter what and no matter where they are, users can determine whether or not they've found the subject they want. Label or caption major areas.

Make sure users can tell they are looking at help, not the application itself.

- Use a distinctive border.
- Display the word *help*.
- Adopt a distinctive color or type style.

Leave plenty of room around the information. Material on screen needs to be surrounded with plenty of unused space. Plan to leave between a third to a half of the screen area blank. The more you pack onto a display, the more difficult it is to read, and the more oppressed readers feel.

Lay out and format visual elements so they emphasize, group, distinguish, and represent information. To group related information, use lines, boxes, and borders. To indicate different levels of importance (major heading, minor heading, text, note), use variations in type size, font, and placement.

- Use underlining sparingly for emphasis.
- Avoid overprinting, strikethrough, and italics (too hard to read on the screen).
- Do not resort to all-capital letters for emphasis.
- Don't use blinking for anything other than the cursor. Too many blinks, and people respond like deer in headlights.

Use color with restraint. Color, used in conjunction with some other visual element such as position, helps people recall information more accurately than black and white alone can. But when you use more than half a dozen colors, people have trouble seeing the point of each one and get lost in the rainbow. So use color sparingly to highlight areas and emphasize your structure. Another reason not to rely on color by itself to make an effect: 8% of your male audience and 0.4% of your female audience cannot easily distinguish red and green.

Set up a palette of usable colors and assign a purpose to each.

- Use background colors to group items.
- Use variations in saturation of one hue to group items while providing cues about structure.
- Don't use multiple colors in running text.

Watch out for cultural associations to a color. In finance, red means loss; in politics, radical; in temperature, warm; in traffic, stop. The cultural context may support your idea or defeat it.

Keep users informed

This is the golden rule of interfaces. The look of each object in your interface should express its purpose. For instance, buttons should say, *sotto voce*, "Press me." Clearly identify which objects a user can act on and provide feedback as soon as possible after they are used. Keep users informed of the results, too. For instance, if a task will take more than a few seconds, displaying a clock helps reassure the user that the system has not frozen.

Step 3: Structure the content of help

The way you structure the content is even more important in online help than in a book.

- On the screen, users receive unfamiliar cues to their place, and they may receive fewer of them.
- Users cannot locate themselves with reference to the beginning or ending.
- Users cannot form a conception of the size of the help facility.
- Boundaries between sections of information are often not as recognizable.

More familiar with books, people are more forgiving of sloppy organization in them. And many people have developed techniques that compensate for the sloppy organization, such as browsing, grazing, and flipping through pages.

Structure help clearly so users can grasp your organization quickly and reliably

The more complex the subject, the more your structure determines whether or not users can find and understand the information they need. Sometimes you can use the organization of existing good manual as a rough spec, but do not limit yourself to that. If the manual organization is weak or does not match your help content outline, use it as a reference only.

Make a Content Outline—a structured organization of topics

The basic unit of information is the topic. Topics are units of meaning (thoughts, concepts, facts) rather than arbitrary presentation units (volumes, pages, panels, windows).

- Include information in a topic that users think of as a unit, want to see at one time, and refer to as a whole.
- A single topic should answer one specific question. It can contain different amounts of information.
- Keep topics brief, but don't carve them up into chunks so small that no one chunk means anything.
- Recognize that what looks at first like a topic may turn out to be a group of topics—a category.
- Divide topics into smaller chunks than you would for a paper manual.
- Include topics of concern to every type of user, such as a command summary for expert users or pop-up definitions in quick help for beginners.
- Answer questions.

This type of question	Is best answered by…
How do I…?	Procedures for performing a task
What is …?	A definition in a glossary, command reference, index, pop-up in help, or quick help
What's wrong…?	If the product detects an error, start with a message and a reference, or provide a real set of diagnostics
What's new?	If appropriate, add a section on what's new in this version of the product

Group topics as users expect to find them. Arrange the groups of topics in hierarchies to offer information gradually. For more information about grouping topics, see Chapter 3, "Understanding Your Audience and Their Work."

Be slow to exclude any information. Make cuts only after outlining everything you think a user needs. Cutting and making help smaller is easier than squeezing in more data and enlarging help. Later, severe space constraints often lead to cuts of whole categories, such as command reference, or troubleshooting. But you cannot apply real size constraints until you know exactly how much each display costs on average, after taking advantage of all the compression and tricks available, usually during a beta phase.

Step 4: Prototype and test a sample

Once your content outline and help design have been accepted, you can create a working sample. The sample implements representative sections so you can test the help facility user interface, the links between and within parts, and the content itself. You will make extensive changes after testing, so don't mock up the entire help system. Implement sections that refer to parts of the software that are already working (if any).

Use the sample screens to estimate the number of screenfuls of information to give you an idea of the total size of the help facility.

Create menus from the content outline

Your prototype should have a complete menu system, even though most choices haven't any content. You want to be able to test out the scale of your help facility. At first you'll probably have many levels. But you should aim for fewer, so people can make decisions faster.

Put more topics on the first level. List 12 to 15 topics in a first-level menu to help users choose the right information category the first time. More topics mean more differentiation among categories, and that helps beginners quickly and accurately recognize the needed topic.

Include all major objects that users work on, such as text or graphics, and all major actions, such as formatting or editing text.

Combine action and object for greater precision by offering topics such as sending files, receiving files, and converting files.

List fewer topics on lower-level menus. That encourages people to feel as if they are narrowing down their search, proceeding from many to few, from complex to simple. Limit lower-level menus to five to seven items.

If possible, show lower-level menus at the same time as the first-level menu so a user can quickly see the relation between major topics and subtopics.

On all menus

- Don't number the individual topics.

- Give each topic a short, meaningful name.

- Offer topics and subtopics—nouns, gerunds, maybe a few adjectives. Help menus should be different from those in the application, where each command is a verb in a sentence in which the selected object is the subject. And don't use the same terms as the application menu—that would really confuse users. For instance, if the application menu has a command Attach, then the related topic on the Help menu should be something like Attaching a File.

- You needn't make every menu item short—sometimes brevity can be cryptic.

- Use parallel form when you can.

Here's a first-level menu for the help facility of an editing utility, with the Spelling submenu open.

Help Menu

Counting words

Grammar-checking

Idiom-searching

Layout verification

Opening and closing documents

Printing the results of an editorial pass

Proofing

Punctuation-checking

Sorting

Spelling

     Checking a selection

Continued

Continued

Here's a first-level menu for the help facility of an editing utility, with the Spelling sub-menu open.

Checking the whole document
Installing a dictionary
Switching a dictionary
Troubleshooting
Using the Thesaurus

Draft contents for every type of help display

To test every aspect of your help facility, create prototypes of every possible display:

Procedures: at least one group
Command reference: one related group
Glossary: enough items for one or two letters
Index: enough items for one screen or letter.
Table of contents/menus: enough to test all levels. Exception: You may need to provide complete tables of contents or menus to give reviewers a sense of the scope (breadth and depth) of the help facility.

Create a style guide for writing the content of the help facility

Begin by revising the one you use for paper manuals to ensure that both kinds of documentation appear to come from the same company.

Spell out the style requirements for help, and make clear how and why they differ from those for the paper documentation. When you hand off the completed help facility, the people responsible for maintaining, revising, and updating it will need to know why you made the choices you made and how to make changes consistent with it.

Test the prototypes

You should administer the test to subjects who resemble your real audience. Others do not know the prototype and interface as well as you do and so will take longer to recognize significant data. (See Chapter 17, "Getting Feedback," for advice on running user tests.)

Have professional testers check the help facility for performance and robustness.

- Confirm precision of searches.
- Do some destructive testing, but don't spend a lot of time on this. Everything is fragile.
- Create a database of bugs, problems.

Revise the working sample

Focus on large issues first. Solving a big organizational problem can simplify the writing at the lowest level.

Revise all the documents and create the final help specification.

- The help environment
- Audience profile
- Product profile
- Platform profile
- Information profile
- Content outline
- Help user interface specification

Step 5: Write and design the content

Base your text on the manual, if it is well organized. If the manual organization is weak or does not match your help outline, use it as a reference only.

Avoid book writing onscreen

In a book you can count on people reading one paragraph after another, but in help, all you can count on is that people have chosen to read one particular paragraph. Here's how to avoid thinking like a book writer.

- Expect that users will jump in the middle.
- Title every topic to make the subject instantly obvious.

- Stick to one topic per display.
- Separate categories of information clearly; for instance, distinguish between a definition and an example.
- Make transitions crisp and obvious, not gradual and unobtrusive.

Condense carefully

People get more impatient reading long, tangled text on the screen than when reading it in a book.

Trim or cut lengthy material that can be skipped easily on paper, such as

- Elaborate introductions
- Summaries
- Explanations after steps in a procedure (don't eliminate, though)

Break apart long sentences, but avoid the telegraphic style when compressing text to go online. Do not suppress subordinating conjunctions and connectives, articles, or parts of verbs.

Judith Ramey, a professor who has researched the impact of excessive brevity, speaks of the "Escher effect" of such telegraphic writing, because like the artist's etchings, these displays force you to keep looking at the context to get your perspective, "rather than simply taking in the information offered. They force users to analyze particular phrases and sentences."

Make sure the meaning survives. Mechanical shortening can inadvertently create ambiguities when secondary meanings are cut.

- Extra words may have been included to rule out misunderstandings.
- Preserve illuminating details, such as those that set the purpose and context of a task. ("If you need to do x, y, or z…")
- Have the original writer review the edit to assure that the original meaning survives (or write both yourself).

Make graphics central, not just decorative

Make pictures the starting point for text, not the other way around. They communicate better than text on the screen, and they can

- Show what you mean in context
- Emphasize important features
- Motivate and attract users

Add text to the graphics. Embed captions and callouts in illustrations, rather than in running text referring to the picture. Do not refer to illustrations that aren't on the screen. Use pop-up definitions to keep text out of sight until needed.

Use simpler pictures than in a book. Fine details can get lost on low-resolution screens. When you face severe limits on memory, avoid large, detailed pictures because they take up more room. Zoom in, use closeups, and blowups for easy recognition.

Keep the transitions consistent

Without knowing it, we all have picked up the conventions of film and television. We can't quite explain why, but we recognize the meaning of a cut, a zoom, and a fade, and we get used to the way a particular director uses those transitions. If you use the same transition for the same purpose, you give people a feeling of stability; but if you become inconsistent, people begin to feel anxious without knowing why. For example, using a cut to move back from one display and to zoom in on a detail in another subtly confuses people brought up on TV.

Use animation to show change and movement

Animation can show abstract changes, such as movement of data through a process, development over time, or the workings of some complicated machine. The main reasons against animation are memory and size constraints and making the viewer a captive audience. If you use animation, make it an option so people who don't want to watch don't have to, and provide a means for cutting the animation short.

Checklist

☐ Take a diagnostic approach

☐ Incorporate help into the flow of the user's work

Specify the help environment

☐ Describe the hardware and software platform in a platform profile

☐ Describe the place of the help facility in relation to all the other means of providing information about the product

Design the help user interface

☐ When appropriate, create a metaphor for the help facility

☐ Provide the means for users to employ their favorite strategies for acquiring information

☐ Create direct, memorable routes to relevant information

☐ Keep users from getting lost in the help facility

☐ Let users navigate quickly and surely in the help facility

☐ Let users resume their work gracefully

☐ Design for the screen, not for paper

☐ Keep users informed about what they see happening onscreen

Structure the content of help

☐ Structure help clearly so users can grasp your organization quickly and reliably

☐ Make a content outline—a structured organization of topics

☐ Be slow to exclude any information

Prototype and test a sample

☐ Create menus from the content outline

☐ Draft sample contents for every type of help display

☐ Begin a style guide for writing the content of the help facility

Write and design the content

☐ Avoid "book" writing on the screen

☐ Condense without becoming telegraphic

☐ Make graphics central, not just decorative

☐ Use the same type of transition for the same purpose

☐ Use animation to show change and movement

PART THREE

Revising

Getting Feedback

But I was anxious to make my book as good as I could and I hoped to benefit by his criticisms. They were in point of fact lenient . . . . As I listened to my don's remarks I could not but think how much better I should write now if in my youth I had had the advantage of such sensible, broadminded and kindly advice.

—W. Somerset Maugham

To revise, you need feedback from the product team, from an editor if there is one, from other writers—and most importantly, from your audience. Feedback isn't criticism; it's information you can build on. During the 1980s, developers and designers learned that users should participate in the design of a human interface and test the usability of a series of evolving prototypes. The same is true for manuals. With a series of reviews, plus the results of a number of user tests, you can refine a manual to increase its usability. Revising this way involves several steps and takes some time.

17

Solicit reviews from the team

If you had enough time, you could wait a few months until you cooled off and distanced yourself from all the half-conscious decisions you made as you wrote. Then you could pick up the manual Good rewrites depend on good reviews—not rave notices but thorough, intelligent, constructive commentary that clarifies troublesome passages and points the way toward solutions.

So you need help from the rest of the team. You depend on their comments, meetings, and decisions. Here's how to work together on revisions.

Decide which groups should review your draft

When you're working for a small organization, either as an employee or as a contractor, the responsibility for deciding who reviews a draft will often be yours. In a large organization a manager will usually designate reviewers. Whether you're working with a manager or not, make sure the reviewers represent every department with a stake in the documentation.

- **User testing.** As your most important source of information, users tell you whether or not your approach is working. Are test subjects able to follow your instructions?
- **Quality assurance.** These trained professional testers go through the manual line by line to verify it.

- **Customer support.** These are the people who will have to answer customers' questions if the answers don't appear in the manual.

- **Research and development.** The engineers who created each module, and integrated the product can tell you, to the last jot, how things work.

- **Marketing.** The product manager and any international marketers can make sure that your tone and contents are right for the customers.

- **Legal.** Have them look carefully at trademark notices, copyright notices, and Federal Communication Commission boilerplate.

Listen to every relevant point of view for every draft. If you don't, at the last minute, just as you're putting the finishing touches on the final draft, you're liable to hear that marketing thinks you've given short shrift to some features highly prized by customers— and you'll be faced with a major rewrite.

Don't circulate more than three drafts. You can wear reviewers out, particularly when they are not deeply involved in the project, so don't overload them with too many revision cycles. People read most attentively the first time through. From then on they tend to look only at areas they're anxious about. And after several drafts many people skim so fast that they miss the fact that pages 20 to 30 appear behind page 79.

State your needs in a cover letter

A reviewer's job seems simple, but comments don't come easily from most people. Help team members out by writing a cover letter suggesting what to look for, what to say, and when.

The letter that accompanies the very first review draft sets the stage for all subsequent reviews. Remind everyone that the more effort they put into reviewing this draft, the more likely it will be that later drafts will get done quickly, smoothly, and on schedule. Warn them that when you get to the beta draft, you're planning not to change much, unless they object to something violently. Explain that at final draft, it's too late to change anything except what one writer calls deadly technical errors. Repeat these cautions and suggestions in each subsequent cover letter.

Educate your reviewers before they review.

Make your assumptions explicit. Summarize the goals of the documentation, who you are writing for, and what approach you've adopted, so reviewers don't go off on a tangent and waste their efforts critiquing from a point of view that would seem utterly alien to your customers.

Target the subjects for review. Ask them what's missing, what's undecided, what's wrong. If you have specific questions about a chapter, put those in. Point out what you've guessed, particularly if you're not sure everyone agrees.

Lower their expectations. Point out that you have tried to make the manuscript accurate throughout, but that there may be a number of outstanding questions, undecided issues, or fluctuating specifications. Ask people not to expect perfection. Wherever they know better, ask them to tell you the details.

Set a date you need responses by. Whenever you send out a draft, set a deadline for return with comments. Emphasize the dates when you will need their photographs, illustrations, prototype hardware or software, specifications—whatever. Emphasize how much the schedule for the manual will slip if you don't get those on time.

Specify the medium for responses. If you're still a paper and pencil person, have them mark up a paper copy of the draft. If you prefer electronic files—and they know how to use them—get them to send you a separate file with their ideas. Better yet, get them to add their comments to the file as annotations and collect everyone's comments in one file, so people argue with each other, not you. Prior comments stimulate their thinking and conserve their efforts by letting them avoid duplication. Also, you won't have to collate so many sets of comments.

Distill the comments

Expect a wide variety of reviews. Some people make very detailed notes, others slight and glancing. A few reviewers, obsessed with one or two pet issues, overwhelm you with suggestions about them.

Recognize that a reviewer can point to a problem, but may not come up with a good solution. The solution is still up to you. Don't just cave in and take a comment as gospel.

Here's a sample cover letter.

Dear Reviewers,

Here's the beta draft of the user guide for our new Network Mail product. Please return your comments on this copy by next Monday, the 15th.

Please let me know

- What should be corrected—and how. (Please write the facts in the margin.)
- What should be added. (Have I covered all important tasks a customer would want to do? All features, at least lightly?)
- What should be cut.
- Marketing folks: Does the benefits section correspond to your evolving brochure and ad campaign?
- Engineers: Is the material on setup and installation, in Chapter 2, still valid?

As we all agreed when we finalized the documentation plan, I envision two main audiences for the guide: people who have already been using our current mail product, and people who are new to the product and perhaps to the whole idea of electronic mail.

To address the first audience, we have included a "What's New" section; and for the second audience, we have expanded the first chapter to include a conceptual overview of the way electronic mail works, with many illustrations.

The bulk of the book is devoted to ordinary tasks most customers want to carry out using our product. You'll note that the reference section, as planned, is extremely spare, almost a quick reference. We have expanded the glossary, though, to include examples and fuller definitions than before, because customer support got a lot of calls asking about terminology.

Some sections (such as the ones on remote access and UNIX terminals) reflect guesses and approximations. If you know the facts, please, please write them in.

Please write your comments on the manual itself, or if you prefer, use a word processor, noting the page number of each passage you are referring to, and give me the hard copy.

Thanks a lot for your help. Your comments can make this manual a lot more useful for our customers!

Collate all the comments. After all the comments come back, Rani Cochran, a writer who specializes in international manuals, takes the marked-up manuals and lays them out on a large table.

I copy the comments from page 1 of all 15 manuals, and then I turn a new leaf on my nice new copy and do page 2. I put down everything. When I just made a clear error or some dumb typo, I only have to write down one thing. But when the question is one of style or approach or organization, I often get four or five conflicting comments. I make a note of all of them and attribute each one, because it's my duty to sort them out. Often I'll have to negotiate on matters of content and audience.

Locate the most helpful reviewers and concentrate on their comments. Connie Mantis, who has written manuals on word processing and telecommunications packages, says,

> Some people actually think up solutions. I decided to pinpoint my best reviewers, the ones that really seemed to know what they were doing. For instance, there's one guy who not only catches the technical stuff, he notices a lot of the grammatical stuff that nobody else caught. So I said, "He's my prime guy." Plus he offers solutions. So I said, "I'll always do his first, then I already have a lot of questions answered." I knew that by the time I got to somebody else's comments, who had just written "Huh?", it was already rewritten, or I knew how to fix it.

Pinpoint disagreements between team members. If you foresee a messy period of resolving ambiguities and differences, go through your collated comments and make a list of questions and open issues needing resolution. Use an outliner so you can easily organize the questions in a meaningful sequence. Numbering them will help you refer to a specific question during the many phone conversations you're about to launch into.

Here's a set of notes on open issues.

Open Issues

1. Removing internal packing materials; replacing dust filter

    1.1 Does the front panel of the computer have to be removed?

        NO.

    1.2 What must be removed to get at filter?

        LID ONLY

2. Ethernet—"The internal EtherTalk card is configured to use thin Ethernet cable and Ethernet Phase I or II. If you want to connect to a system using thick Ethernet cable, you will need to move a pair of jumpers on the card."

    2.1 Is the computer set up for thick and thin Ethernet or must it be changed to thick?

        THIN.

    2.2 Do we need to say more about thick Ethernet?

        NO.

    2.3 A terminated BNC T connector must be installed for the computer to boot.

Continued

Continued

Is this for thin Ethernet only?

NOT RELEVANT.

2.4   Is anything needed for thick Ethernet installation? What?

NOT RELEVANT.

As the open issues get resolved, record the answers in the electronic file along with the original questions. Use capital letters or boldface to make the answers stand out. Then circulate the questions along with the answers to ensure that everyone on the team knows what you consider the answers to be.

Call a team meeting to go over the reviews

When several different reviewers disagree, invite them to a review meeting. Between the review comments and the meetings, you should be able to resolve outstanding differences. This helps your style. When you're writing to accommodate three or four interpretations, you get ambiguous. Once the team decides what they want to do, you can say it straight.

Margot Forrest, who has created dozens of manuals, says,

> We routinely hold these meetings—page-by-page walkthroughs of manuals with every member of the product team—and they are very successful. We get accurate manuals, and engineers begin to feel documentation is part of the product.

Arrange for food. Start off on a convivial note. Forrest says meetings go a lot smoother since her company began providing food.

Get someone else to facilitate. If you're an employee, get your manager to run the meeting; if you're an independent contractor, ask a partner, associate, or editor to do it. They can help you maintain your objectivity if some commentators are critical, and they leave you free to write notes you'll be able to make sense of later.

Focus on major issues and general comments. You can waste hours, even days, if you just plod through the manuscript paragraph by paragraph. Usually you can handle the major questions in two or three hours. After that, people begin to fade anyway. Minor comments can usually be left for you to read and correct on your own.

Don't take criticism personally. Keep your goal in mind: You want to write the best manual possible. Others are helping you do this.

Get a definite commitment from someone to make a decision by a certain date. Announce what you are going to do until you have different information or are told to take a different action by a manager. That way you're more likely to get fast action on resolving a disagreement. If you don't take any action, others often see no need to take any action of their own.

Record all decisions. Circulate a memo afterward, showing what you understand you are to do. Thank the reviewers. If you decide not to follow someone's suggestions, you might send a note explaining why. You don't have to defend every decision you make, but you do want to be sure you have dealt with each issue that's been raised, no matter how tiny.

Ask for reviews by another writer and an editor

Unlike members of the product team, another writer and an editor can examine the manuscript as writing, not documentation. You receive more comments on style and organization than on factual accuracy, and you'll be reminded of the places where you wandered away from departmental formatting standards—all useful information but possibly more painful to hear than the news that you got a dip switch setting wrong.

Meet with your colleague or editor to go over the documentation plan and whatever questions you want advice about. Make sure they know what stage the manuscript is at so that they can do an appropriate level of edit. (Show them our Chapter 21, "Reviewing Someone Else's Manual.")

Listen rather than defend yourself. Make sure you understand what changes the person is asking you to make; don't settle for hazy suggestions. You should have the final say, but don't just nod and pretend to listen, and then go your own way. Recognize that although the reviewers may have come up with some poor solutions, they were pointing at passages that seemed awkward, rough, or wrong.

Test the manual on customers

The product designers may have a good idea of what their customers want to do, but few designers can recognize all the possible problems a customer may encounter. In the same way, experienced writers and editors can spot the places where you deviate from good practice, but they cannot know where users will get into trouble. Cognitive psychologist Don Norman says,

> Innocence lost is not easily regained. The designer cannot predict the problems people will have, the misinterpretations that will arise, and the errors that will get made.

That's why you need to have your customers—or even people who are similar to your customers—try out your manual. You see if they really can find and use the information you've packed into the manual. And this kind of testing exposes many problems that your team of subject-matter experts missed, because they already know the subject too well. As the writer Neal Margolis says,

> I can observe patterns of usage, learn what works and what doesn't, and polish my skills based on real information about how customers use my manuals and what they like and don't like. I can generalize from what I learn. Testing lets me avoid mind-reading. I don't have to guess what readers want or anticipate their needs on an uncanny sixth sense.

Testing the manual on users differs from other forms of review.

It's not quality assurance. Professional testers usually go through the whole manual, verifying every statement by trying it out on the software. They do have one major limitation: Since they are expert computer users, they are very adept at avoiding trouble—unlike ordinary users.

It's not formal research. You aren't producing a case study, an ethnographic report, or an academic essay. You need to find out fast what to change in this particular manual. You do not need to make generalizations that stand up in every circumstance. To real researchers your testing will be anecdotal, limited, ad hoc. But for you that's good enough.

It's not applying standards or formulas. Readability formulas attempt to predict how well your audience will be able to understand prose. Unfortunately, in actual tests such formulas often fail.

Assess your situation

You may have to do all the testing yourself, or you may simply stand aside and make recommendations while an official testing team goes to work.

If you're part of a large organization or contract with one, your manuals may receive some empirical user testing. The quality assurance or testing group will probably prepare the test plan, administer the tests, evaluate them, and make recommendations. You should participate in the process, identifying test subjects, deciding what needs to be tested, creating test problems, and observing the tests.

If you're writing for a small organization or a large organization that hasn't gotten around to testing manuals yet, it's likely that some or all of these tasks will become your responsibility. Be sure, however, that they are indeed part of your job and that you've budgeted time and money for them.

In either case you'll want to test enough to come to some firm conclusions. You aren't testing the whole manual, just key tasks that users must perform correctly to make the product successful.

Decide what you want to learn from the test

Whether you're preparing or just contributing to the test plan, you should start by defining what you want to find out. Here are some general objectives:

- Can people find out what they want? How quickly?
- When people get into trouble, can the manual help them out?
- After using the documentation can users really do something they couldn't do before?
- Is there enough detail?
- What has been left out?
- What's poorly explained?
- What's just wrong?
- Did the table of contents and index help people find what they needed, or did they have to skim?
- Did the art and text work together to communicate?

- How many times did a test subject have to ask questions of the tester?
- How many people achieved success at the assigned tasks?
- How long did test subjects take to complete the assigned tasks?

Decide when to test

The earlier you test the better. Test the early drafts, picking only topics referring to functioning parts of the software. Consider this testing part of your design process, not a verification of your accuracy. By testing repeatedly you build on what you have learned and gradually reduce the distractions and obstacles inherent in your approach.

Test the beta manual against beta software (software in which the interface has been frozen and most features work at least a little). At this point you should get the most detailed ideas for change. After beta you don't have time to make anything but small changes, so you hope that at beta you will catch any major difficulties.

Test the final manual against the release software. At this point you can't afford to make many changes, but you may be able to correct a few of those small but embarrassing gaffes that seem to creep past the eyes of dozens of reviewers.

If your company considers so much testing a luxury—as many do—make sure you at least test your beta version, because you still have a chance to make major changes then, if you have to. At final you are so pressured by the schedule that you write too fast and make too many wild guesses to produce a reliable manual.

Create test problems that focus on typical tasks

A good way to test manuals is to pose some problems for people to solve. The problems should require test subjects to use the major functions of the product—some simple, some complex. If you select the problems carefully, you can find out whether your subjects can locate the basics, find some obscure facts, and make use of advanced features. Their solutions provide proof at the end that they have actually succeeded.

Create a scenario explaining what peoples' roles are during the test. Provide whatever data they should manipulate, such as the figures to put in a spreadsheet or the names and addresses to add to a database. You may also need to create some sample files.

Make up a list of tasks involved in solving the problems. As you write up these tasks, you may want to leave out any mention of the manual in some scenarios, to see how the test subjects can handle the interface and structure of the software without documentation. You can suggest they use the manual in other scenarios, and for questions about specific passages, require that they use the manual.

Here are three challenges posed to a group of subjects who will test a database product.

Using the Contacts database, look up the California phone number of a business called Cozbiz, with offices in California, New Mexico, Massachusetts, France, and Japan. Write the California number here. _____

Locate all the contacts in Canada, and print out a list showing their names, addresses, and phone numbers, sorted by postal code. You may want to turn to the chapters in the manual on finding information, sorting, and printing.

Find out what the command Match (on the Utilities menu) can do for you, using the Glossary and Index of the manual. Write the answer here.

_____

Circulate the test scenarios among other members of your product team, particularly people from marketing, to make sure they agree that your tests focus on the most significant tasks. Try out the scenarios yourself to see if they can be done and to get an idea of how much time is required. Based on that experience, figure the number of hours you expect to have each person testing.

Decide how to collect the information

You should plan to be present during the tests, taking notes of what people say and do. Your impressions, and their comments, provide you with a lot to rethink and revise.

Have people tell you what they are thinking and doing as they do it. Observe them as they work. Afterward debrief them by asking a few planned questions and then opening up the discussion so you can find out what they recall, what they think was most difficult, what they suggest. Karen Schriver, who has done many user tests, points out several benefits of this approach:

- You learn the location and nature of the difficulty immediately.
- You may get a diagnosis of the problem.
- You can see if the problem stems from some jarring interplay between graphics and text, rather than one or the other.
- You discover many more omissions than you would any other way.

If you want to study the comments, you can audiotape them. But to avoid having to type up an entire transcript, make notes during the session so you need to replay only key segments. That transcript is sometimes called a protocol. Researcher John Carroll says,

> One of the important points about this method is that the protocol is produced at the same time as the experience it describes. Thus we do not ask participants to summarize their reactions to the task of learning a computer application (that is what you might read in magazine reviews of a computer product), we asked them to verbalize the experience itself. This method produces vivid glimpses of human problem-solving and learning, and a very rich qualitative survey of phenomena and problems in a task domain.

You may want to have a second person observe more objectively, recording the length of time it takes each participant to complete a task, noting the number of errors on each task, the number of keystrokes or screens each participant had to use to accomplish a task. From such numbers you can create home-brew statistics—the kind that won't pass muster in a scholarly journal but will show you whether or not you're making substantial improvements in a series of tests.

Use objective recording methods when you need to resolve debates about the organization of the material, to settle on a page layout, or to provide information about problems that are highly unusual and difficult to pinpoint. Videotaping or using software to capture a log of the entire session lets you replay a test situation over and over until you figure out what happened and why.

Recruit subjects who resemble the customers

Recruit people who are similar to your target audience. You want people who might actually use the program, not professional test subjects. Listed in order from best to OK, here are people to recruit:

- Real users. Use the installed base for a previous product, whenever possible. Margot Forrest says,

  We often test our hardware or software documents on our current users. They loved giving us input into the "product," and one writer walked away with a $30,000 order as a result of the usability test. They'll usually do it for free, too.

- Outside test subjects, such as paid temporary employees from an agency. You can arrange for a variety of temps with different skills and different levels of ability to suit your testing needs.
- Company employees not working on your project. Choosing in-house personnel avoids confidentiality and security problems.
- Family and friends. They've got your best interests at heart, so confidentiality is usually not a problem. Make sure, though, that they'll really report what's wrong.

Decide how many people you can watch at once. We emphasize watching them personally because you'll find out much more than you do sending them home and asking for comments or letting someone else take notes. Few of us can pay attention to more than two or three people at one time. The best is one-to-one.

How many people should you test at any given course of tests? Half a dozen or a dozen is sufficient. You'd need more people than that to reach statistical significance, but even with three or four people, you begin to see patterns emerging that tell you baldly, sometimes painfully, what needs to be fixed.

Develop the test materials

Testing takes a lot of preparation. Here are a few things you should get ready:

- Your schedule, with a list of the test subjects
- Instructions to the people who will be testing the manual, including all your test problems

- Copies of the manual (for them, for you, and any other observers)
- Copies of the software
- The right hardware, in working condition, plugged in, alive
- A reserved room, with enough space to walk around without getting in people's way, and perhaps a separate room for interviews
- Lunch, if people are going to be there all day
- A set of questions you want to ask everyone in the follow-up interviews

Conduct the test

In the weeks before you have other people test your manual, you should be testing it yourself. Make sure that every step of the tutorial matches the way the software really behaves. Then try it out on resident experts—people who know the program or people who know how to put a manual through its paces. The purpose is to clear all the irritating mistakes out of the manual before you put it in front of people who represent the users. (Otherwise you're wasting their time and your own.) If a test subject gets started and your tutorial crashes the program, you can be sure you haven't done your homework.

Relax. On the big day, calm down. To get the most out of testing, you want to be receptive. A former teacher and writer Meg Beeler says,

> Remind yourself that the purpose of this exercise is to get information and to make the manual better. You won't facilitate the process at all if you're defensive or attached to your manual. If you have trouble with that, you might pretend that the manual is someone else's. If people sense that you don't want to hear what they have to say, then they're not going to tell you.

Explain what you want your subjects to do. Emphasize that you are looking for problems in your manuals. If they don't understand something or get stuck or confused, it is probably the fault of the book.

When you talk to people before they begin testing your manual, Beeler says,

It's crucial to tell them that the purpose is to find your mistakes. You should discuss this the first time you talk to them, and repeat it when they're about to begin testing. Say, "We don't want you to know anything; it's fine; we're not looking for what you know, we're trying to find our problems."

Tell them that you want them to speak up, whenever possible, if something seems wrong, or if they have suggestions.

Remember, most people have been trained in school never to make marks in their books, never to object to some confusing passage, always to blame themselves if something goes haywire. Many people also come to the computer with a legacy of computerphobia: "I'll never understand computers. And if I can't follow the directions there's something wrong with me." You may need to overcome years of indoctrination so you can persuade them to tell you when something's inaccurate or obscure.

Watch carefully. You may be surprised at what you discover—steps you left out, tricky or ambiguous passages, descriptions that no longer match the words on the display, phrases that make some readers guffaw, perhaps even a few outright mistakes.

Watch what each test subject does. See if people get lost, see if they hunch over or start fidgeting or sit there for a long time staring at the main menu. Beeler says,

> Especially when they first start, they're very reticent. They'll just sit there reading an obscure page over and over again.

You get a lot of nonverbal clues you would never get from just talking to them afterward. Think of odd behavior as a symptom. To find out what's really bothering them, though, you may have to ask.

Make notes as you go. You may think you'll remember everything that's important, but use a pencil and paper to help. Sometimes you'll be able to reorganize a section or some steps on the spot. Other times you won't have time to do anything besides mark the spot where someone got stuck or make a few cryptic notes to yourself.

Ask, don't argue, and get out of the way. Ask what's bothering them, what's confusing. Make a note in that part of your copy of the manual. Beeler says,

> When you see someone stopping, you need to ask them why. They may not know why they have stopped, but what they say will give you some clues. I've also found that right there on the spot they can give you good ideas for fixing problems. Otherwise, you'd have to go home and sit down and think about it for three hours before you knew what to do.

You may feel like defending yourself. Don't. What you meant doesn't matter; if a reader doesn't understand, it's your fault. So shut up and take notes.

Don't make the test "successful" by offering the advice or the procedural step that isn't in the manual. Step in with a suggestion only when the test grinds to a halt and there's no way a subject can continue without your help. Then get out of the way and let them continue.

Don't take Helpful Harrys too seriously. These people spend their time going off on tangents, being picky, not really trying to do the work you've outlined. They spend more time rewriting than performing. These people are too conscientious to make good test cases. (Ordinary users don't spend their time figuring out how to rephrase your first paragraph.)

Don't set too rigorous a schedule. If you put too much stress on people, they flake out. Encourage them to go at their own pace.

Debrief your subjects afterward. Hold individual interviews or a general discussion at the end. When people have finished going through particular steps, they can tell you how they reacted to the program and the manual in general. You might start with a broad-based questionnaire to get people thinking, then launch into a free-wheeling discussion.

Apply the results

In early stages you turn up as many problems with the software's interface as with your manual. Pass those along quickly to the engineers.

Later the finger turns toward you. Sort through all the comments, and focus on those that raise major questions of access, organization, tone, or approach. Decide what changes you think should be made, and then get the team's agreement before proceeding.

Leave the nits for later. Many disappear when the organization shifts, and the remaining ones can be cleared up in a few keystrokes. If you have time, make a complete list; if you don't have time, just march through your notes, page by page, making the changes.

Checklist

- ☐ Decide which groups should review your draft
- ☐ State what you need from reviewers in a cover letter
- ☐ Collate and distill all the comments
- ☐ Meet with the team to resolve open questions
- ☐ Decide what you want to learn from the test
- ☐ Begin testing as early as you can
- ☐ Focus test problems on typical tasks involving the major functions of the product
- ☐ Be present at the tests to collect information
- ☐ Test subjects who resemble the endusers as closely as possible

Rewriting Drafts

*Every difficulty slurred over will be a ghost
to disturb your rest later on.*

—Chopin

Like housework, revising is never done. You polish one spot, scrub another, wash away smudges, patch rough surfaces, and find in a few days that you've got to do it all again. In fact, revising is what you'll do most as a technical writer. You're constantly cleaning your own or somebody else's manuals—from quick fixes to wholesale rewrites.

The most obvious demands for rewriting come from your reviewers, but your own eye will spot plenty of passages that need revision. William Zinsser, author of *Writing to Learn*, says,

> After a lifetime of writing I still revise every sentence many times and still worry that I haven't caught every ambiguity; I don't want anyone to have to read a sentence of mine twice to find out what it means. If you think you can dash something off and have it come out right, the people you're trying to reach are almost surely in trouble. H. L. Mencken said that "0.8 percent of the human race is capable of writing something that is instantly understandable." He may have been a little high. Beware of dashing. "Effortless" articles that look as if they were dashed off are the result of strenuous effort. A piece of writing must be viewed as a constantly evolving organism.

Make major changes first

When you've collected the reactions of everyone on the product team, another writer or two, and perhaps an editor, plus the results of many user tests, you may feel snowed under. Resist the temptation to start clearing away details. Look first at the lay of the land and consider structure before style. One organizational change may solve a lot of tangled syntax in sentences that you wrote to excuse the disorder.

Focus on structural changes

Think of structure as a series of promises to the readers. Does your content deliver what your headings promise? If so, your structure probably makes sense. But if you keep jumping back and forth, think about rearranging the sections and subsections. Consider alternate structures **before** rewriting anything. Whenever a problem crops up, focus first on its cause, and then on its cure.

- In a reference organized around major functions, test subjects had a hard time finding information about particular commands. The solution: Organize around menus instead, and move all the overviews about functionality into a large part called "What the Software Does."

- In a set of procedures, test subjects could not find out how to start the software. That information appeared at the end of the second chapter, "Installing the Software." The solution: Make "To Start the Software" the first procedure in the set of procedures.

- In a tutorial, customers were told to print a report before they had been walked through the actual printing process. During testing many users got stuck. The solution: Move the module on printing forward and rewrite it to apply to the report.

Add missing sections first. Then put together sections that collect material currently scattered throughout the manual, so you can assess the impact of this reordering on the rest of the book before you tinker further.

Look at any transitions that have caught several reviewers' eyes. Sometimes that means that you've got topics out of order and couldn't quite justify the mess. So don't rewrite until you are sure the paragraphs are really in the right sequence.

Make sure your overviews still introduce

Reconsider your introductions to chapters and sections. Lots of chapter overviews get written before the chapter is complete, so the introduction hardly mentions two-thirds of the topics to come. Such an overview is more of a glimpse than a view.

The original introduction repeated the major marketing claim, but overlooked the fact that the rest of the chapter explained the interface.

The Mapper lets you modify detailed street-by-street sections of maps of the largest 100 cities in the United States.

The revised introduction suggests what people can get out of the rest of the chapter, making it easier for them to skip the chapter if that's not what they want to learn.

The Mapper lets you modify detailed street-by-street sections of maps of the largest 100 cities in the United States. In this chapter you'll learn how to

- Launch Mapper
- Use the mapping tools
- Issue commands

Watch the smaller introductions, too—the sentences that lead up to lists. The items in the list may have been shuffled, added to, or subtracted from so often during your writing that the lead-in sentence no longer makes sense. This is the kind of problem reviewers often miss.

Decide exactly what to change in your style

If you've gotten a smattering of comments about your style, ask yourself which traits people noticed. Often people hit on one mannerism and mark it throughout. But they may well be bothered by a general tone of which that trick is just a symptom. Don't rush to revise your style. Instead, ask yourself a few questions first.

- **How many people want me to change my style?** Consider whether the request comes from a majority of your reviewers. If it's a weird minority, listen, but don't be too quick to act on their advice.

- **Do people asking for a change represent real users?** If not, thank them and forget it.

- **Do comments focus on one particular stylistic tic?** If so, just fix it throughout, in one pass.

- **Are reviewers reacting to the overall tone and approach?** If so, you and your reviewers may not agree on the audience. Reevaluate your audience and get agreement from the team. This rethinking usually means detailed rewriting, so warn people that it will take longer than an average revision.

- **Identify patterns and solve dozens of problems at once.** To avoid the anxious feeling that you have 400 hours of work to do in a week, get an idea of the main types of stylistic changes you want to make before you become overwhelmed by the sheer number. They usually fall into categories, and once you've decided what you want to do about each, your job is a lot less complicated.

Correct the corrections

As you make changes to your draft, you shake up the old structure, dislocate connections, intrude on sequences that made sense. Overviews that once predicted the contents of a chapter or section no longer apply. Incorporating an engineer's paragraph may put a metallic clank in a section that used to run smoothly. Here are some tips on revising your revisions.

Be thorough

If you make a change in one place, be sure you make it everywhere. To keep track of changes and apply them consistently, you can make a review matrix with a column for each chapter and a row for each change.

Confirm all cross-references. Make sure all your references are up to date. If you change the names of chapters and sections, search for the old names in other parts of the manual, and replace them with the new names. But don't make the change globally; take the time to look at each one. If you've used standard introductory phrases such as "Please see," or "Turn to," you can search for them to review your cross-references.

Renumber steps in procedures. If you add a step or delete one, make sure you renumber the steps. (Many outliners do this automatically.)

Adjust for agreement. When you switch from using the code name to the real product name, make sure sentence structure agrees with the name change.

When a new subject crops up, define its terms. You may already have defined most of the concepts you introduced in the beginning of a chapter, but during the review meeting, the team asked you to add another idea. Take the time to define that, too. And add it to the glossary.

Review the table of contents after you add headings. Make sure that all the headings in one section are parallel in form, and that all items of the same kind (individual procedures, syntax descriptions) appear at the same level throughout the manual.

Here reviewers pointed out that the first procedure takes only one step and applies only when you're in the middle of creating a switch. They suggested cutting it. They also pointed out that the headings were not consistent.

Generating a Switching Diagram

Impact of Deselection, Selection, or Non-Selection of a Format

Changing Default Parameters for Generation

Execution of the Switch Compile Command from the Electric Menu

Use of the Switch Compile Tool from a Tool Palette

Switch Diagram Report

Log of Work Session

Listing of Switch Generation

In the rewrite the first procedure changes to a step. The other headings become gerund phrases.

Generating a Switching Diagram.

Setting the Parameters

Starting to Generate the Switch with a Tool

Starting to Generate the Switch with the Switch Compile Command

Examining the Switch

Reviewing the Work Session

Reviewing the Code Generated During the Creation of the Switch

Revise the reviewer's prose

Most engineers learn a peculiar prose in graduate school and stick with it throughout their careers. If they hand you "stuff to put in the manual," rewrite the material before including it.

Change the point of view first. Most engineers write specs describing what will happen if a user happens to press a button or choose a command: "If the user inputs a certain command, the following 18 things must happen." But customers only want to use the command when they intend one or more of those 18 things to happen. So start with the purpose, and only then turn to the relevant command. That's adopting the user's point of view.

Here's a note handed to the writer of the reference section.

Issuing the Options command brings up an option sheet that displays various nonstandard schema grids, described in their horizontal and vertical axes. Selecting one of these and clicking OK applies it to the current drawing. Selecting Cancel puts away the option sheet without applying any nonstandard schema grid.

The writer rewrote the command reference…

Options Command: Lets you pick one of the following nonstandard schema grids:

1.25" x 2"

1' x 2'

10" x 20"

The horizontal unit appears first, the vertical second. The units of measure depend on what you have specified in Preferences.

…and added a new procedure to the cookbook section.

To use a nonstandard schema grid

1. **Click Options on the Grid menu.**
   You see the Options sheet.

   (Art)

   For each grid the first number represents the horizontal unit, and the second represents the vertical unit. The units of measure are those you selected in Preferences.

2. **Select the grid you want and click OK.**
   If you decide you don't want a nonstandard schema grid, click Cancel.

Simplify on your own

Reviewers who are not writers or editors often ignore small or subtle variations in format. During revision you have a chance to clear away some of the unnecessary distinctions and sophistications that you put into the draft, out of either zeal or carelessness.

Limit the number of typographic formats. For instance, in your first draft you may have boldfaced every glossary term every time you used it, adding italics if the term was a function, and all caps if it was a command. The effect: a jazzy page. Even though no one objected, you might calm the pages down by boldfacing only the first use.

Limit the types of notes. As you write, you often insert a variety of notes, by-the-ways, cautions, important notices, and flags. If you have more than one kind of note, serving different purposes, look at each one and make sure it serves the same function as the others. For example, you might limit warnings to circumstances in which a user might get hurt, cautions to situations in which a user might lose data, and notes for special additional information that will help a user perform the task. Trimming from half a dozen to a few kinds of special notices helps the reader know what to expect in each.

Turn one clotted paragraph into several simple paragraphs. Sometimes you have said a lot, even too much, in one paragraph; the reader gets bumped this way and that and wonders what your point is. Slow the pace and devote one paragraph to each topic.

Reviewers who read this paragraph got confused about exactly what to do when.

During the processing of the Init command, the software consults the library of databases and draws down the requested schematics, with whatever views you asked for. A schematic gives a symbolic view of the design; the other views are hierarchical and literal. Before you can issue the Init command, you need to clear the currently active window. That completes the actions you have been carrying out and cancels any currently operating commands. You can issue the Init command in the Prompt Window. The software displays a form in which it asks you to list the schematics and other views you want. When the software finishes processing the Init command, along with your requests, you see the top-level schematic and, behind it, windows with each of the other views.

The writer carved up the material, devoting one paragraph to the prerequisites, one to issuing the command, and another to the results.

If you want to bring up one or more schematics, along with some associated views, you must finish what you're doing in the current window. Clear the window first; that completes any actions you've been carrying out and cancels any currently operating commands.

You request the new schematics and views by typing *Init* in the Prompt Window. The software displays a form in which you can enter the names of the schematic and views you want.

When you OK the form, the software consults its library of databases and draws down the schematics and other views. You see the top-level schematic in the front window and, behind it, windows containing the other views.

When you get stuck...

Sometimes you rewrite a sentence ten different ways and every version sounds wrong.

Ask someone else to take a try. He or she probably will not come up with a perfect solution but is likely to ask you some questions that force you to think about the whole issue differently.

Back off from the subject. Read everything that comes before and a little of what comes after, and without looking at the trials you've already made, summarize the key idea you want to get across. Ignore the particular words; get at the gist.

Put it on the back shelf. If you still dislike what you come up with, turn to another task for an hour or so. Count on your unconscious to emerge with a solution while you work on something else. After lunch the passage will look different, and if you're lucky, a new approach will pop into your mind.

Encourage reviewers

Show reviewers that their comments have made a difference. Return their marked-up copy, with your revision. That way they can compare line by line to see how you acted on their advice—if they have time. Write a memo to each reviewer, summing up the ways you have followed their ideas, or disagreed—and why.

To:	Maude	
From:	Mel	

Here's how I used your suggestions for revision.

Page	Subject	Action Taken
1	Title	Yes, I agree. A Grand Tour is a little grand. I've replaced that with "Introduction."
1	Keycaps	I agree. This material belongs later in the chapter.
2	Equipment	No. Our audience will react to "Configuration" as engineering jargon.

Prepare for the next edition

As soon as you finish your manual it becomes a candidate for someone else to rewrite. You can help another writer with those revisions or updates by the way you handle some parts of the manual—and by writing notes directly to that writer.

Create your own reader response card

In the back of your manual, ask the readers to help by sending you detailed comments. We don't like the standard cards that ask for general praise: "Do you like the style of writing in this manual? What do you like most about this manual?" The answers to these kinds of questions are no help to a writer.

Make up a reader response card that will elicit useful answers. Most pollsters find that people take a long questionnaire as evidence that you will actually use their responses rather than throwing them in the trash. So go through each chapter.

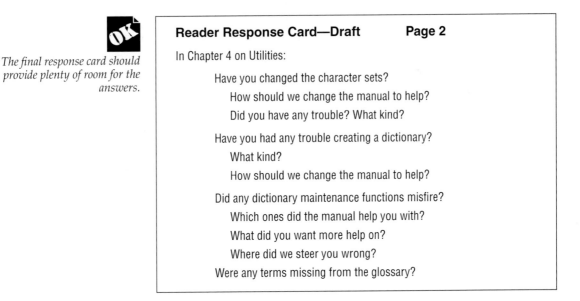

The final response card should provide plenty of room for the answers.

Reader Response Card—Draft   Page 2

In Chapter 4 on Utilities:

    Have you changed the character sets?

        How should we change the manual to help?

        Did you have any trouble? What kind?

    Have you had any trouble creating a dictionary?

        What kind?

        How should we change the manual to help?

    Did any dictionary maintenance functions misfire?

        Which ones did the manual help you with?

        What did you want more help on?

        Where did we steer you wrong?

    Were any terms missing from the glossary?

Make the card as long as you need. If this example seems too specific, try listing all your major headings along the left, and then provide a series of columns in which people can write comments. Possible column titles include

- What did you look for in this section, but not find?
- What should be added?
- What could we do a better job on?
- What was confusing?
- Was there something you particularly liked in this section?

Make an archive to hand off to the next writer

When you complete your manual you may not feel like thinking about it a minute longer. But take some time to help the next writer—the one who will have to revise it later. You can provide

- **A letter from you**—one writer to another, saying what you would do differently, what you like best and worst, what got skimped on or left out, what to watch out for.
- **A style guide**—if there is one.
- **A copy of the printed manual**—with notes on everything you'd change, if you could, from typos, illustrations, and errors to whole sections you would add or subtract.
- **A copy of your electronic version, plus a paper copy**—with all last-minute changes marked on it. That way the new writer won't have to proofread 100 pages to locate 18 corrections.
- **A filenames guide**—the names of all text and graphics files, as well as an explanation of the naming conventions you used.
- **Notes on the tools you used**—any special hardware and software (word processor, graphics software, screen capture program).
- **Old memos**—the ones that explain the reasoning behind the design and approach you took.

Checklist

☐ Focus on structural changes first

- ☐ Make sure your introductions to chapters and sections still introduce the relevant topics
- ☐ Decide exactly what changes to make in your style
- ☐ Review the revisions and corrections to make sure you integrate them seamlessly with the material you keep
- ☐ Revise the reviewer's prose
- ☐ Simplify the formatting and content of the manual
- ☐ If you're stuck, back off from the subject and get help from reviewers and editors
- ☐ Create your own reader response card
- ☐ Make an archive to hand off to the next writer

Refining Your Style

That must be wonderful; I have no idea what it means.

—Molière

19

Some writers work hard to present themselves as complex, occasionally brilliant, well-armored, overplumed, and ready to fight anyone who laughs. But you probably want the style of your manuals to be friendly. That often requires an extra effort.

After you've done every draft, prowl through the manuscript looking for stylistic tangles—constructions that could trap, mesmerize, or even terrify your readers. Some of these snafus look so odd that anyone can see the danger; others are so familiar that you pass right by them, ignoring what they might do to readers who follow you.

Train yourself to recognize these messes. The more you get used to spotting them and transforming them into simple prose, the easier it becomes to sidestep them when you are writing new material. What you learn as you revise will gradually seep into your fingers, so that you no longer create Double No-Nos and One Bite Intros.

Write clearly

In general, begin with what you know is familiar to your readers, and then introduce the new and unknown, one step at a time. Point out how a new idea resembles or differs from an old one. In this way readers can assimilate the new without fearing it, apply their accustomed ways of thinking to the new subject, and gradually expand their conceptual model to include the topic you're introducing.

Many of the worst problems readers face in technical prose stem from poor organization within a chapter, paragraph, or sentence. Straightening up the organization will go a long way to making your prose clear. Whenever you sense that a passage is unclear, look at its basic structure first. Is it inconsistent, incomplete, or just plain incoherent? Does it show any of the following signals of imminent disintegration?

Flowering inconsistency

Calling a rose a shrub in one place, a vine in another, and a flower in another makes readers wonder if you are talking about one plant or three. Be consistent. A rose is always a rose is always a rose.

To a beginner these phrases suggest three different actions. Which is the right one?

- Exiting
- Leaving the program
- Returning to the operating system

Use one word for one action.

Quitting

Follow a consistent task-action grammar. For the same task, go through the same sequence of actions each time, rather than creating elegant variations.

First you select, and then you act on the selection—that's the task-action grammar of many programs.

Double-click the paragraph to select it, and then choose Bold from the Format menu.

Before the before

Imposing antecedent upon antecedent, gives readers a dizzying feeling that time has dissolved. The paragraph backs into the present, crying, "Before that, but before that, but before that." Results from not organizing the material in time sequence.

Here the writer jumps around in time confusingly.

Before you go on to the detailed explanation concerning the function you are about to study, you should first load the SET UP file. If you have not already created that, see APPENDIX A for the procedure.

Remember, as a preview to the SET UP file, you must insert the SYSTEM disk and reboot. Before you do that, be sure to save your material on the disk.

Sort out what the user has to do first, second, and third.

1. **Save your current work to disk.**
2. **Eject the disk, insert the SYSTEM disk, and reboot.**
3. **Load the SET UP file.**
   Now you're ready to go on to the details concerning the function.

Trailing off

A sentence that starts off crammed with ideas but ends up in a ditch is usually an accident caused by impatience. The writer hurries the main point of a sentence into the first few words, and then wonders how to end it all.

- Report generation to specified requirements can also be accessed.
- A function known as CATALOG, which displays the volume number and list of all files on a given diskette, also exists.
- The requirement for at least one completed form cannot be gotten around.

- You can also specify the way you want reports generated.
- To display the volume number and a list of all the files on a given diskette, use the CATALOG function.
- You must have at least one completed form.

Put the most significant or the most interesting information, the very reason for the sentence, at the end.

Parallels that aren't

Jolting readers in the middle of a list by shifting the way you present items (switching from a series of nouns to a verb, for instance) startles readers, forces them to go back to reread, and raises questions about how to understand you.

The list began as a series of noun phrases; later the writer remembered that you need a printer, too, and just added a sentence.

- An RS 232C interface
- An Axoltl III computer
- You have to have a printer, too
- Don't reconfigure your system yet, though

The last sentence is another afterthought. The result: two noun phrases and two sentences. Using this list, readers cannot quickly see if they have all the equipment.

Whenever you have a list, keep all the parts of it in the same grammatical form.

- An RS 232C interface
- An Axoltl III computer
- A Mk IV printer
- A current system file

Half a contrast

Implying a contrast but depriving readers of the other half suggests some other possibilities that are never spelled out. Heavily emphasizing words such as **only** and **not** leaves readers with unanswered questions.

What else might the reader think of using?

- Only RAM may be used for this operation.

Well, if it doesn't discuss those questions, what will it talk about?

- This chapter will not cover questions of bad disks.

- On the one hand, such errors may lead to system failure, incorrect data, or in some cases, disk erasure. Next we will discuss pathnames.

On the one hand this, but on the other hand, what?

Often you don't really have a contrast in mind. If that's the case, wipe out the signals that tell a reader a contrast is coming.

- For this operation you must use RAM.
- This chapter shows how to make sure your disks work properly. If you think you have a bad disk, turn to Appendix A for help.

When you are thinking of a contrast, envision a seesaw. You've gotten the child on one end up in the air, now give the kid on the other side a turn.

- On the one hand, such errors may lead to system failure, incorrect data, or disk erasure. On the other hand, these errors may not cause you any problems at all, if you have used the right pathname.

Plump paragraphs

They start off in one direction but end up detouring off the main road, visiting a few small towns, traipsing back to a different highway, and then suggesting that you consult the map if you have any questions. They often result from a writer rushing to complete a section, and dumping every known fact into one paragraph without figuring out what should come first, second, and third, and without separating different topics into different paragraphs.

Rewriting often leads to several paragraphs, as you expand the ideas that got compressed into the original. Upon analysis, some distinctions made in the original may turn out to be pointless and can be omitted.

Here the writer has collected several facts that may belong in the same chapter but don't fit together to make a coherent paragraph. The effect is jumpy, chaotic.

The property list contains the optional characteristics you have assigned to an object, text block, or graphic. You can set default properties globally in your library, and you can override those on an individual basis. Overriding can be done manually or automatically. Graphics generally come with attributes, that is, preassigned characteristics, plus some default properties, and text blocks come with some attributes and some default properties that you can change or omit. You will find a list of default properties and standard attributes in Appendix A.

The distinction between graphics and text turned out to be nonexistent and got dropped. The real subjects emerged: What is a property, how is it different from the very similar attribute, and how can you change them?

Properties are characteristics you can assign to an object, text block, or graphic. Unlike attributes, properties are purely optional; if you wanted to, you could have an object devoid of properties. It would still have some inherent attributes, such as height, width, and depth.

You can change properties or attributes. To change them for all objects, text blocks, or graphics, use your library. To change them for a particular object, text block, or graphic, you select it, and then use a command on the Options menu. The standard attributes and default properties appear in Appendix A

Prose that clanks

Using phrases and whole paragraphs that you've read five times before in the same manual is a rigid and repetitive way to describe similar phenomena.

This an accurate but lazy way to introduce two different functions. Readers begin to feel that a machine is doing the writing.

- FITR is a command. This command dictates parameters for the R files. The parameters involved are described below. This command should be invoked only by a systems analyst or supervisor.
- RAXR is a command. This command dictates parameters for the XR files. The parameters involved are described below. This command should be invoked only by a systems analyst or supervisor.

Here the writer provided a table listing the commands.

You should only issue the following commands if you are a systems analyst or supervisor:

Command	Dictates Parameters for
FITR	R FILES
RAXR	XR FILES

To avoid mechanical prose, combine whatever can be combined so you say it only once. Use tables and lists. Condense any material that must be repeated, so you repeat only a sentence or phrase, not a whole paragraph. But don't slip into elegant variations to escape mechanicality. You may make readers think two commands are very different when they're not.

Write actively

Active sentences keep people alert. People understand them faster and remember them more easily than passive sentences. To avoid ambiguity, listlessness, and the tedium of bureaucratic prose, use active verbs, use *you* when you need to, and watch out for the following symptoms of fading energy.

Passive nobody

A passive construction implies that events take place without anyone doing anything. The passive nobody moves files, desks, and ideas without any assistance from a human being. It makes readers wonder whether they should be doing something—or just sitting there waiting for the system to perform. Actions turn into states of being.

Does the system do this? Do I do this? Who's responsible around here?

- The filenames can be removed when the RFIL command has been entered and accepted.
- Potential sources of trouble may be discovered during the system's startup phase.
- An option is preselected; if approval is granted, that option is initiated.

All forms of the verb *to be* turn other verbs passive: is, are, was, were, has been, have been, had been, will be, won't be, shouldn't be, and haven't ever been.

- To remove filenames, enter the RFIL command.
- You may discover potential sources of trouble during the system's startup phase.
- To initiate a preselected option, you grant approval.

Concentrate on actions. Who changes or does what, how do they do it, and when? Assign responsibility to the system, to the program, or, if necessary, to the reader. If you have to tell people to do something, don't pussyfoot around—tell them. (Are you slipping into the passive because you don't dare to order readers around?)

You can see that sometimes to make your prose active, you have to address the customer directly. Instead of saying, "This option is user controlled," say, "You can exercise this option yourself." Like the imperative, *you* makes clear who should do what. *You* is somebody.

Its Its

This crowd of neuters—nonpersons who investigate, judge, and find guilty without ever appearing—are puzzling because they might refer to a reader, to the writer, or to some computer system.

Who determined that? Who thinks it's clear? Who ever thought that?

- It has been determined...
- It will be clear that...
- It is often thought that...

- We determined...
- You will see...
- People often think...

When the air grows thick with these *its*, get out your wand and turn them into people. Don't write as if the program thinks.

The dead hand

When you make a perfectly human action into an idea or object, you mummify that action. The dead hand turns *"I decided"* into *"The decision was made to...."*

These verbs are well buried in their noun forms. To revive them, rethink what you meant.

- The insertion of new channels by means of digitization and modulation or a combination of the two can mean an increase in cost-effectiveness and a utilization of previously idle time frames.
- Transmission via satellite requires frequent resynchronization due to the satellite's attraction to the sun and the moon.

Turn these clunky nouns back into verbs. You can reveal who does what and make your point clearer.

Note that only real rewriting can resuscitate the verbs.

- When we insert new channels by digitizing and modulating signals, we save money because we can use more of the carrier more of the time.
- The sun and the moon draw the satellite out of its circular orbit, so you have to keep changing your aim when you transmit.

Clichés

Old and tired and flat, a cliché sounds like it means something, but just what isn't clear anymore—it has been used to mean so many different things. Readers may nod understandingly because they recognize the cliché, not because they know what you mean. And if you go on using clichés, the nodding may continue until your readers are asleep.

- This is a user-friendly program.
- When you're interfacing with the system…
- What's the bottom line?

Clichés often get into your prose when you're puzzling about what to say and a prefab phrase rises in your mind. Experiencing relief, you figure the phrase more or less covers what you want to say. And you know your audience will recognize it, so that establishes some kind of bond, right?

Watch out for that feeling of relief. It's a sign you've taken the shortcut to a meaning that's more convenient than accurate.

False good cheer

Party smiles. Routine congratulations. Trained welcomes. Rehearsed enthusiasm.

That's engineered, not friendly.

Isn't calculating fuel burn patterns over the Atlantic fun?

You want to sound encouraging, open, human. But don't try too hard. Watch out for excessive jolliness—when you're forcing yourself to be cheerful.

Bloodless writing

Some writers give you the impression they have no senses. Touch is unknown to them, and taste and smell are taboo. Evidently they never hear or see anything that's not already in the program or the equipment.

As a result, readers get none of those helpful asides that tell them that the disk drive will make noises, but the whirrings they hear are OK. Readers may begin to think the writer has no feelings. And as people with operative senses, they intuit that behind the manual there is no one alive.

Consider what the customer may notice and worry about—not only if it indicates trouble, but also if it might look or sound like trouble when it's not. For instance, a particular noise may not worry you, but it could frighten an anxious beginner. Here are examples of a writer considering the customer's experience.

In the installation section, when customers have just turned on their hard disk drive for the first time.

> You now hear a low whirring noise; that is the fan cooling the disk drive. In a few moments you may hear some low clicks as the drive mechanism starts reading information from the disk.

In the troubleshooting section, when customers have been using the drive for a while.

> **Symptom:** a high-pitched whine.
>
> **Diagnosis:** Your drive may have been affected by static electricity passed from your hands or clothes. This should not damage your data or the drive if you act promptly.
>
> **Solutions:** Turn the drive off, then on again. From now on, before touching the drive, tap a metal object to discharge any static electricity. If possible, remove any heavy carpeting under your desk.

So describe. Admit what you go through. Confess to hunches and physical reactions. Stop every once in a while to say what you notice about the display, the monitor, the keyboard, the drives. That will help readers imagine what you're doing—and who you are.

Break the rules to clarify your prose

Back in high school, Krinkow the pedagogue drilled us all in a bunch of rules that didn't make much sense to us. They were designed to keep us from making horrendous blunders. We learned to follow the letter of the rules, not the spirit. So we still misapply them.

In following Krinkow's rules, we often make our prose ten times more complicated than it needs to be. Here are some of the rules—with our reasons for breaking them.

Rule #1: Never start a sentence with **because**

Krinkow said this because many of us wrote things like, "I like jam. Because it is sweet." But that's no reason to change *because* to *due to* or *as* or *since*, when those just add ambiguity. For instance, substitute *because* as you read these examples.

Because makes a better beginning after all.

> - Due to the fact that the file is now empty, you can delete its name from your directory without harm.
> - As the disk is formatted, you may proceed to enter the following text.
> - Since you have inserted the Utilities disk in the built-in drive, you can hear a whirring noise.

Rule #2: Never say **I**

Krinkow thought you should only tell objective truth—or at least you didn't put subjective truth on paper.

> - One can easily see....
> - The writer's own experience can testify....
> - It is obvious that....

When you're writing a manual, you usually don't need to mention yourself. But if you do, admit it's you.

Rule #3: Never use about

Krinkow objected to all inaccurate guesses, hating it when we wrote that the baseball game lasted "about two hours." So we learned to leave that dangerous word out, substituting much longer but safer phrases like these:

- In the approximate vicinity of…
- Relating to the subject of…
- In reference to…
- With respect to…

Write *about* things, and if you have to indicate that statement is fuzzy, say something like "It takes about two hours." We know what you mean. If you're still uncomfortable about being imprecise, say why you cannot be more precise.

Rule #4: Don't use then so often

The pedagogue hated paragraphs that went like this:

We ate lunch. Then we played ball. Then we had a snack. Then we went out in the woods. Then we saw a snapping turtle.

We didn't understand why Krinkow disliked *then* so much, but we learned to use lots of longer phrases instead. (We also got rid of *now* for the same reason.)

- At that point in time...
- During that previously mentioned period...
- Within that time frame...

Use *now* and *then*. They're short, but they do the job. And if you're using them too often in a paragraph, don't blame them—it's just you getting repetitious.

Avoid impenetrable words and phrases

Customers encounter many indigestible lumps in manuals—weird all-capital gibberish, unfamiliar terms, ornate Latinate phrases, and just plain jargon. Most writers justify all these lapses in the same way they defend the use of jargon.

Jargon, the in-language of the expert, can sometimes give extra precision to your descriptions, but make sure your audience really needs to make such fine distinctions. Often jargon just prevents people from understanding the basic idea, without helping them understand the subtle ramifications that the professionals care about.

We're most likely to slip in a bit of impenetrable prose when we're tired and our minds keep ratcheting back to words and phrases whose use has become automatic for us—or when we just don't understand what we're writing about.

Noun clump

Creating a string of nouns is a clumsy way of avoiding two or three phrases or clauses. It's confusing because readers lose track of the point and wonder when it will ever end. It's ambiguous because people can read several nouns as an adjective phrase and get one picture of the subject, then, looking again, see several other nouns as a descriptive phrase, and end up with yet another view.

Is the first item a manual for people who manage office designers? In the second, who's controlling the monitor? Where do the hyphens go in the last?

- The Office Design Management Worksheets User's Manual
- The Microcomputer System Development Monitor Control Program Manual
- The Run Time System Options Menu prompts...

If you find you've spawned a noun clump, take a deep breath and give it some air.

- The Office Designer's Manual
- Using the Control Program to Monitor the Development of your Microcomputer System
- The messages that prompt you to choose one of the commands from the Options Menu on the Run Time System...

Whazzat

An unfamiliar term that leaps out at a reader and often appears in introductory material. Never mentioned before, it makes readers question their memory or their competence.

What's boot? Have readers done it before? Do they need reminding? Do they realize they've already initialized? And what are all those functions? Should readers already know them?

- Then boot your system again.
- Reinitialize.
- Your word processing package lets you use one of the 13 programmable function keys to perform functions such as block moves, maskmaking, zero slashing, right justification, and fractional spacing.

If they don't know what zero slashing is, are they such klutzes that they ought to stop right now before damaging such a sophisticated system? Or did the writer describe all these before, and they just forgot? Maybe they'd better turn back a few pages.

To wipe out Whazzats, go through the manuscript looking for terms you may not have defined earlier. Find the first mention of the term and add an explanation. And if you've mentioned something 20 pages ago but not since then, remind readers that they've heard the term before and tell them, gently, what it means. In material designed for lookup rather than sequential reading, define the term unobtrusively each time you introduce it in a new topic, because people may not have read the earlier topic.

Doohickeys

Unpronounceable or indecipherable words or phrases are often borrowed from professional journals. Sometimes they start out as pieces of home-grown terminology that the engineers have been using for months. These terms may even appear in released software where they mystify customers.

> • Invalid parameter
> • Carrier undetected
> • Mail merge

Replace in-house or in-group terminology with language that's familiar to the customers. Whenever possible, get the software itself changed.

> • Pick 1, 2, or 3
> • Phone connection broken
> • Adding addresses to form letters

Long words

Sometimes you can't avoid a long word. It may be the only precise way to describe something. But a long word can act as a big club, threatening some readers.

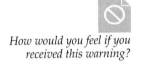

Finalization of these requirements is a condition of commencement of utilization of the system.

How would you feel if you received this warning?

You must do this before you can start using the system.

Here's a translation.

Often you can find a short word that does just as well as the long one. Even a series of short words will be easier to understand. In several studies, customers with widely different levels of experience and education all agreed that they preferred language at the fifth-grade level. We all used to get extra points in English class for calling lying *tergiversation*, but we're not in English class now.

Abbr.

Avoid unnecessary abbreviations and acronyms; over-abbreviation can confuse readers.

If CPU ops generates an IDL EM on the CRT, SD PDQ.

If the computer's operating system displays a message announcing an imminent data loss, shut down immediately.

Writing for international audiences

There are few tested rules for making sure that your prose can be transported easily and accurately across national boundaries. Some writers avoid contractions, on the theory that these will be difficult to translate. But this theory, like others we've heard about writing for multiple audiences, seems to assume that you will be at the mercy of a lousy translator, in which case nothing you do will matter anyway.

We're left with common sense. Clear prose is easier to translate than ambiguous prose; acronyms that form a word in English won't act as a mnemonic in Hindi; examples that depend on your own culture won't travel; and anything that smacks of an in-joke will cause anguish or confusion among the translators. Most of your puns, turns of phrase, and double entendres will get lost, or worse, turned into a puzzling mess in transit. Humor, like poetry, is what does not get translated.

And translation is often not enough, particularly when sending your manual to countries outside of North America and Europe. Hiraku Amemiya, a lead writer for an independent technical writing group in Japan, says that even the manuals that Americans consider excellent end up being constricted, and of limited use, when simply translated into Japanese. What's needed is a new manual, not a word-for-word translation. Most of the general principles of technical writing apply around the world; but you need to give the local writers the freedom to organize and write in a way that seems natural for their audiences.

Checklist

- ☐ Write clearly
- ☐ Write actively
- ☐ Break the rules to clarify your prose
- ☐ Avoid impenetrable words and phrases

Updating a Manual

When you say something, make sure you have said it. The chances of your having said it are only fair.

—E. B. White

Updates begin when a manual has already gone to press or even been released with the product, and you discover serious inaccuracies, topics left out, and various undocumented "improvements" to the software made by the engineers.

Updating is a special form of revising in which you have less freedom to maneuver, less time, and less opportunity to make dramatic improvements.

- You're usually making changes to someone else's manual, so the organization and style seem odd, like a shirt that doesn't fit.
- You're often given very little time in which to make the changes, and you may be told explicitly to leave large portions of the manual untouched, so you have to fit in as best you can.
- Updating the manual usually means rewriting some but not all of the manual—adding and subtracting pieces.

In updating you have to live with another writer's structure and style but not be overwhelmed by it. And the production budget looms over you, urging you to perform only the most delicate surgery, so that you won't have to send lots of pages back for reshooting by the printer.

Deciding to update

You don't make the decision to create an update alone; in fact, such decisions often emerge from meetings among executives and drop onto your desk without much discussion. As the program gets fixed or improved, your original manual becomes outdated. There are three major reasons for updates:

- Customers have encountered serious problems with the software, and the current manual can't help them solve the problems.
- People have discovered errors and omissions in the original manual.
- The software itself has changed—new features, new functionality under old commands, new interface (new command names, dialog boxes, icons).

Errata sheets and change pages

If there's a danger to users' health or data, you'd better let them know fast. You don't have time at first to revise the whole manual, but you do have time for a quick fix or an errata sheet (an admission of error). Sometimes you have a few days to print a sheet that corrects a few serious mistakes—nothing more.

> **Correction**
>
> The total number of characters you can place in a Text field should be 64,000, not 6400, as stated on page 23 of the manual.

If your company still sends out three-hole-punched change pages (users are supposed to substitute those for the unfortunate originals), recognize that most people will stuff them in a binder somewhere and lose them. Very few change pages reach their destinations.

Recognize when to rewrite from scratch

Sometimes what starts out as an update turns into a brand-new manual. The whole organization needs to be changed. There are so many little changes that you cannot just make a thousand patches. You feel cramped and embarrassed when you try to make "little" changes. These are all signs that you can't preserve the original; you have to go beyond "an update" to a complete rewrite.

That's an important decision. Rani Cochran, who once began by revising a computer manual and finished up by writing a whole new manual, says,

> I wasted a lot of time when I first began revising, trying to retain the structure of the old manual, trying to respect the original writer's style, trying to fit in. Finally I got my courage and just did it my way.

If the software or hardware has changed a lot, you face that kind of decision. Remember that your manual is often just part of a series. So you must decide whether all of these manuals need to be rewritten. At first the team may resist such an idea since it takes time and money, but in many cases it makes more sense.

Learn what needs to be changed

You'd think that if your manager assigned you to update a manual, someone would know exactly what needs to be updated. Sometimes yes, sometimes no. Usually, there are half a dozen key corrections or new subjects that everyone on the team agrees need to be taken care of. But beyond that there may be dozens of other little subjects, plus ripples from the major topics in parts of the manual no one suspected. So you need to draw up a list of the errors in the old manual and changes to the software.

Gossip and collect specifications

The engineers may have continued to improve the software's speed, robustness, and occasionally its set of features and its interface. As a writer you don't have to worry about the product's efficiency, but as soon as the team adds features or changes the interface, they have outdated the original manual.

Collect any descriptions of the changes. In large companies, engineers have to propose changes and get them approved. These engineering change orders leave a trail you can follow. In smaller companies you need to hang out at the soda machine to find out what the engineers have been up to.

You should also play the new software against the current manual to see if you can spot any other little changes no one told you about.

Skim published reviews

Reviews rarely yield much you can actually use in an update. Few devote enough room to the documentation. If the reviewer dismissed the manual as useless or messy, you should probably think about a complete revision, not just a touch-up.

Read the reader response cards and letters

If the manual included a detailed questionnaire soliciting help from the readers, it may provide a lot of information about what went wrong with the original manual—places people found confusing, information they could never find, errors. Read a few hundred, and you will see definite patterns emerging, like vote totals.

On the other hand, if the reader response card is the traditional marketing blurb ("Did you like this manual? Please say why, and return this card."), you won't get anything except indigestion from reading a few hundred.

Talk with customer support

Find out from customer support what the main questions and problems have been. Often these are so extensive that you can simply list them, along with the affected page numbers of the manual, as an argument for a total rewrite. But since management often ignores the need for major revisions, you should ask customer support to prioritize their list of problems so you can address the top half dozen.

The best run documentation groups meet regularly with the customer support people to hear the latest wave of questions and discuss the best way to answer them. But in many companies the two groups are kept tidily apart, so contact has to come from lunchroom conversations. It's worth sitting down at the unfamiliar table. A manual that includes news from real customers solves problems before they arise.

Swap notes with the writers of the current manual

Often the writers recall the areas in which they had insufficient information—because the software was still changing as they went to press, because no one on the team agreed on what to say, or because someone overrode the common-sense approach. The original writers can also explain some of the reasoning behind their organization, so you can adapt to the plan or change it sensibly. By now they may have regrets, too—sections they wish they had omitted or passages they're embarrassed to admit they authored. Asterisk those passages in your copy as candidates for revision.

Control the damage

Sometimes you can slip updates into the running text without throwing off the pagination or disturbing the layout. That's rare. For circumstances where you have to change more than a word or two, here are some tips.

Limit the effects of your changes

Where possible, keep the changes confined to a particular page so that the rest of the chapter does not have to be repaginated. If you don't, your printer will have to reshoot the next eight pages just because a few paragraphs spilled over and changed their layout.

Always write briefly. Include the minimum. Add an item to a list rather than throwing in a new paragraph. Add a phrase to a sentence rather than making up a new sentence. Distill a half hour conversation with the marketing whiz into two sentences, and promise to expatiate on the glories of the feature later, when you get to rewrite the whole manual.

Pick target chapters, and try to put most changes there. If possible, avoid making changes to overviews and introductions.

Include comparison tables (before and after)

Dick Leeman, a writer who worked on an update of a language designed to accommodate new hardware and to expand some of the features, figured that readers would have already read the original manual. But he had to review some of the material in that manual to show how changes affected the language so readers could see how things worked and why—before and after the changes.

He set up a series of tables summarizing how the system worked in each version, like this

Version 1.0	Version 1.1
Allows 2 libraries per program	Allows up to 6 libraries per program
PROGRAM LIBRARY FILE:	PROGRAM LIBRARY FILE:
Limit: one per program	Limit: one per program
Same directory as program	Same directory as program
Takes name of program	Takes name of program
Cannot be shared	Cannot be shared
	OR REPLACE THE PROGRAM LIBRARY FILE WITH...
	LIBRARY FILE NAME:
	Lists pathnames of up to 5 library files
	Limit: one per program
	Same directory as program
	Takes name of program
	Cannot be shared
SYSTEM.LIBRARY	SYSTEM.LIBRARY
Must be on system disk	Must be on system disk

To show how these features affected every stage of a programmer's work, Leeman added a chapter of running commentary. He says,

> This takes the user, a professional program developer—perhaps someone who hasn't been doing it that long—through the complete program design, development, coding, compiling, and executing of one application, so that you can see in particular how the new features work. It's deliberately conversational, as if I were looking over their shoulder.

Such tables and the accompanying commentary help summarize all the changes in one place.

Devote a separate booklet to new features

If the product is going to be revised again soon, you may not want to disturb the original manual. Sometimes a *What's New* booklet describing the new features may be enough. If the new features require extensive documenting, you may need to write and format the booklet exactly like the original manual. In either case arrange the booklet around real customer tasks and show illustrations.

What's New booklets often serve as marketing blurbs more than real documentation. The fanciest features tend to drift to the front. When you can't avoid doubling up, group the changes around the major activities users carry out, and explain the improvements in terms of what someone can do better now.

Don't confuse things, though, by using such a booklet to correct errors in the original manual. Leave those for errata sheets, change pages, or a separate booklet.

Checklist

☐ Use errata sheets to inform users of a few errors in the documentation

☐ Use change pages when you can replace originals in a binder

☐ If the rewritten document turns into a patchwork quilt, rewrite from scratch

☐ Learn what needs to be changed

☐ Limit the effects of your changes

Reviewing Someone Else's Manual

Be slow of tongue and quick of eye.

—*Miguel de Cervantes*

When you're asked to review someone else's manual, you may feel like a street cleaner. You may think you're supposed to march through the pages straightening syntax, drawing clarity out of chaos, filling in holes, and cutting away tangles so people won't slip or get lost.

Actually you're entering into a collaboration with the writer to produce the best manual possible. Each of you has a different task.

21

Define your goals

Part of what you're doing is critical, like the work of an editor. You must think like a user and act as a representative for the people who really will have to use the manual later. Talk to the writer, and reread the audience profile and documentation plan to understand what the different audiences need from this manual and to see what approach was planned.

Part of your task is creative. You may scribble in better phrases and snappier openings or write up your general conclusions in a way that will be useful to the manual's writer.

When you review a manual, you should have these aims:

- To clear away stumbling blocks and unnecessary distinctions from the paths of readers
- To spot the writer's messy habits so they can be cured before they irritate readers
- To ensure that the manual's organization makes sense, leads readers gradually through the instruction, and provides various paths through the reference material
- To establish a reassuring record of consistency and accuracy

Every writer needs a reviewer. Leslie Liedtka, who edited dozens of manuals, once argued that like an editor, a reviewer can provide another set of eyes.

> When you're looking at something you've written yourself, you don't always notice your problems; you don't notice you've made an error. You thought it was such a great idea, and you wrote it down, and you may not notice that you've got a split infinitive and a word misspelled and you're not following any standard.

Don't be doctrinaire

You may have certain rules you always follow when you write. It's tempting to apply them everywhere, even when they don't really apply.

Instead of trying to make the other writer measure up to your ideas, stick to your role as stand-in for the users. As Liedtka says,

> Try to forget everything you know about the computer. Read the manual as if it's the first time you've ever read one, so you say, "Now wait a minute. They're telling me I'm supposed to be using this file, but I didn't even make it yet."

You may encounter passages that puzzle you but don't seem to violate any known standards. When something just doesn't sound right, follow your instincts and raise the red flag. You needn't have a solution to raise a question.

Edit, don't rewrite

As a writer, you may be tempted to jump in and start rewriting the whole manual. But your job is to edit it. You are supporting, not replacing, the writer.

- Do not make changes just to keep your pencil busy. If you see a passage that doesn't present a real problem to the customer, leave it alone.

- Leave the final decision up to the writer. Take this attitude when you write comments, so you don't sound dictatorial.

- Empathize with the problems the writer may have faced— inconsistent information from the engineers, rapid changes in the software, time pressure. Keep these in mind so you don't make comments that imply the writer's a fool, or worse.

On the other hand, don't just mark "Awkward" on a paragraph and fly on. If you can think of a better way to organize it, do so. If you come up with a better phrase, write it down. Just don't act as if that's the perfect solution.

Traditionally editors wrote everything in the margins. But then some of their comments found their way into print, so editors began typing up pages and pages of separate notes, often keyed to the page numbers of the manuscript. Today, if you are handed the writer's file, you can use software to make revisions directly on the screen and add notes on the spot. Depending on the software you use, you can mark your suggested revisions with change bars, add voice commentaries, stick notes in a pop-up window, put your comments in "hidden text" that the writer can choose to show or hide, or completely rework the piece and leave the chore of comparing the original with the new to a document comparison application. Whatever technique you use, the process comes close to rewriting, so you need to work out a convention by which the writer can distinguish your changes from the original and decide what to do about your suggestions.

At each stage, make several passes

What you look for depends on what stage the manuscript has reached.

- When the writer has prepared a table of contents and perhaps a rough draft of a chapter or two, you should do a **developmental edit**, aimed at improving the organization before the writer gets stuck in a structure that leads to massive duplication, confusing jumps, or gaps.
- When the writer hands you a working draft (an alpha or beta or anything before the supposedly perfect final draft), you need to do a **regular edit**. Of course, there's no such thing as a regular edit, because each person, and each company, does this chore differently. Other names for this include literary edit, alpha or beta edit, and draft review.
- When you are looking at a final draft, one about to be handed off to the production team and printer, you should focus on the 1001 formal issues, such as the capitalization of number three heads, in a **preproduction edit**.

When you wade into the manuscript, you'll find hundreds of potential problems to watch out for. You cannot expect to read a first-draft paragraph and catch all the mistakes at once. Try to pick a few related issues, such as formatting of headings, and read through a whole chapter looking for those; your success rate will be much higher because you won't be distracted by a dozen other issues that leap up. As you grow more experienced in editing, you can cover more issues in a single pass. But a reasonable review may involve half a dozen passes, looking for problems in the organization, style, grammar, format, fact, and overall meaning.

Reach an agreement with the writer about exactly what you should look for—and when. If you must return the manuscript by tomorrow, you can't agree to do as much as you could if you had a month. Avoid the disappointment that comes when the writer expects one level of edit and you provide another.

Your review should address writing; other reviewers should be checking the manual for accuracy. Usually you should not have to test the product to make sure that the writer has described it accurately; often, in fact, the writer is imagining what will happen based on some specifications and gossip.

Do a developmental edit when you can still make a difference

As soon as the writer has a well-thought-out table of contents—and perhaps a chapter or two—do a developmental edit. At this point you can still make major changes to the structure without forcing the writer to rewrite chapter overviews, transitions, cross-references, and subsection introductions. If you wait until the writer has worked for months fleshing out a particular table of contents, the writer will resist any changes because they require too much rewriting—and that would torpedo the schedule.

A developmental edit focuses first on organization. Meaning springs first from organization, and readers care more about meaning than style. Make sure that the structure of the book is clear to anyone who cares to look, appropriate for the subject, and efficient. Only when you have tested the structure should you turn to the writer's tone and style.

Interrogate the organization of the manual

To develop the manual, look at the table of contents—the skeleton of the book, without the flesh. Is the head in the right place? Do both legs have feet? Look at the chapter topics first, then the sequence of major headings within a chapter, and finally, within each major section, the flow of minor headings. At each level ask yourself these questions:

- Is the logic behind the organization apparent?
- What is redundant and should be cut? (Depending on the situation, you may not be able to get rid of all redundancy.)
- What is missing? (This is very difficult to guess, even when you are familiar with the product, but keep in mind what the customer needs, and you may find some surprising lapses. Often, for instance, the first table of contents omits any mention of how to start the product.)
- Does the book hang together? Can you see why the writer included all this material here, rather than leaving some of it for other manuals?
- At any given level (chapter or first-level heading, for instance), are most topics of about equal importance? You want to make sure that no trivial topics have floated up to a high level, exaggerating their significance and challenging the reader to understand why they are emphasized so strongly.

By the end of this review, you should come up with a new table of contents, one about which you can confidently state

- **The organization makes sense.** It is clear why each section follows the one before, and it can be understood without a lot of reading.
- The organization seems to accommodate the needs of average readers.
- **What should come first comes first.** Readers don't have to jump forward and backward in the manual to figure out how some function works.
- **The organization goes no deeper than it has to.** Readers have trouble seeing the difference between a fourth-level head and a fifth-level head, so the fine distinctions get lost in a welter of indentations and minor variations in type size and style. Simplify. A shallow organization works best for any book other than an extremely technical reference tome for advanced professionals to consult for an occasional fact or two.

Make the style fit the audience

If you have a rough draft of some chapters, look at the tone to make sure it seems appropriate for the audience. You needn't make lots of specific comments on the prose because much of it will change in future drafts, but you should pick out specific passages that illustrate what you think works, or does not work, in the style.

Writers are touchy about style because they often identify a particular style as theirs. In making suggestions about the style, then, keep the focus on what the audience needs. You are trying to reach agreement on the way the writer will write from now on, in this manual. Check to ensure that

- **The level of detail seems right for the audience.** Remember that different chapters may be aimed at different segments of the audience, and that early chapters often need to sketch ideas broadly before filling in the details in later chapters.
- **The style gets out of the way of the audience.** If the audience needs a lot of explanations, an elaborate style may be just what they need. For an experienced audience, such prose slows them down.
- **The tone matches the audience's expectations.** From one company, readers expect a folksy, friendly approach; from another a cool-as-steel neutrality. Some experts expect a tough, stripped-down, but logical approach, while beginners often yearn for more support.

To show the kind of changes you have in mind, take a few specific passages and rewrite them. If you think the problem is general, then list a series of places where you think the same change should be made. Stress your general strategy rather than specific revisions. You are really addressing the writer's attitude toward the audience, not a particular phrase.

Do a regular edit for sense

When a writer hands you a manual at one of the regular milestones—a beta draft, for instance—you should plan to look at the whole book with one major question in mind: Does this make sense?

As you begin a regular edit, you'll probably notice stylistic problems first: passages of jargon, haste or slowness, changes in tone, lack of variety in sentence structure, passive verbs spreading their rot, peculiar personal quirks, blind spots, and odd twists of phrase.

Don't get lost in correcting these awkward stretches. You can become so involved in style that you lose track of the way you are moving forward through the text. You will have ceased being a stand-in for readers, who care more about finding topics of interest and understanding what's said.

Make the organization economical

Insist on getting a complete table of contents, and use that to make sure that the headings communicate the reasoning within the organization rather than defying understanding. (Who knows what logic lies behind topics that fall into chapters named Chapter One and Chapter Two?) In this sense you are asking the same questions you would during a developmental edit, and you hope that the answers don't point to a drastic reordering of topics.

Cutting is easier than adding, so pray you find more redundancies than gaps. Consider moving small sections around, but hesitate before suggesting whole chapters be merged or transformed.

Untangle the prose

Unknotting clots of language appeals to writers. In your comments, try to state a general rule that you are applying before you suggest a revision.

Every writer has a set of bad habits you'll learn to spot after a chapter or two. Here's a list of potential stylistic messes to watch out for:

- **Disagreement**—singular subject followed by many prepositional phrases containing plural objects, then a plural verb; or combinations such as "Everyone...they," or "The customer... they." (This failing is one of our own bad habits.)
- **Irrelevancies**—examples that don't match what was said about them, illustrations that don't illustrate.

- **Lack of energy**—sentences that trail off, parallels that are set up but not completed, contrasts that aren't carried out.
- **Negative thinking**—paragraphs that start with a caution or restriction, double negatives, statements that could be phrased in positive terms.
- **Noun clumps**—grab-bag sequences of three or more nouns in a row that make the reader wonder which words should be considered together and which should be thought of as forming a modifying phrase.
- **Passive voice**—the verb *to be* should signal trouble; read carefully any sentence that contains some form of *is*. The sentence may turn out OK, but probably not.
- **Sequential goofs**—paragraphs that don't follow chronological sequence, are missing steps, have topics that get in the way when you expect to go from Topic A to Topic B.
- **Sexism**—any use of *he* or *she* should trip the alarm.
- **Unclear references**—a *that* clause that appears long after the object it refers to, dangling modifiers, pronouns without clear references.
- Unexplained terms, abbreviations, and acronyms.
- **Future tense**—usually not needed and has less energy than present tense. It creeps in by accident or through laziness.
- Verbosity and pomposity.

Campaign for consistency

Here is where your critical facility becomes most important. Watching for absolute consistency of references, for instance, seems to require a different way of thinking than writing does. But consistency is important for readers. When a writer uses three different terms to refer to the same object, some readers will imagine three different objects. As editor Jon Thompson says,

> When all the lists are punctuated differently, and *database* is spelled as two words in one place and as one word in another, and there are serial commas in one place and not in another, after a while there's a cumulative effect.

At first this inconsistency just confuses readers, who begin to think there's some significance to the variations and try to figure out what they mean. Then inconsistency begins to sap their confidence in the reliability of the manual.

You're making the manual consistent in several ways:

- **With the product.** This is the minimum requirement. You should use the manual and see if it really describes the product accurately.

- **With other manuals in a series.** The same standards should apply to the current manual as the others in a suite of manuals.

- **With its own terminology.** Don't use ten different names for *computer*. Pick one name and use that over and over.

- **With its own organizational principles.** If one section is organized with definition first, then example, then procedure, all similar sections should be, too—or have a good reason not to be.

- **With its own design.** If the writer uses marginal glosses for definitions in five sections, and then starts using marginal glosses as if they were subheadings, make a note. Readers' expectations have been set up—and frustrated. Also, keep an eye peeled for inconsistent application of formatting standards.

- **With its own style and tone.** Beware of extreme gyrations of tone. These often occur if the writer wrote sections at different times under different pressures.

Check the English

Don't assume the writer has run a spelling checker. If you have time, check the spelling yourself. Remember, though, that spelling checkers are just computer programs, and as long as *lead* appears in their dictionary, they have no idea that the writer meant *led*.

Even if you are just reading for sense, circle any typos. Look for repeated words ("the the" is easy to miss), the same word spelled two different ways (gray and grey), grammatical goofs, and those odd twists of phrase that make you shake your head because they just don't sound right, even though they are grammatically OK. Those often turn out to be nonidiomatic combinations or two idioms bumping into each other and canceling each other out.

With a professional writer you should be able to point out problems without correcting them all. For an occasional writer, though, you should offer the correction.

Police the format

Here's an area most writers are glad to leave to someone else—a production team or a professional editor. But even if your company has someone to correct the final draft for formatting errors, you can clean up the manuscript a lot by pointing out problems you spot in this draft. Use your company style guide, if you have one, to find out what font, size, style, spacing, color, and position each element such as a level one head should be.

Take individual passes through the manuscript to check the formatting of elements, such as

- **Art.** Does every piece have a caption? Are the callouts in the right font and position? Is all the art the same size or one of the authorized sizes?

- **Headers and footers.** Are they in the right place? Are they styled correctly? Is the right information in them? Do the page numbers jibe?

- **Headings.** Are they all capitalized the same way? Do all the headings of the same level look the same? Are any headings placed at the bottom of the page, announcing nothing but the footer?

- **Lists.** Are all items punctuated the same way (beginning with a capital letter or not, ending with a period or not)? Do all lists use the same indentations, bullets, numbering, or do they follow the company policy (which may assign different formats to different types of lists)?

- **Product names.** Are they all spelled and capitalized the right way? Do trademarks appear where they should (usually after the first reference to the product in the book, but your lawyers may disagree)?

- **Punctuation.** Are there spaces before some periods or commas? Too many spaces after a period, comma, colon, semicolon, dash? Hyphens used in place of dashes? Periods used in some areas, but not others?

Doing a preproduction edit

If your company uses some form of desktop publishing, you get paper copy that looks like a photocopy of a finished book. You can do a thorough review in a few days, looking at both contents and layout before turning it over to the author or the production team, who note your suggested changes, make a few of them, then send the files off to be photocopied or typeset and printed.

You no longer have any time to make large-scale changes to the organization or even to make more than a few changes to style. You are now dealing with the manual as a book headed for production, and you can no longer pay much attention to the actual contents. You've got to assume the book communicates.

In separate passes, examine these:

- **Access.** Make sure people can find their way around the book using tables of content, headers and footers, page numbers, and the index.

- **Completeness.** At this point, a book is a collection of pieces. Is all the art really here? Is every appendix really in place? It's astonishing how many little parts can turn out to be half done, mysteriously missing, or "still to come."

- **Cross-references.** Once you have completely prepared pages, you need to make sure that the table of contents' headings and page numbers match those of the document, that figure numbers match references, that the index sends people to the right place.

- **English.** You need to check spelling, grammar, and punctuation even more carefully than you may have done for a regular edit. Use a spelling checker on the file, if you have the file available, but recognize that even the best dictionaries don't recognize the misuse of a correctly spelled word. Watch for popular confusions, such as *its* and *it's*, *effect* and *affect*.

- **Formatting.** Again, you have to review the formatting of each element separately, even more painstakingly than you may have done for a regular edit.

- **Front matter.** No one likes to read copyright notices, manual part numbers, legal disclaimers, official FTC notices, and lists of trademarks, but you should confirm that these are included and that they are up to date. Make sure that your company's address and phone number are correct, too.

- **Gaps in sequence.** Are any steps missing? If the paragraph announces three items, does the bulleted list have three items? Do the figure numbers proceed in order? Check pagination and any alphabetical or numbered sequences to make sure there are no gaps. (Gaps creep in when the writer deletes one item without renumbering the rest.)

- **Typos.** They're usually lurking in the big type, such as the book title, chapter titles, and major headings, which every other reviewer has skipped, assuming that anything that large must be right. Typos also tend to cluster at the tops and bottoms of pages and in closing paragraphs.

- **Pages as wholes.** Whenever you get to look at made-up pages, scan for irregular spacing between paragraphs, between headings and text, between the headers and footers and the rest of the text. Make sure no page has a widow or orphan—a page break that leaves a heading at the bottom of the page, with no following text, or that abandons a paragraph's last line at the top of the next page. Make sure that every time a reader opens the book, the two facing pages work together or at least don't conflict with each other.

Meryl Natchez, who has worked with dozens of editors, and hundreds of writers, says, "Editing and proofing are an art. Some people can't do it at all, others are experts. Find a true artist and put your faith in their work."

Communicate with the writer

As you write your comments, show your sympathy for the writer. Imagine how you would react to expressions like "Terrible!" scratched in the margin. The writer has enough work to do in fixing the passage without being burdened by resentment as well. Be polite.

Write as an ally, not a grader

You aren't grading a paper; you're helping a coworker.

Write a cover letter. This is a digest of your main ideas. Keep the focus of your comments on the manual, not the writer.

Summarize the pluses before the minuses. Praise before you criticize. Show that you recognize the good work the writer has done. Don't be impatient to jump into your own suggestions.

Identify any troublesome patterns. Take the time to sum up the patterns you've spotted and state the general change you suggest. Then the writer will be able to see that all those red marks are really instances of only six mistakes multiplied throughout the pages. Six well-considered decisions can solve a hundred problems.

Use your imagination. Imagine why a writer might be making the same goof over and over. Once you have an idea about the writer's point of view, you can make suggestions for new ways of thinking. Here's how manager and editor Jon Thompson would put it to a writer:

> You have a tendency to use the passive voice, and here's an example of it, and here's why I think you may be falling into the passive voice. Possibly you're thinking more about the product than about the reader, so you tend to say, "the disk can be booted by inserting it," as opposed to saying, "You can boot the disk." Once you get consciously thinking about the user, instead of the product, that will help.

Be specific. Provide details that will help somebody to rewrite— exactly what bothered you, which phrase derailed you, what word sounded sour. Make all suggestions as specific as you can.

Talk in person

Whenever time and circumstances permit, talk with the writer before returning the marked-up manual. Make your points out loud so they're more likely to be understood when read. Also you can lessen the inevitable shock (we always think our latest manuscript is nearly perfect) of all those marks by talking about what you like and showing you have confidence in the writer's ability to make improvements in the draft.

Solve problems together. Focus on improving the manual. Be prepared to admit that you may have gone too far, or misunderstood the context, or just plain made a change for the sake of change. If you still think your idea clarifies the passage for the reader, don't back down, but leave the final decision to the writer. If the writer suggests some change to the department approach, and you agree, then join the writer in proposing it to whatever group sets the standards.

Checklist

- ☐ Define your reviewing goals
- ☐ Act as a stand-in for users
- ☐ Edit, don't rewrite
- ☐ For each review, group related issues, and make a separate pass through the material for each set
- ☐ Do a developmental edit when the writer has a well-thought-out table of contents and a chapter or two
- ☐ Do an edit for sense at each major milestone draft
- ☐ Do a preproduction review to fine-tune the manuscript
- ☐ Communicate with the writer to make your intent and your suggestions clear

For More Ideas and Information ...

Setting the Scene

Illich, Ivan Tools for Conviviality. Harper & Row, New York, NY, 1973.

Chapter 1, The Project Cycle—What You Do at Each Stage

Brockmann, R. John, Writing Better Computer User Documentation: From Paper to Hypertext. John Wiley & Sons, New York, NY 1990.

Brooks, Frederick P. The Mythical Man-Month: Essays on Software Engineering. Addison-Wesley, Reading, MA, 1982.

Casey, Steven M. & Simpson, Henry. Developing Effective User Documentation. McGraw Hill, New York, NY 1988.

Freiberger, Paul & Swaine, Michael Fire in the Valley. Osborne/McGraw-Hill, Berkeley, CA, 1984.

Jaques, Elliott Requisite Organization: The CEO's Guide to Creative Structure and Leadership. Cason Hall, Arlington, VA, 1988.

Kidder, Tracy The Soul of a New Machine. Little Brown, Boston, MA, 1981.

Chapter 2, Gathering Information

Gross, Ronald The Independent Scholar's Handbook. Addison-Wesley, 1982.

Gross, Ronald The Lifelong Learner. Simon & Schuster, New York, NY, 1977.

Marshall, Catherine and Rossman, Gretchen B. Designing Qualitative Research. Sage Publications, Newbury Park, CA, 1989.

Miller, Delbert C. Handbook of Research Design and Social Measurement, 5th ed. Sage Publications, Newbury Park, CA, 1991.

Mortimer J. Adler & Charles Van Doren How to Read a Book. Simon & Schuster, New York, NY, 1940, 1972.

Patton, Michael Quinn Qualitative Evaluation and Research Methods, 2nd ed. Sage Publications, Newbury Park, CA, 1990.

Spyridakis, Jan H., Wenger, Michael J., and Andrew, Sarah H. The technical communicator's guide to understanding statistics and research design. Journal of Technical Writing and Communication 21, no. 3 (1991) pp. 207-219.

The Economist Numbers Guide. The Economist Books, Ltd., London, 1991.

Van Wicklen, Janet. The Tech Writing Game. Facts on File, New York, NY 1992.

Yin, Robert K. Case Study Research: Design and Methods. Sage, Newbury Park, CA, 1984.

Chapter 3, Understanding Your Audience and Their Work

Anderson I.H. Studies in the Eye Movements of Good and Poor Readers. Psychological Monographs 48, no. (1937) pp. 21-35.

Carroll, John M. Paradox of the Active User. in Interfacing Thought: Cognitive Aspects of Human Computer Interaction, John M. Carroll ed., MIT Press, Cambridge, MA, 1987, pp. 80111-80.

Charney, Davida Comprehending Non-Linear Text: The Role of Discourse Cues and Reading Strategies. in Hypertext '87 Papers. University of North Carolina, Chapel Hill, North Carolina, 1987, pp. 109-120.

Charney, Davida H., Reder Lynne M., & Wells, Gail W. Studies of Elaboration in Instructional Texts. in Effective Documentation: What We Have Learned From Research, ed. Stephen Doheny-Farina, MIT Press, Cambridge, MA, 1988.

Cuff. R. N. On casual users. International Journal of Man-Machine Studies 12, no. 2 (1980) pp. 163-187.

De Bono, Edward Practical Thinking. Penguin Books, New York, NY, 1976.

Golinkoff R.M. A Comparison of Reading Processes in Good and Poor Comprehenders. Reading Research Quarterly 11, no. (1975-1976) pp. 623-659.

Hill, William C. & Miller, James R. Justified Advice: A Semi-Naturalistic Study of Advisory Strategies. Microelectronics and Computer Technology Corporation (1987).

McKoon G. Organization of Information in Text Memory. Journal of Verbal Learning and Verbal Behavior 16, (1977) pp. 246-260.

Newell, A, & Simon, H.A. Human Problem Solving. Prentice-Hall, Englewood Cliffs, NJ, 1972.

Norman, Donald A. Learning and Memory. W. H. Freeman, New York, NY, 1982.

Norman, Donald A. Models of Human Memory. Academic Press, New York, New York, 1970.

Pritchard R. The Effects of Cultural Schemata on Reading Processing Strategies. Reading Research Quarterly 25, no. 4 (1990) pp. 273-295.

Reynolds R.E., Taylor M.A., Steffensen M.S., Shirey L.L., and Anderson R.C. Cultural Schemata and Reading Comprehension. Reading Research Quarterly 17, no. 3 (1982) pp. 353-366.

Spyridakis, Jan H. & Wenger, Michael J. Writing for Human Performance: Relating Reading Research to Document Design. Technical Communication 39, no. 2 (1992) pp. 202-215.

Steffensen M.S., Joag-Dev C., and Anderson R.C. A Cross-cultural Perpespective on Reading Comprehension. Reading Research Quarterly 15, no. 1 (1979) pp. 10-29.

Tesler, Larry, Enlisting User Help in Software Design. SIGCHI Bulletin (1983) pp. 5-7.

Turkle, Sherry. The Second Self: Computers and the Human Spirit. Simon&Schuster, New York, NY 1984.

Zuboff, Shoshana In the Age of the Smart Machine. Basic Books, New York, NY 1988.

Chapter 4, Learning the Product

Norman, Donald A. The Psychology of Everyday Things. Basic Books, New York, NY, 1988.

Papanek, Victor and Hennessey, James How Things Don't Work. Pantheon Books, New York, NY, 1988.

Chapter 5, Planning the Documentation

Bandes, Hanna Defining and Controlling Documentation Quality: Part 1. Technical Communication 33, no. 1 (1986) pp. 6-9.

Bandes, Hanna Defining and Controlling Documentation Quality: Part 2. Technical Communication 33, no. 2 (1986) pp. 69-71.

Carroll, John The Nurnberg Funnel: designing minimalist instructions for practical computer skill. MIT Press, Cambridge, MA, 1990.

Daniel B. Felker (ed.) Document Design: A Review of the Relevant Research. American Institute for Research, Washington, D.C., 1980.

Doheny-Farina, Stephen ed. Effective Documentation: What We Have Learned From Research. MIT Press, Cambridge, MA, 1988.

Fuqua R.W. and Phye G.D. The Effects of Physical Structure and Semantic Organization on the Recall of Prose. Contemporary Educational Psychology 3, no. (1978) pp. 105-117.

Guillemette, R. A. Prototyping: An Alternate Method for Developing Documentation. Technical Communication 34, no. 3 (1987) pp. 135-141.

Horton, William Illustrating Computer Documentation. John Wiley, New York 5, 1991.

Huston, Kathy and Southard, Sherry G. Organization: The Essential Element in Producing Usable Software Manuals. Technical Communication 35, no. 3 (1988) pp. 179-187.

James, Geoffrey Document Databases: The New Publications Methodology. Van Nostrand Reinhold, New York, New York, 1985.

Ramey, Judith Developing a Theoretical Base for On-Line Documentation, Part I: Building the Theory. The Technical Writing Teacher 13, no. 3 (1986) pp. 302-315.

Redish, Janice C, & Battison, Robbin M. A Document Design Model Applying Research to Technical Writing. in Proceedings of the 30th International Technical Communication Conference. Society for Technical Communication, Washington, D.C., 1983, pp. 58-60.

Savage, Charles Fifth Generation Management: A touchstone for teamworkers. Digital Press, Bedford, MA, 1992.

Sheppard, Sylvia B, Bailey, John W, & Bailey, Elizabeth Kruesi An Empirical Evaluation of Software Documentation Formats. in Human Factors in Computer Systems. Ablex, Norwood, New Jersey, 1986.

Southard, Sherry Practical considerations in formatting manuals. Technical Communication 35, no. 2 (1988) pp. 173-178.

Waite, Robert Making Information Easy to Use: A Summary of Research. in Proceedings of International Technical Communication Conference. Society for Technical Communication, Washington, D.C., 1982, pp. 120-123.

Chapter 6, Developing a Schedule and Estimating Costs

Caernarven-Smith, Patricia Annotated Bibliography on Costs, Productivity, Quality, and Profitability in Technical Publishing, 1956-1988. Technical Communication 37, no. 2 (1990) pp. 116-121.

Chapter 7, As You Write—Working Methods

Albers, Josef Intgeraction of Color. Yale University Press, New Haven, CT, 1963.

Arnheim, Rudolf Visual Thinking. University of California Press, Berkeley, CA, 1969.

Benbasat, I., Dexter, A. S., & Todd, P. An experimental program investigating color-enhanced and graphical information presentation: An integration of findings. Communications Of The ACM 29, no. 11 (1986) pp. 1094-1105.

Benson, P. J. Writing visually: Design considerations in technical publications. Technical Communication 32, no. 2 (1985) pp. 35-39.

Bertin, Jacques Semiology of Graphics. University of Wisconsin Press, Madison, Wisconsin, 1983.

Bruno, Michael H. Principles of Color Proofing. GAMA Communications, Salem, NH, 1986.

Ellis, Clarence A., Gibbs, Simon J., & Rein, Gail L. Groupware: Some issues and experiences. Communications Of The ACM 34, no. 1 (Jan 1991) pp. 38-58.

Farkas, David K. Online Editing and Document Review. Technical Communication 34, no. 3 (1987) pp. 180-183.

Fish, R., Kraut, R., Leland, M. & Cohen, M. Quilt: A collaborative tool for cooperative writing. in Proceedings of the Conference on Office Information Systems. Association for Computing Machinery, New York, NY, 1988, pp. 30-37.

Greenbaum, Joan & Kyng, Morten. Design at Work: Cooperative Design of Computer Systems, Lawrence Erlbaum & Associates, Hillsdale, NJ, 1991.

Irene Greif, Editor Computer-Supported Cooperative Work. Morgan Kaufmann, Palo Alto, 1988.

Jonassen, David, & Hawk, Parmalee Using Graphic Organizers in Instruction. Information Design Journal 4 (1986) pp. 58-68.

Kosslyn, S.M. Information Representation in Visual Images. Cognitive Psychology 7 (1975) pp. 341-370.

Lay, Mary M. & Karis, William M., editors. Collaborative Writing in INdustry: Investigations in Theory and PRactice. Baywood Publishing Company, Inc. Amityville, NY 1991.

Marca, David & Bock, Geoffrey Groupware: Software for Computer-Supported Cooperative Work. IEEE Computer Sopciety Press, Los Alamitos, CA, 1991.

Maughm, W. Somerset The Summing Up. Doubleday and Company, Inc., New York, NY 1938.

Olson, M. H., Ed. Technological Support for Work Group Collaboration. Lawrence Erlbaum Associates, Hillsdale, NJ, 1989.

Schrage, Michael Shared Minds: The New Technologies of Collaboration. Random House, New York, NY 1990.

Schrank, Robert Ten Thousand Working Days. MIT Press, Cambridge, MA, 1978.

Sirkka L. J., & Dickson G. W. Graphics and Managerial Decision Making: Research Based Guidelines. Communications Of The ACM 31, no. 6 (1988) pp. 765-774.

Tufte, Edward R. The Visual Display of Quantitative Information. Graphics Press, Cheshire, CT, 1983.

Tufte, Edward R. Envisioning Information. Graphics Press, Cheshire, CT, 1990.

University of Chicago The Chicago Manual of Style. University of Chicago Press, Chicago, IL 1982.

Weiss, Edmond H. The Writing System for Engineers and Scientists. Prentice-Hall, Englewood Cliffs, NJ, 1982.

White, Jan. V. Graphic Design for the Electronic Age. Watson-Guptill Publications, New York, NY, 1988.

Chapter 8, Openers—Tables of Contents and Introductions

Mandler G. Words, Lists, and Categories: An Experimental View of Organized Memory. in Studies in Thought and Language, ed. J. L. Cowan, University of Arizona Press, Tucson, AZ, 1970.

Williams, Thomas R. Can Introductions Provide "Prior Knowledge': Some Evidence from the "Advance Organizer" Literature. Conference Record, International Professional Communication Conference 1992, IEEE Professional Communication Society, Piscataway, NJ, 1992, pp. 135-139.

Chapter 9, Getting Users Started

Southard, Sherry Introduction. Technical Communication 35, no. 2 (1988) pp. 167-168.

Chapter 10, Tutorials

Alvermann D.E., Smith L.C., and Readence J.E. Prior Knowledge Activation and the Comprehension of Compatible and Incompatible Text. Reading Research Quarterly 20, no. 4 (1985) pp. 421-436.

Campbell, Gwendolyn The Effectiveness of a Keystroke Line in Interactive Tutorials. Sigchi Bulletin 20, no. 2 (1988) pp. 27-29.

Chapter 11, Computer-Based Training

Ambron, Sueann & Hooper, Kristina, editors. Interactive Multimedia: Visions of Multimedia for Developers, Educators, & Information Providers. Microsoft Press, Redmond, WA, 1988.

Carroll, J. M. Minimalist training. Datamation 30, no. 18 (1984) pp. 125-136.

Christ, R. E. Review and analysis of color-coding research for visual displays. Human Factors 17, no. 6 (1975) pp. 542-570.

Czaja, S.J., Hanmmond, K., Blascovich, J.J., & Swede, H. Learning To Use a Word Processing System as a Function of Training Strategy. Behavior and Information Technology 5, no. 3 (1986) pp. 203-216.

Duin, Ann Hill Implementing Suggestions from Current Research: An Investigation into Transforming Computer-Assisted Instruction. in 34th International Technical Communication Conference Proceedings. Society for Technical Communication, Washington, D.C., 1987, pp. 29-32.

Fisk, A. Relative Value of Pictures and Text in Conveying Information: Performance and Memory Evaluations. in Proceedings of the 30th Annual Human Factors Society Meeting. Human Factors Society, Santa Monica, CA, 1986, pp. 1269-1272.

Gaines, Brian R., & Shaw, Mildred L.G. The Art of Computer Conversation: A New Medium for Communication. Prentice-Hall, Englewood Cliffs, NJ, 1984.

Gould, J. Why is Reading Slower from CRT Displays than from Paper. in Proceedings of the 30th Annual Meeting of the Human Factors Society. Human Factors Society, Santa Monica, CA, 1986, pp. 834-835.

Haeusing, M. Color Coding of Information on Electronic Displays. in Proceedings of 6th Congress of the International Ergonomics Association. International Ergonomics Association, 1976, pp. 210-217.

Hollan, J. D., Hutchins, E. L., & Weitzman, L. STEAMER: An advanced computer-assisted instruction system for propulsion engineering. Proceedings of Summer Computer Simulation Conference (1984) pp. 400-404.

Kearsley, Greg Embedded Training: the New Look of Computer-Based Instruction. Machine Mediated Learning 3 (1985) pp. 279-285.

Marcus, Stephen The Host in the Machine: Decorum in Computers Who Speak. IEEE Transactions on Professional Communication 28, no. 2 (1985) pp. 29-33.

Wärn, Yvonne Cognitive Aspects of Computer-Supported Tasks. John Wiley & Sons, New York, NY, 1989.

Chapter 12, *Procedures*

Booher, Harold R. Relative comprehensibility of pictorial information and printed words in proceduralized instructions. Human Factors 17 (1975) pp. 266-277.

Bradford, Annette Norris Conceptual differences between the display screen and the printed page. Technical Communication 31, no. 3 (1984) pp. 13-16.

Coveillo, John W. Development of Troubleshooting Material: The Technical Part of Writing. Proceedings of the 34th International Technical Communication Conference (1987) pp. 149-152.

Dixon P. The Processing of Organizational Information in Written Directions. Journal of Memory and Language 26, no. (1987) pp. 24-35.

Jones S. The Effect of a Negative Qualifier in an Instruction. Journal of Verbal Learning and Verbal Behavior 5, no. (1966) pp. 497-501.

Miller G. The Magical Number Seven, Plus or Minus Two: Some Limits on our Capacity for Processing Information. Psychological Review 63, no. 2 (1956) pp. 81-96.

Odescalchi, Esther Kando Productivity Gain Attained by Task Oriented Information. in 33rd International Technical Communication Conference Proceedings. Society for Technical Communication, Washington, D.C., 1985, pp. 359-362.

Sides, Charles H. Writing Instructions for Computer Documentation: an Annotated Bibliography. Technical Communication 35, no. 2 (1988) pp. 105-107.

Southard, Sherry Special Section: Usable instructions based on research and theory: Part 2. Technical Communication 35, no. 3 (1988) pp. 167-193.

Southard, Sherry Usable Instructions Based on Research and Theory: Part 1: Introduction. Technical Communication 35, no. 2 (1988) pp. 89-90.

Southard, Sherry Usable Instructions Based on Research and Theory: Part 2: Introduction. Technical Communication 35, no. 3 (1988) pp. 167-168.

Southard, Sherry Usable instructions based on research and theory: Part 1. Technical Communication 35, no. 2 (1988) pp. 88-105.

Wieringa, Douglas, Moore, Christopher, & Barnes, Valerie Procedure Writing: Principles and Practices. Battelle Press, Columbus, OH, 1992.

Wurman, Richard Saul. Follow the Yellow Brick Road. Bantam, New York, NY, 1992.

Chapter 14, *Indexes and Glossaries*

Dansereau, Mary E. Creating an Online Index. in 34th International Technical Communication Conference Proceedings. Society for Technical Communication, Washington, D.C., 1987, pp. 105-107.

Frisch, Kathryn L. The Convex Info System—An Online Information Index. in 34th International Technical Communication Conference Proceedings. Society for Technical Communication, Washington, D.C., 1987, pp. 108-110.

Chapter 16, Online Help

Apple Computer, Inc. Macintosh Human Interface Guidelines. Addison-Wesley, Reading, MA 1992.

Barrett, Edward The Society of Text: Hypertext, Hypermedia, and the Social Construction of Information, The MIT Press, Cambridge, MA 1989.

Barrettt, Edward, editor Sociomedia: Multimedia, Hypermedia, and the Social Construction of Knowledge. The MIT Press, Cambridge, MA, 1992.

Barrett, Edward, & Pardis, James The On-line Environment and In-House Training. in Text, ConText, and HyperText: Writing with and for the Computer. The MIT Press, Cambridge, Massachusetts, 1988, pp. 227-249.

Bolter, Jay David. Writing Space: The Computer, Hypertext, and the History of Writing. Lawrence Erlbaum & Associates, Hillsdale, NJ 1991.

Borenstein, Nathaniel S Help Texts vs Help Mechanisms: A New Mandate for Documentation Writers. in SIGDOC 85 Conference Proceedings. Association for Computing Machinery, New York, NY, 1985, pp. 8-10.

Cohan, L.A., & Newsome, S.L. Navigational Aids and Learning Styles: Structural Optimal Training for Computer Users. Sigchi Bulletin 20, no. 2 (1988) pp. 30-32.

Dean, Morris How a Computer Should Talk to People. IBM Systems Journal 21, no. 4 (1982) pp. 424-453.

Dorazio, Patricia A. Help Facilities: A Survey of the Literature. Technical Communication 35, no. 2 (1988) pp. 118-121.

Fischer, Gerhard, Lemke, Andreas, & Schwab, Thomas CHI '85 Proceedings. in Knowledge-Based Help Systems. Association for Computing Machinery, New York, NY, 1985, pp. 161-167.

Horton, William Designing and writing online documentation: help files to hypertext. John Wiley, New York, 1989.

Lakoff, George & Johnson, Mark Metaphors We Live By. University of Chicago Press, 1980.

Laurel, Brenda. Computers as Theatre. Addison-Wesley, Reading, MA, 1991.

Laurel, Brenda, editor The Art of Human-Computer Interface Design. Addison Wesley, Reading, MA, 1990.

Mason, R.E.A., & Carey, T. T. Prototyping Interactive Information Systems. Communications Of The ACM 26, no. 5 (1983) pp. 347-354.

NeXTSTEP User Interface Guidelines. Addison-Wesley, Reading, MA, 1992.

Nielsen, Jakob Hypertext and Hypermedia. Academic Press, Inc., Boston, MA, 1990.

Petrauskas, Bruno F. Online Documentation: Putting Research into Practice. in 34th International Technical Communication Conference Proceedings. Society for Technical Communication, Washington, D.C., 1987, pp. 54-57.

Shneiderman, Ben Reflections on Authoring, Editing, and Managing Hypertext. in The Society of Text: Hypertext, Hypermedia, and the Social Construction of Information. MIT Press, Cambridge, MA, 1989.

Shneiderman, Ben Designing the User Interface: Strategioes for Effective Human-Computer Interaction, 2nd ed. Addison-Wesley, Reading, MA, 1992.

Tognazzini, Bruce Tog on Interface. Addison-Wesley, Reading, MA, 1992.

Chapter 17, Getting Feedback

Craig, John S. Approaches to Usability Testing and Design Strategies: An Anotated Bibliography. Technical Communication 38, no. 2 (1991) pp. 190-194.

Mills, C. B., Panel organizer and moderator Usability testing in the real world. SIGCHI Bulletin 19, no. 1 pp. 43-46.

Schriver, Karen A. Writing for Expert or Lay Audiences: Designing Text Using Protocol-Aided Revision. Technical Report No. 43 (July 1989) Communications Design Center, Carnegie-Mellon University, Pittsburgh, Pa.

Chapter 18, Rewriting Drafts

Doyle, Michael & Straus, David How to Make Meetings Work. Playboy Paperbacks, New York, NY 1980.

Hildick, Wallace Word for Word: The Rewriting of Fiction. W.W. Norton, New York, NY, 1965.

Lanham, Richard A Revising Prose. Scribner's, New York, NY, 1979.

Schriver, Karen A. Moving from Sentence-level to Whole-text Revision: Helping Writers Focus on the Reader's Needs. in Expanding the Repertoire: An Anthology of Practical Approaches for the Teaching of Writing, ed. McCormick, K. Center for the Study of Writing, Berkeley, CA 1989, pp. 46-57.

Zinsser, William Writing to Learn. Harper and Row, New York, NY, 1988.

Chapter 19, *Refining Your Style*

Britton B.K., Glynn S.M., Meyer B.J.F., and Penland M.F. Effects of Text Structure on the Use of Cognitive Capacity During Reading. Journal of Educational Psychology 74, no. (1982) pp. 51-61.

Clark H.H. and Sengul C.J. In Search of Referents for Nouns and Pronouns. Memory and Cognition 7, no. 1 (1979) pp. 35-41.

Coleman E.B. The Comprehensibility of Several Grammatical Transformations. Journal of Applied Psychology 48, no. 3 (1964) pp. 186-190.

Dobbs A.R., Friedman A., and Lloyd J. Frequency Effects in Lexical Decisions: A Test of the Verification Model. Journal of Experimental Psychology: Human Perception and Performance 11, no. 1 (1985) pp. 81-92.

Ehrlich K. Comprehension of Pronouns. Quarterly Journal of Experimental Psychology 32, no. (1980) pp. 247-255.

Flesch, Rudolf The Art of Plain Talk. Macmillan, New York, NY 1951.

Flesch, Rudolf How to Write, Speak, and Think More Effectively. Harper&Row, New York, NY, 1960.

Garnham A. and Oakhill J. Interpreting Elliptical Verb Phrases. Quarterly Journal of Experimental Psychology 39, no. (1987) pp. 611-627.

Herriot P. The Comprehension of Active and Pasive Sentences as a Function of Pragmatic Expectations. Journal of Verbal Learning and Verbal Behavior 8, no. (1969) pp. 166-169.

Hudson P.T.W. and Bergman M.W. Lexical Knowledge and Word Recognition: Word Length and Word Frequency in Naming and Decison Tasks. Journal of Memory and Language 24, no. (1985) pp. 46-58.

Irwin J.W. The Effects of Explicitness and Clause Order on the Comprehension of Reversible Causal Relationships. Reading Research Quarterly 4, no. (1980) pp. 477-489.

Loman N.L. and Mayer R.E. Signalling Techniques that Increase the Readibility of Expository Prose. Journal of Educational Psychology 75, no. 3 (1980) pp. 402-412.

Pound, Ezra ABC of Reading, New Directions, New York, NY 1934.

Spyridakis J.H. and Standal T.C. Signals in Expository Prose: Effects on Reading Comprehension. Reading Research Quarterly 23, no. 3 (1987) pp. 285-298.

Strunk, William, Jr. & White, E.B. The Elements of Style. Macmillan, New York, NY, 1979.

Tabossi P. Effects of Context on the Immediate Interpretation of Unambigius Nouns. Journal of Experimental Psychology 14, no. 1 (1988) pp. 153-162.

Young, Matt. The Technical Writer's Handbook. University Science Books, Mill Valley, CA, 1989.

Chapter 21, *Reviewing Someone Else's Manual*

Gross D., Fischer U., and Miller G.A. The organization of Adjectival Meanings. Journal of Memory and Language 28, no. (1989) pp. 92-106.

Tarutz, Judith A. Technical Editing, Addison-Wesley, Reading, MA, 1992.

Index

C

shortcuts 254, 295
 table 255
 visual overview of controls 250
 warnings 254
competitive analysis 66
completeness
 editing for 399
 in drafts 140-141
 in installation guides 172-173
CompuServe 125
computer phobia 34
computer-based tour 183
computer-based training
 behaviorist boredom 215
 benefits 211-212
 carrying on a dialog in 222
 compared with paper tutorial 191, 211-212
 condensing text 222-223
 distinguishing the training from the product 220
 formatting for screen 223
 free play, if possible 219
 imitating the real software 221
 in documentation plan 84
 in suite of documentation 211
 learning objectives 212-213
 menus 213-214
 navigating through 213
 pointing to the next activity 224
 remediation 217-218
 responding to the user 218-219
 screen constraints 220
 steps and explanations 221
 summarizing 224
 tables of contents 213-214
 testing afterward 216-217
 text area 221
 tone 222-223
computer-supported collaboration 125
concepts
 in audience profile 32, 38
 learning about product 65-66
condensing text
 in computer-based training 222-223
 shrinking paragraphs 365-366
consistency 361-2, 396-397
constraints on help 304-305
context
 for command reference 253-254
 for language reference 259
 in glossary definitions 288
context-sensitive help 309
contractor
 costs 117-118
 documentation plan 6
 doing a rough estimate 4
 proposal 4
contrasts 364-365
controls, documenting
 bulletted lists in 255
 charts 255
 command description 253-255
 context 253-254
 defining 253

shortcuts 254, 295
table 255
visual overview of controls 250
warnings 254
competitive analysis 66
completeness
    editing for 399
    in drafts 140-141
    in installation guides 172-173
CompuServe 125
computer phobia 34
computer-based tour 183
computer-based training
    behaviorist boredom 215
    benefits 211-212
    carrying on a dialog in 222
    compared with paper tutorial 191, 211-212
    condensing text 222-223
    distinguishing the training from the product 220
    formatting for screen 223
    free play, if possible 219
    imitating the real software 221
    in documentation plan 84
    in suite of documentation 211
    learning objectives 212-213
    menus 213-214
    navigating through 213
    pointing to the next activity 224
    remediation 217-218
    responding to the user 218-219
    screen constraints 220
    steps and explanations 221
    summarizing 224
    tables of contents 213-214
    testing afterward 216-217
    text area 221
    tone 222-223
computer-supported collaboration 125
concepts
    in audience profile 32, 38
    learning about product 65-66
condensing text
    in computer-based training 222-223
    shrinking paragraphs 365-366
consistency 361-2, 396-397
constraints on help 304-305
context
    for command reference 253-254
    for language reference 259
    in glossary definitions 288
context-sensitive help 309
contractor
    costs 117-118
    documentation plan 6
    doing a rough estimate 4
    proposal 4
contrasts 364-365
controls, documenting
    bulletted lists in 255
    charts 255
    command description 253-255
    context 253-254
    defining 253

D

Q

R